THE CHILD

A C.G. JUNG FOUNDATION BOOK
Published in association with Daimon Verlag
Einsiedeln, Switzerland

The C.G. Jung Foundation for Analytical Psychology is dedicated to helping men and women grow in conscious awareness of the psychological realities in themselves and society, find healing and meaning in their lives and greater depth in their relationships, and live in response to their discovered sense of purpose. It welcomes the public to attend its lectures, seminars, films, symposia, and workshops and offers a wide selection of books for sale through its bookstore. The Foundation also publishes *Quadrant*, a semiannual journal, and books on Analytical Psychology and related subjects. For information about Foundation programs or membership, please write to the C.G. Jung Foundation, 28 East 39th Street, New York, NY 10016.

THE CHILD

Erich Neumann

Translated by Ralph Manheim
Foreword by Louis H. Stewart

SHAMBHALA
Boston
1990

SHAMBHALA PUBLICATIONS, INC.
Horticultural Hall
300 Massachusetts Avenue
Boston, Massachusetts 02115

9 8 7 6 5 4 3 2 1

First Shambhala Edition
Printed in the United States of America on acid-free paper
Distributed in the United States by Random House
and in Canada by Random House of Canada Ltd.
Library of Congress Cataloging-in-Publication Data

Neumann, Erich.
    [Kind. English]
    The child / Erich Neumann: translated by Ralph Manheim.
        p. cm.
    Translation of: Das Kind.
    Reprint, with new foreword. Originally published: New York:
Published by Putnam for C.G. Jung Foundation for Analytical
Psychology, 1973.
        "Published in association with Daimon Verlag Einsiedeln."
        "A C.G. Jung Foundation book."
    Includes bibliographical references.
        ISBN 0–87773–570–0 (alk. paper)
        1. Mother and child. 2. Ego (Psychology) 3. Personality in
children. I. Title.
    BF723.M55N48513   1990   89-29752
    155.4′182—dc20   CIP

CONTENTS

FOREWORD

It is a pleasure to write an introduction to this new edition of Neumann's *The Child*, which has been out of print for some time. This book was first published in a German edition in 1963 and appeared in English translation in 1973. Neumann's all-embracing archetypal perspective continues to inspire and inform depth psychological studies in child development.

Neumann is widely known and respected for his writings on creativity, culture, and the moral sense, but the book of his that has had the greatest impact on analytical psychology is no doubt *The Origins and History of Consciousness*. There Neumann took on the daunting task of discerning in ancient mythology evidence of the development of human consciousness. "It is the task of this book," he writes in the introduction, "to show that a series of archetypes is a main constituent of mythology, that they stand in an organic relation to one another, and that their stadial succession determines the growth of consciousness." Neumann goes on to say that "the individual ego consciousness has to pass through the same archetypal stages which determined the evolution of consciousness in the life of humanity. The individual has in his own life to follow the road that humanity has trod before him, leaving traces of its journey in the archetypal sequence of the mythological images." In this statement we recognize the task that Neumann set himself in *The Child*: to show how the development of the child's ego-consciousness recapitulates the same archetypal stages and symbolic images that appear in ancient mythologies.

This idea is already implicit in Jung's theory of analytical psychology, but *The Origins and History of Consciousness* and

The Child were the first attempts to demonstrate the hypothesis. In retrospect, we can see that *The Child* was a natural outgrowth of *The Origins and History of Consciousness*. It is apparent that, from the beginning, the themes of these two books were inextricably entwined in Neumann's thought.

In a foreword to *The Origins and History of Consciousness*, Jung expressed his great admiration, and perhaps a tinge of envy as well, for what Neumann had accomplished. The book begins, he says, "just where I, too, if I were granted a second lease of life, would start to gather up the *disjecta membra* of my own writings to sift out all those 'beginnings without continuations' and knead them into a whole." Jung notes that Neumann begins "at the very place where I unwittingly made landfall on the new continent long ago, namely the realm of *matriarchal symbolism*; and, as a conceptual framework for his discoveries, the author uses a symbol whose significance first dawned on me in my recent writings on the psychology of alchemy: the *uroboros*."

Without a doubt Jung would have been just as pleased with *The Child*. For it also exemplifies a concept that Jung expressed early on but, caught in the onrush of his creative *daimon*, unavoidably left undeveloped—the mother-child relation as a *participation mystique*. For Neumann the terms *participation mystique* and *unconscious identity*, which come from Lucien Lévy-Bruhl, express the quality of union or merger that characterizes the mother-child relationship in the earliest period of infancy, the uroboric stage. He concludes that "formulated in these terms the psychic situation of the infant is interpreted not as an *act* of identification, but as an unconscious identity, that is, as a passive state" (*The Child*, p. 15). The mother, he says, "dominates the early development of the human individual just as the matriarchal world, in which the unconscious is paramount and ego-consciousness is still undeveloped, dominates the psychology of primitive cultures" (p. 7). The uroboros, the mythological image of the snake with its tail in its mouth, "as the Great Round, in whose womb the ego-germ lies sheltered, is the characteristic symbol of the uterine situation in which there is not yet a clearly delimited child personality confronting a human and extra-human environment. This undelimited state characteristic of the uterine embryonic situation is largely, though not fully, preserved after birth." (p. 10).

Fundamental to Neumann's archetypal theory is the mother's innate, instinctive response to the infant, not only in humans but in the mammalian species as a whole. For Neumann the mother-child relationship is, from the beginning, "a relationship between two living beings whose instinctive tendency impels them to seek fulfillment in each other and who, just as in the instinct-directed drive of man and women to unite, are oriented toward one another" (p. 83). However, it is the mother's instinctive reactions, he says, which are the foundation of the primal relationship: "They guarantee the stability and self-evident character of the Eros-bond attaching the mother to her child" (p. 24). This is so throughout the animal world, in which the female shows "tenderness, readiness to make sacrifices, and the will to defend the life of the young" (ibid.). The instinctual basis of this response seems to lie in the proportions of the baby's head and in its helplessness. Neumann quotes Niko Tinbergen: "a short face in relation to a large forehead, prominent cheeks" (ibid.). Important also are the infantile body movements. The presence of these features, even in young animals, releases tender parental feelings, and where such features are lacking this reaction does not occur.

It is of equal importance, of course, that there be an innate response of the infant to the mother. As the Divine Child is constellated in the mother, so also is the mother archetype constellated in the infant. At around one to three months of age the infant smiles for the first time with clear-eyed recognition of the mother's face, and frequently of her voice as well. There are, of course, other indications of the child's "expectations" of a mother. The infant "roots" for the mother's nipple and sucks on it, and within hours or days it has recognized the mother's smell. Thus Neumann was on solid ground when he wrote many years ago:

The mother constellates the archetypal field and evokes the archetypal image of the mother in the child psyche, where it rests, ready to be evoked and to function. This archetypal image evoked in the psyche then sets in motion a complex interplay of psychic functions in the child, which is the starting point for essential psychic developments between the ego and the unconscious. These developments, like those embedded in the organism, remain relatively independent of the mother's individual behavior, provided that the mother lives with her child in accordance with her archetypal role. (p. 24)

Neumann was perhaps the first depth psychologist to grasp the full significance of the extra-uterine period, the first twelve to fourteen months of the newborn infant's life. He emphasized the important fact, often neglected by students of child development, that the human infant is born approximately a year early in comparison to the maturity at birth of other higher primates. To achieve a comparable degree of maturity at birth the human infant would probably have to spend at least another year in the womb. This neotony—retarded development—is related to the evolution of the brain. The brain of the human fetus has grown so large by the end of the third trimester of pregnancy that birth must occur at that time. As a consequence of its "premature" birth, the human infant must acquire during its first year of life many of the adaptive skills that other primates have at birth, such as the ability to walk and cling to the mother.

Archetypal development begins in the nurturing, protective atmosphere of the womb and then, following birth, continues in what Adolf Portmann has dubbed the "social womb" of the mother-child relationship. Just as development in the womb takes place in universal stages of physical and neurological growth, the mother-child relationship is programmed to continue the archetypal development of the child, although now with the additional impact of social and cultural factors. By adopting Portmann's term, the *social womb*, Neumann wished to emphasize this important fact.

The evolutionary significance of neotony seems to be linked to the social nature of the mammalian species. With the appearance of the emotions as a more flexible instinctual system, there was an increasing need for the adaptation of infants to the social life of the group, upon which their survival depended. Prolonged infancy provides this opportunity for maturation within the social group. The human infant must learn all the skills that prepare it for a human life of cultural as well as "natural" development. Neumann highlights the significance of human neotony with respect to the social collective:

> In the latter part of its embryonic life the human child is withdrawn from the maternal hands of nature and entrusted to the human mother. The child's primal relationship to its mother is more than a primary relationship, for thanks to this relationship the child, even before its "true" birth at the age of one year, is molded by human culture, since the mother lives in a cultural collective whose language and values unconsciously but effectively influence the child's development. (p. 8)

Having established the reciprocal archetypal responses of mother and infant as his basis, Neumann could now follow the course of the child's development within the primal relationship of mother and child.

Sad to say, owing to Neumann's untimely death in 1960, this book is unfinished. The editors decided, wisely I believe, to leave it in its first-draft state with all the virtues and the faults inherent in such a manuscript. On the one hand, we have the rare opportunity to experience the enthusiasm and driving energy that often characterize a first, unedited draft. On the other hand, we are left with the inevitable repetitions and incomplete treatment of certain issues. Notably lacking is a full treatment of the specific character of feminine development. The editors did, however, add a very brief and general summary of this topic, drawn from the author's other writings on the subject. Neumann was well aware that understanding the archetypal differences in the development of males and females is of great significance. He realized that the girl's relationship to the mother is in fundamental ways different from the boy's, and he had planned to write more about this: "The difference in the development of the girl will at least be touched upon in a later section of this book, since special importance must be attached to the mother-daughter relationship as the first phase of the specifically feminine development" (p. 95).

In view of the book's unfinished form, a few hints and guidelines that have been helpful in my reading of the book may also be of some assistance to the reader. First, a few suggestions on how to read Neumann. The approach is through the imagination as well as the intellect. When Neumann says that the mother-child relationship is archetypal, he is saying: imagine the field of psychic energy that is elicited between the mother and the child and see what images come to your mind. He encourages us to return as best we can to the state of mind that Gaston Bachelard calls poetic revery, and this we shall find is as close as we can ever get to the original state that Neumann calls the matriarchate, in which Eros and the imagination hold sway. Fantasy reigns, he says, so free up your own images of that first stage of the mother-child relationship.

> The matriarchal consciousness of the child is most clearly revealed by the role of fantasy and its close relative, play. Fantasy is by no means identical with a wishful inner pleasure principle; rather, it is an inner sense organ that perceives and expresses inner worlds and laws as the outward sense organs perceive and express the outside world and its laws. The world of play is of extreme importance not only for children but also for the adults of all cultures; it is not a world to be transcended. It is especially important for children. Only an individual embedded in this symbolic reality of play can become a complete human being. (p. 70)

This quotation encapsulates clearly and fully Neumann's deep understanding of the inestimable importance of play and fantasy in the life of the child and the adult.

Neumann asks us to imagine: what has been set loose between the mother and child? The infant evokes the child archetype in the mother and the mother evokes the mother archetype in the infant. The mother is seized by loving, nurturant feelings for the helpless, adorable infant, and the infant is seized by the instinct to root for the nipple and then to swallow the mother's milk. But within one to three months the infant has a startling revelation. It discriminates, out of the void of unconsciousness, the sound of the mother's voice and the sight of her face, and responds with its first clear-eyed smile of recognition. We may imagine that, for the infant, this is a vision of great beauty and wonder, a revelation of the visual-auditory archetypal image of the mother, the Great Goddess, a vision our dreams ever seek to recover. This revelation signals the approaching end of the earliest uroboric state, and leads on to the ensuing stages of development.

It is important to keep in mind that, for Neumann, the primal relationship of mother and child is the basis for all successful normal development, and, as well, for the ways in which pathological development may occur (leaving aside, of course, genetic inheritance of defects, traumatic events, and the like). In the first four chapters he is primarily occupied with the infant's development from birth to around twelve to fourteen months of age, although he edges toward the time when the integral ego and the Self are constellated, around two years of age. The emphasis in these early chapters is almost totally on the mother-child relationship in its normal development, in its disturbances, and in the gradual transition from the matriarchate to the patriarchate. I would draw the reader's attention to the fact that these first four chapters are concerned not so much with ego development as with "the relation, not of the ego, but of the total Self to body, mother, and mother as representative of the world." The emphasis here is on what may be called the "Self functions," that is to say, centroversion, automorphism, and the ego-Self-axis of identity.

The stages of ego development are taken up in chapter 5, which is in part a recapitulation of the first four chapters, as well as an extension into later stages of development. For a frame of reference I would direct the reader's attention to the little outline of stages of ego development on page 139. Two useful additions to this list would be some guidelines as to the child's approximate age at each of these stages, and the inclusion of the earliest pre-ego substage of development. Neumann makes it clear that as he sees it, the first stage—the phallic-chthonian with its two substages—encompasses the period from birth to twelve to fourteen months of age. It would be appropriate to add the uroboric state as the first of *three* substages of the phallic-chthonian. We then would have the substages: (a) uroboric from birth to two or three months, (b) vegetative from two or three months to six or seven months, and (c) animal from six or seven months to twelve to fourteen months. As for other age dating, I might suggest that the magic-phallic is roughly sixteen months to four years of age, while the magic-warlike is approximately age four to six or seven years. The solar-warlike and the solar-rational encompass the periods of seven to twelve, and twelve through adolescence, respectively. These age datings are approximations and may vary considerably in individual cases.

Many of Neumann's terms are, of course, taken from mythology as well as archaeological and religious historical sources. They are evocative on the one hand and off-putting on the other. For example, the symbol of the uroboros is most often represented by the circular image of a snake with its tail in its mouth. But in *The Origins and History of Consciousness*, the frontispiece, entitled "The Uroboros," shows the infant god Vishnu holding his foot to his mouth as he sucks on one of his toes. It suggests that the infant while sucking its fingers or toes incarnates the image of the mythic uroboros. As a symbol of the remote past the uroboros represents the "wholeness" of that state of consciousness in which self and other are undifferentiated, a state characteristic of the initial pre-ego stage. In the same light we may understand the infant's behavior in the discovery of sucking its thumb as representing the first synthesis of the psyche following upon the rude disruption of life within the womb, an existence that had represented a paradisiacal absorption in the purely unconscious processes of life. The natural process of uniting thumb and mouth seems to be an important early developmental event. Not only the mouth, but the thumb, too—inner and outer—reverberates to the pleasurable, self-comforting sensations of rhythmic sucking.

Following the uroboric state (birth to two or three months) are the later phallic-chthonian stages, the Mistress of the Plants and the Mistress of the Animals. These terms may easily evoke images of the early stages of infancy when the child is at first in a largely vegetative state and then gradually becomes more active and is able to sit up and eventually to walk. On the other hand the term *phallic-chthonian*, which encompasses these two substages, is hardly an everyday term and requires the definition and amplification that Neumann provides. Still it remains an unwieldy phrase, not immediately evocative of the child's overall behavior during that period of development. Similarly with the *magic-phallic* stage. This term is evocative in its magical implications, which are readily recognized in the behavior of the child as it progresses from the stage of consciousness of "pretend," around fourteen to sixteen months of age, to the stage of development of the symbol at about age three. As we know, this stage includes the beginings of such "magical" fantasies as the imaginary or symbolic companion. But here too implications of the term *phallic* may not be immediately self-evident to the observer of an infant's behavior. Connections to the mythological image of the phallus can be made if we follow Neumann's interpretations, though, and without question we can support the choice of the term by examples. (One of the most famous in depth psychology is Jung's dream at around four or five years of age of an "underground phallus on a golden throne.") The enormous creativity that children show once they have become conscious of their imagination is, of course, reason enough for a term that emphasizes <u>fecundity.</u> Moreover, once we have Neumann's concepts in mind, our understanding of the child's behavior may actually be enriched. It is at just such places in the book that we become aware of how much Neumann's perspective is influenced by his investigations of the mythological images reflecting the phylogenetic stages of development in human consciousness. Nothing I could say in further explication could be more productive than for the reader to turn to Neumann's *The Origins and History of Consciousness*. A perusal of that book in parallel with *The Child* could be particularly illuminating. Perhaps this little excursion into Neumann's mode of presentation throws some additional light on one of the more important qualities of this book, and of Neumann's approach to his subject: he seeks always to keep the reader in touch with the enormous significance he gives to the archetypal viewpoint and its representation in the images of mythology. The effort required of the reader is well worthwhile.

The Child offers an unexcelled opportunity for coming to grips with Neumann's basic viewpoint. The rewards are great, for in this work the ground plan for a comprehensive archetypal theory of human development has been laid down. In closing I can only agree with his lifelong friend and colleague Gerhard Adler, who wrote in the foreword to Neumann's *Creative Man*: "His work did not spring from his intellect [alone] but from a deep and living connection with the unconscious sources of creativity."

Louis H. Stewart

CHAPTER ONE

The Primal Relationship of Child to Mother and the First Phases of Child Development

The mother dominates the early development of the human individual just as the matriarchal world, in which the unconscious is paramount and ego-consciousness is still undeveloped, dominates the psychology of primitive cultures.

One of the fundamental characteristics that distinguish man from even his closest relatives among the animals, is that the human child, to employ Portmann's terminology,[1] must go through an extra-uterine as well as an intra-uterine embryonic phase. The young of the higher mammals are born in a state of relative maturity; either immediately or shortly after birth they are small adults which not only wholly resemble adult animals but are also capable of living unaided. In order to attain a similar state of maturity the human embryo would require a pregnancy of from twenty to twenty-two months. In other words the human child, after the nine months it spends in the womb, requires another year to attain the degree of maturity that characterizes the young of most other mammals at birth. Thus the whole first year of infancy must be assimilated to the embryonic phase. In addition to the one embryonic phase in which the child is psychically and physically integrated with the mother's body, there is a second, post-uterine, post-natal embryonic phase, in which the child has already entered into human society and, as its ego and consciousness begin to develop, grows into the language and customs of its group. This phase, which Portmann has termed the social uterine period, is characterized by the dominance of the primal relationship with the mother, who is at first the child's entire world and environment but, little by little, opens up new aspects of the world to the child's experience.

This basic phenomenon, specific to mankind, places the development of the child in a human context from the very start. The dependency of human existence is unique, because in the latter part of its embryonic life the human child is withdrawn from the maternal hands of nature and entrusted to the human mother. The child's primal relationship to its mother is more than a primary relationship, for thanks to this relationship the child, even before its "true" birth at the age of one year, is molded by human culture, since the mother[2] lives in a cultural collective whose language and values unconsciously but effectively influence the child's development. The attitude of the collective toward the child, its sex, individuality and development, can be a matter of life and death. The fact of being a girl, a boy, or a twin, the child's appearance, or the circumstances of its birth can, if negatively evaluated by the collective, prove just as disastrous to its future as an organic or psychic malformation.

Thus already in the pre-natal phase there is an evident adaptation to the collectivity with its attitude of acceptance or rejection toward the individual. But, side by side with this tendency to adapt, we encounter from the very outset the automorphism of the individual, his need to fulfill his constitutional and particular nature within the collectivity and if necessary independent of, or in opposition to it.

In attempting to formulate the laws governing the development of the personality, analytical psychology must devise a new terminology, because borrowing terms created by Freud and his school tends to blur the profound differences between our thinking and theirs. Up until now this need has been neglected by analytical psychologists, and the consequence has been a loss of clarity. Such corrections in terminology are necessary on theoretical grounds and moreover, the use of inadequate terms often leads to reductive interpretations of psychic phenomena and hence to misunderstandings which make a sound therapeutic approach difficult if not impossible.

In our endeavor to throw light on the primal child-mother relationship, we come to grips with the interconnection, central to child psychology, between the development of the ego and the development of the total personality.

Any discussion from the standpoint of analytical psychology of the development of the personality – and especially of the child personality – must start from the assumption that the unconscious comes first and that consciousness follows. The total personality and its directing center, the Self, exist before the ego takes form and develops into the center of consciousness; the laws governing the development of the ego and consciousness are dependent on the unconscious and on the total personality, which is represented by the Self.

We give the name of centroversion[3] to the psychic function of the totality, which in the first half of life leads, among other things, to the formation of a center of consciousness, which position is gradually assumed by the ego-complex. With this formation of a center, the Self establishes a "derivative" of itself, an "authority," the ego, whose role it is to represent the interests of the totality over against the particular demands of the inner world and the environment. Symbolically, the relationship of the ego to the totality-center is that of a son. In its relation to the development of the ego, the totality-center, or Self, is closely bound up with the parent archetype. In the first half of life, the psychology of the ego and consciousness predominates and the personality is centered in the ego and consciousness. In the individuation process of the second half of life there is a shift of accent from the ego to the Self. All these processes, as well as the amplification and synthesis of consciousness and the integration of the personality, come under the heading of centroversion.

Whereas the concept of centroversion applies to the interrelation of the personality centers, the concept of automorphism[4] embraces the development not so much of the psychic centers as of the psychic systems: consciousness and the unconscious. It concerns their relation to one another; for example, the compensatory relation of the unconscious to consciousness, and also the processes that take place only in the unconscious or only in consciousness but serve the development of the personality as a whole.

The primal child-mother relationship determines the first months of the child's life. It is the period in which the child ego is formed or at least begins to develop, in which the ego-nucleus, which was present from the start, grows and achieves unity, so that we may ultimately speak of a more or less unified child ego.

This earliest, pre-ego phase of existence is accessible to the adult only as a borderline experience, for our adult experience is normally an experience of the ego, contingent on the presence of consciousness, whereas the undeveloped state of the ego in this early period seems to make experience impossible. Only when the relations between ego and Self have become clearer, will it be understood that even in this earliest phase experience is possible and moreover that this early experience is of crucial importance for mankind as well as the individual.

We have elsewhere[5] described this phase as mythological reality and attempted to elucidate the symbols connected with it. The term uroboric has been selected for the initial pre-ego state, because the symbol of the uroboros, the circular snake, touching its tail with its mouth and so "eating" it, is characteristic of the oppositionless unity of this psychic reality. Thus the uroboros as the Great Round, in whose womb center the ego-germ lies sheltered, is the characteristic symbol of the uterine situation in which there is not yet a clearly delimited child personality confronting a human and extra-human environment. This undelimited state characteristic of the uterine embryonic situation is largely, though not fully, preserved after birth.

In the embryonic phase, the mother's body is the world in which the child lives, not yet endowed with a controlling and perceiving consciousness and not yet ego-centered; moreover, the totality-regulation of the child's organism, which we designate by the symbol of the body-Self,[6] is, as it were, overlaid by the mother's Self.

At the same time, those factors in the embryo that we look upon as constitutional and individual develop in accordance with the autonomy of the child's individual Self; but this automorphic development is embedded in the alien reality of the mother, which acts upon the embryo as a superordinate reality. It is only with the conclusion of the post-uterine embryonic phase that we can demonstrate the full establishment of the authority which analytical psychology terms the individual Self.

To the earliest biologically grounded manifestation of the Self we have given the name: body-Self. It is the delimited and unique totality of the individual, now freed from its embeddedness in the maternal body; it comes into being with the biopsychic unity of the body.

With the birth of the body the child's bond with its mother is in part severed, but the significance of the second embryonic phase specific to man is precisely that after birth the child remains in a sense an embryo, in other words, that it remains partially captive to its primal, embryonic relationship to its mother. It has not yet become itself. The child becomes fully itself only in the course of this primal relationship, which process is normally completed only after the first year of life.

In the pre-ego stage characteristic of earliest childhood, in which the ego and consciousness are still in the process of development, the polarized experience of the world with its subject-object dichotomy is not yet present. This childhood experience, which is that of every individual, is the ontogenetic embodiment of the primal unitary reality in which the partial worlds of outside and inside, objective world and psyche do not exist. In this post-natal embryonic phase the child is still contained within its mother though its body is already born. In this phase there is a primary unity of mother and child. In coming-to-itself the child emerges from this unity with its mother to become an individual subject confronting the world as thou and as object.[7]

But this reality encompassing mother and child is not only a psychic reality but also a unitary reality, in which what our differentiating consciousness terms "inside" and "outside" are identical for the child. Just as for the ego, for example, there is an immediate connection between the will to perform a movement and its execution, so for the child a need or a discomfort such as hunger or cold is linked to its satisfaction or appeasement by the mother. This unity on which the child's existence depends consists in a biopsychic identity between body and world, in which child and mother, hungry body and appeasing breasts, are one.

Normally the child rests secure in this unitary reality. When a tension arises, it signals by screaming; the need is more or less quickly satisfied and the tension relieved, whereupon the child sinks back into sleep.

Even later, during the first month of life, as the ego more and more frequently achieves an insular consciousness – first for brief moments, then for longer periods – and gets its bearings in the world, there is still no differentiation between its own body and the mother who brings pleasure and dispels displeasure. For the child ego, with its experience of pleasure and displeasure, world-experience *is* experience of the mother whose emotional reality determines its existence. For the child in this phase the mother is neither outside nor inside; it does not experience her breasts as alien and outside, or its body as its own. As in the uterine phase, child and mother are still so intermeshed as to be one; they form a dual union.

In mythological terms, the ego is still contained in the uroboros, and the environing mother is, for the embryo, containing vessel and world in one.

The child's still undifferentiated body image is as large and un-delimited as the cosmos. Its own sphere is so fused with the world and hence with everything that we call the outside, that it may well be termed cosmic in scope. Only as its ego develops, does the child gradually come to differentiate its own body image, and concomitantly the world takes on clarity, as an object confronting the ego. In his *Notes on the Body Image and Schema*, Clifford Scott writes: "A part of the body image is a constantly changing world schema, whose extreme limits must concern themselves with what can only be termed the limits of space and time."[8]

The dual union of the primal relationship is cosmic and trans-personal because the child has neither a stable ego nor a delimited body image. It is a unitary reality not yet separated into inside and outside, subject and object. It is all-encompassing. In this primal relationship the mother, too, lives like the child in an archetypally determined unitary reality, but only a part of her enters into it, because her relationship with her child governs only

a part of her total existence. The infant, however, is totally embedded in this realm, in which the mother represents for it both
world and Self.

With the observation that in the embryonic phase the mother is
also the child's Self, we come up against a difficulty: we are
obliged to assume that in the first phase of the primal relationship
there is — from the standpoint of our consciousness — a two-fold
child-Self. If we take the notion of a post-natal embryonic phase
seriously, we are obliged to say that the child becomes a Self, an
individual totality, only at the end of a year, at the end of the
entire intra- and extra-uterine embryonic stage. Until then, because of the child's containment in the unitary reality, we have a
situation that is paradoxical from the standpoint of consciousness.

On the one hand, there is the child's body-Self,[9] determined by
the species and arising concomitantly with the individual body-
totality; on the other hand, the mother, in the primal relationship,
not only plays the role of the child's Self, but actually *is* that Self.
But the body-Self also has the character of a totality and should
not be taken as a mere physiological entity, for bodily disposition
and psychic disposition, hereditary constellation and individuality,
are already present in the biopsychic unity of the body-Self.

From the standpoint of our differentiated consciousness, the
structure of the adult Self always implies an I—thou relationship.
The ego experiences the Self as an opposite, which within the
psyche is manifested as the Self center and outside it as world
and fellow man or the projection of an archetypal image. This
means that the Self has an Eros character which determines a
man's entire development and which may be described as individuation, as relation, and as a change of relation. Thus, paradoxically, the Self is that which is most our own, but at the same
time it takes the form of a "thou"; for our consciousness, it is the
individual center of the personality, but at the same time it
possesses a universally human and cosmic character. This paradoxical twofold nature of the Self is manifested in early childhood;
as the child's "very own," the Self is the body-Self as "thou," it
is the mother.

In the first phase of childhood the thou-relatedness of the Self is
"given," and from our standpoint externalized, in the mother — but

here we must bear in mind that this concept of an outside contained in the notion of externalisation is actually inappropriate to the cosmic situation of the child. However, since we can describe the unitary reality of the primal relationship only as a relationship between two persons, mother and child, our formulation cannot be adequate to the actual situation.

Because the early, uroboric phase of child development is characterized by a minimum of discomfort and tension, and a maximum of well-being and security, as well as by the unity of I and thou, Self and world, it is known to myth as paradisiacal. By contrast, the situation of the human adult is necessarily one of suffering. Because the adult ego, as the subject of experience is identical neither with his Self (his own totality), nor with the thou (his fellow men and environment), it must develop amid complex tensions between antithetical poles of Self and thou.

The situation of tension arising from the separation between psychic systems — consciousness and the unconscious — is normal for the adult. Simultaneously with this constellation there occurs a polarization of the total personality between the two centers — the ego as center of consciousness and the Self as center of the total psyche embracing consciousness and the unconscious — and hand in hand with it a polarization of the world into inside and outside. The ego stands between the Self and the world, and the automorphous development of the total personality is dependent on the attitude of the ego toward the inside as well as the outside, toward the Self as well as the world.

But in the uroboric situation of the pre-ego period, in which the ego still lies dormant or emerges only for isolated moments, these oppositions and tensions do not exist. Because, for the embryo, no opposition between ego-Self and maternal environment is possible and the mother is at once thou and Self, the unitary reality of paradise prevails in the early post-natal situation. In the post-uterine as well as the uterine situation the child is sheltered in the containing round of maternal existence, because for the child the mother is Self, thou and world in one. The child's earliest relationship with its mother is unique because here — and almost exclusively here — the opposition between automorphous self-development and thou-relation, which fills all human existence with tension, does not normally exist. Therefore, experience of this phase, which sets its imprint on all future development and is of particular importance for the psychology of creative individuals, is a source of lasting nostalgia, which can have a progressive as well as regressive effect on the adult.[10]

Only if we correctly interpret the symbolism of the uroboric state of containment "in the Round" can we understand why the term autism is inapplicable to this phase. Because the ego has not yet developed, the relatedness and Eros-character of the primal relationship is manifested cosmically and transpersonally and not personally. That is why Paradise and Original Home, Round, Ocean or Pond are among the symbols of the remote past. Containment in this cosmic world is an expression of the embryonic form of pre-ego existence, in which the containing mother is manifested in the symbols of an encompassing reality, namely, the unitary reality. The term autism, signifying a state in which the object is totally absent, is intelligible only from the standpoint of the subject-object relation of the adult ego. It ceases to be correct once we understand the primary unitary reality of the embryonic pre- and post-natal primal relationship. In the post-uterine phase of existence in unitary reality, the child lives in a total *participation mystique*, a psychic mother-fluid in which everything is still in suspension and from which the opposites, ego and Self, subject and object, individual and world have yet to be crystallized. That is why this phase is associated with the "oceanic feeling" which repeatedly makes its appearance even in adults when unitary reality complements, breaks through, or replaces everyday conscious reality with its polarisation into subject and object.

In Psychoanalysis the antithesis between the psychic situation of the infant and the object-relatedness of the later ego is explained with the help of such concepts as "identification" and "primary narcissism." By contrast to these, terms such as "adualism" (Baldwin) and "dual union" (Szondi) express the primary situation of the child with precision. Analytical psychology employs the more universal terms *participation mystique* and "unconscious identity" (Levy-Bruhl). As formulated in these terms the psychic situation of the infant is interpreted not as an *act* of identification, but as an unconscious identity, that is, as a passive state.

We speak of identifications and acts of identification only when a developed ego is already present. Such identifications do actually occur for example in all initiation rituals. The initiating authority consciously brings about an identification with the ancestors, the totem animal, etc. But when we speak of unconscious acts of identification, we unjustifiably project the activity of our ego upon the unconscious, which is in reality characterized by a primary identity, that is, an identity which is simply present as such. In this sense, the dual union of the primal relationship is a constellation of identity, *not* an identification of a not-yet-existing child ego with the mother. This "being-present-as-such" is, precisely, characteristic both of the unitary reality and of existence in a non-subjective cosmic state.

Consequently the primary Eros-character of the primal relationship – in which first an interpretation, then a coexistence and confrontation are inherent in the life of the species, so that the entire existence of the child depends on the realization of this Eros constellation – is the direct opposite of Freud's primary narcissism or of any imaginable narcissism. Cogent as the reasons may seem that led Freud to set up an opposition between narcissism and object-relatedness, he misplaced the accents, for he failed to understand the apersonal relatedness constellation of the primal relationship. This relatedness – and this is what led Freud to formulate an opposition between narcissism and love of an object – is not a relation, for a relation presupposes both a subject and an object. Neither is present in the pre-ego phase of the primal relationship. This is what distinguishes the primal relationship from every other and later relationship. Nevertheless the Eros character of *participation*, or reciprocal relatedness, is stronger than is possible in any relationship that presupposes an opposite.

In analytical psychology, the uroboric stage of child development with all the archetypal implications described in my *Origins and History of Consciousness* corresponds to the phase of primary narcissism, the still objectless state of the infant personality. In the present book, accordingly, I no longer employ the term narcissism positively as well as negatively as I still did to some extent in the *Origins and History of Consciousness*, but reserve it for a specific negative attitude and development of the ego.

In the dual union of the primal relationship there is still no intrapsychic tension between ego and Self. The development of the later ego-Self axis of the psyche and the communication and opposition between ego and Self are initiated by the relationship between mother and Self and the child as ego. At this point, the fusion of mother and child, Self and ego, is dominated by the constellation of mutual relatedness and dependency on Eros. Thus when we speak of a duplication of the Self in the primal relationship, we are attempting to express from the standpoint of our polarising consciousness, the paradoxical situation prevailing in the primal relationship. At the same time we wish to throw light on the dynamic relationship between mother and child and upon the development of the child ego and personality within this relationship.

The primal relationship is the foundation of all subsequent dependencies, relatedness and relationships. Whereas dual union is guaranteed by nature in the uterine embryonic phase, it emerges after birth as the first need of the mammal and especially of the human child. That is why in all living creatures who come into being inside a mother, the dependency of the small and infantile on the large containing vessel stands at the beginning of all existence.

To our differentiating consciousness, the duplication is manifested by the fact that the psychobiological totality of the child, its body-Self, is the automorphous foundation of its development. At the same time the mother's existence is the absolute life-giving and life-regulating precondition of infant existence, which alone makes its development possible.

Here again the concept of unitary reality, a reality transcending the separation into body and psyche, inside and outside, must be invoked. In this sphere the psyche is so linked with the body and the world that psyche, body and world are not yet distinguishable from one another. Thus in the child's primal relationship with its mother, that which consciousness later tries to keep apart and distinguish as opposites – the physical and the psychic, the bio-psychic and the objective – are one. At first sight one might suppose, with Freud, that the body-Self is the representative of the organism and its unconscious, instinctual world, that the unconscious is the representative of the organism,[11] and that the mother represents the world as environment and human society. But in regard to the original situation such a division and classification is impossible. Body-Self and world are just as closely connected as are mother and psyche. What later appears to the ego as the unconscious, represents in equal degree the reaction of the biopsychic organism and the world contained in this reaction, for they are still indistinguishable.

The actual situation is archaic and therefore difficult for our consciousness to understand. We simplify it by separating it into inside and outside which is so satisfying to our consciousness. Only at the end of its post-uterine embryonic development, when the child is definitely born, does it live as an individual endowed with an ego that has already begun to react distinctly in a world separated from it and confronting it. Only then does the mother, as world, become environment or unconscious. But in this phase the individual has already attained his total Self. The body-Self and the relatedness-Self, present in the mother, have become one.

In the course of the child's development the Self incarnated in the mother of the primal relationship, or, to formulate it more cautiously, the functional sphere of the Self incarnated in the mother, which in the primal relationship becomes formative experience for the child, must gradually "move" into the child. The independence of the child as ego and individual, begins at the conclusion of the post-uterine embryonic phase and coincides with its emergence from the strict confines of the primal relationship. The child then becomes open to other relationships, an ego inwardly and outwardly confronting a thou. Only then, with the partial dissolution of the *participation mystique* between child and mother, does the child cease to be merely a body-Self and becomes an individual totality, possessed of a total Self and open to relationships.

With his "true" birth the human individual becomes, quite characteristically, not only an individual of his species but also a part of his group. Not only is the child now "itself," but this "itself" is at the same time manifested both inwardly and outwardly as an I—thou relationship. From now on the ego-Self axis, the relation of the ego to the Self, makes its appearance as a fundamental inner phenomenon of the psyche, while outwardly the separation between I and thou, subject and object becomes discernible both as a relation to the thou and as a relation to the world as an opposite.

For the sake of simplicity we speak of a total Self, which is consolidated only at the conclusion of the embryonic period. In it the unity of the body-Self with the relatedness-Self externalized in the mother is achieved. Thus these are not parts, but aspects of the Self which are present from the outset but become discernible only in the course of development.

Analytical psychology attributes to the Self, as the totality of the individual, the quality of a datum given *a priori* and unfolding in the course of life. This "givenness" of individuality has its parallels in such concepts as entelechy and monad or in the astrological belief that the horoscope determined by the unique moment of birth corresponds to the uniqueness of the individual his constitutional predisposition and his latent possibilities.

This manner of thinking seems to conflict with the genetic, evolutionary view, according to which the personality is an historical product molded by the conditions of its environment. The one view puts the accent on a datum which comes to grips with the outside world, the other on the constitutive action of the environment, which shapes the living creature. Both views are typologically one-sided; only taken together can they encompass the whole truth.

We cannot speak of an identification in the pre-ego and early-ego phase. Likewise we should not confuse the moving of the Self (which has been externalized in the mother) into the child with a process of introjection, even though this phenomenon is the prototype of all subsequent introjective process. In reality, introjection occurs only when the polarization between I and thou, subject and object, inside and outside has developed sufficiently for us to speak of taking in something that is outside. This occurs, for example, when a child who has already developed ego-consciousness — i.e. is in the patriarchal phase — takes traits of the individual, personal father figure and introjects them into its superego. But in the initial constellation everything is present both inside and outside or neither inside nor outside, so that there can be no question of externalization or introjection.

The removal of the mother's Self from the field of unitary reality goes hand in hand with the gradual dissolution of the dual union characteristic of the primal relationship. As the child approaches the end of the post-uterine embryonic phase and becomes a human individual, not only has its body-Self fused with the Self externalized in the mother to form a total Self, but moreover the ego has developed beyond its germinal stage and achieved a certain continuity with the child's developing consciousness.

With the consolidation of its ego, the child gradually enters into the development of consciousness, culminating, finally in the polarization of the adult consciousness. But up to this final stage the child must pass through archaic phases which we can also trace back through the history of all human consciousness. Here, however, we shall not be concerned with this gradual development from archaic-magical to abstract-objectifying thought, but rather with the relationship between the developing ego and the total Self, which has established itself through the union of the body-Self with the Self that was present in the mother.

This relationship between the ego and the Self is of crucial importance for the development and sound functioning of the psyche. We call it the ego-Self axis. When we say that the ego is based on the Self or that the ego is a derivative of the Self, we are again referring to a function of centroversion. In other words, we are stating a condensation of the phenomenon that the total personality (for which the Self stands as a necessarily hypostatized center) directs, controls and balances all the processes leading to the emergence of the child ego and its development into an adult ego.

The child's need to preserve the dual union of the primal relationship is almost identical with its instinct of self-preservation, for its existence is wholly dependent on the mother. But this is not merely organic and material; as we now know, it does not relate exclusively to care and feeding.[12] Loss of the mother or of the person substituting for her is felt less in the bodily than in the psychic sphere. It is also manifested in loss of contact with the world, in impairment of the child's automorphism and instinct of self-preservation, and in the destruction of the first beginnings of an ego-development.

The primal relationship is an expression of total relatedness, as is strikingly demonstrated by the fact that its loss of it can provoke emotional disturbances culminating in apathy, idiocy or even death for a child. The loss of mother is infinitely more than the loss of a source of food. For an infant—even if it continues to be well fed—it is identical with loss of life. The presence of a loving mother who supplies insufficient nourishment is by no means as disastrous as that of an unloving mother who supplies plenty of nourishment.

This has nothing to do with blood kinship, for the true mother is more or less replaceable by a figure playing an analogously affective role. In other words, it is not the personal individual, but the generically maternal that is the indispensable foundation of the child's life. The mother of the primal relationship is the "good Great Mother." She is the being who contains, nourishes, protects and warms the child, and who is affectively bound to it. She is the foundation not only of its physical but also of its psychic existence. She gives security and makes life in this world possible. In this sense she is anonymous and transpersonal, in other words archetypal, as the one part of a specifically human constellation which operates between her and the child. Her unconsciously directed behavior, which enables her to coincide with the mother archetype, is vitally necessary to the normal development of the child.

For this reason excessive individual deviations from the norm, either in a good or in a bad sense, are harmful. The effects of too much or too little attention to the child are equally negative. Disturbances in the mother's life, illnesses, psychological shocks and disorders are deviations from the archetypal constellation of the primal relationship and can impair or halt the child's development. The physical aspect, nourishment for instance, is not a mere symbol for a psychological factor, although in this domain every physical fact is also symbolically significant; nor do psychic factors, such as tenderness, merely stand for the physical, although no psychic factor is without its physical correspondence.

The fusion of the child with the mother in the primal relationship and the cosmic character of the field in which the primal relationship operates have special consequences for the development of the child personality as an individual whole. The primal relationship has as its field a system of relatedness with mother and child as its poles; but in the pre-ego phase of child development this field is also a reality independent of the poles. The primal relationship, as a specifically archetypal constellation, embraces both individuals in its transparent reality, each pole – mother and child – appearing to the other and acting upon it as an archetype. This basic archetypal situation guarantees the formative functioning of the primal relationship with all its vital consequences for child development.

To speak of the cosmic character of the body-image, in which the child is fused into a unity with mother and world, is equivalent to saying that the primal relationship takes place in a unified field where there is no bodily delimitation as symbol of individualization. The *participation mystique* between mother and child orients each through the other. The child unconsciously "reads" the mother's unconscious in which it lives, just as – normally – the mother exerts a regulative action by reacting unconsciously to the unconscious behavior of the child.

Here the psyche is not yet incorporated in an individual body, but is suspended in the field of the unitary reality which contains within it something that is in a sense pre-psychic and pre-physical, that is still psychic and physical in one.

This union with the mother is dissolved only gradually, as the child's individuality and ego-consciousness develop. C. G. Jung attributes many of the disorders of the child psyche to psychic disorders of the parents. This means that, up to puberty, there is normally a partially unconscious union between child and parents, especially the mother.

The situation of *participation mystique* is expressed for example in the fact that a state of anxiety in the mother imparts itself to the child without the need of any direct or indirect communication. Whereas in analytical psychology the identity-constellation of the primal relationship, and the development of the ego out of it, play an important and perhaps crucial role. Sullivan concentrates almost exclusively on the transmission of anxiety from mother to child.[13] Actually this *participation mystique* is manifested in a number of otherwise incomprehensible phenomena that have been reported by patients suffering from schizophrenia.

If, as now seems probable, certain forms of schizophrenia signify a regression to the phase of the primal relationship,[14] we can readily understand why, in states of agitation, schizophrenics should participate in the inner conflicts of those around them,[15] why, as has been widely reported, they show an extraordinary awareness of the therapist's unconscious, and why they are often more capable than normal persons of understanding their fellow invalids' unconscious and its symbolism.[16] This is merely to mention in passing isolated occurrence of authentic parapsychological phenomena in schizophrenia.[17]

These phenomena based on *participation mystique*[18] confirm the Eros-character of this phase in which the centering of the psychophysical individual personality of the child is not yet complete, or, as in regressive psychic disorder, in which it is suspended.

The bond of dual union is a specific situation in which a not yet individualized being in the pre-ego stage is joined with a transpersonally, archetypally functioning being in a unified field.

A mother with her child evokes the image not of an individual woman with her individual child but of an archetype common to all mankind. From time immemorial men have been deeply stirred by this fact and looked upon it as suprapersonal. To the consciousness of the mother, to be sure, a child is of course also something individual which belongs to her own destiny. Yet in the reality of the primal relationship as she experiences it, every mother is *the* mother, every child is *the* child, and the relationship between them is *the* primal relationship, which is "realized" according to an archetypally prescribed pattern.

The fact that the control and regulation of child development are at first exerted exclusively by the mother, who represents the Self, does not refer to the mother as ego and individual. It is precisely her average-human, largely unconscious and instinctive behavior within the primal relationship which guarantee the human development of the child and the child ego. When we speak of the transpersonal role of the mother manifested in the primal relationship, we are referring precisely to her unconscious, instinctive reactions, for instinct is not individual but a product of the collective unconscious. The largely instinctive reactions of the mother are the essential foundation of the primal relationship. They guarantee the stability and self-evident character of the Eros-bond attaching the mother to her child, and even in the animal world express themselves in tenderness, readiness to make sacrifices, and the will to defend the life of the young.

The mother constellates the archetypal field and evokes the archetypal image of the mother in the child psyche, where it rests, ready to be evoked and to function. This archetypal image evoked in the psyche[19] then sets in motion a complex interplay of psychic functions in the child, which is the starting point for essential psychic developments between the ego and the unconscious. These developments, like those embedded in the organism, remain relatively independent of the mother's individual behavior, provided that the mother lives with her child in accordance with her archetypal role.[20]

In man these reactions are also provoked in accordance with the system that largely dominates the animal world: an instinctive process is set up by a specific "stimulus pattern."

Thus it has been discovered that the typical form of the baby's head sets the human parental instinct in motion. The conditions are: "A short face in relation to a large forehead, prominent cheeks, deficient body movements."[21] Where these features are present—even in young animals—they release tender parental feelings; where they are lacking, this reaction is absent. Unquestionably we still have much more to learn about these instinctive phenomena which are always the expression of an archetypally determined relationship between individuals of the same species.

Whereas in the first phase of the primal relationship the mother appears as the containing and nourishing world, the second phase is characterized by the distinctly human form of the mother archetype. Here again, to be sure, the mother is an archetype, not only a personal, individual mother; that is, she is the *Great* Mother and Mother Goddess; but at the same time she has become a human mother. The functions that were previously performed by the anonymous, formless world in which the still undelineated child "floated" – the functions of containing, nourishing, warming and protecting – are now humanized. That is, they are experienced in the person of the mother who, at first in isolated moments, then continuously, is experienced and known as an individual human being. Only gradually as the child slowly develops into a persona- lity endowed with ego-consciousness does it begin to perceive the mother as a personal, individual figure, and become a subject whose object is the mother. Even then the mother remains all-powerful; the primal relationship is still the entire field of the child's life, until the child becomes individualized and its ego develops. Then an I-thou relationship comes into being.

In the cosmic-anonymous phase, the primal relationship wholly determines the child's feeling of existence in the world, but as the mother becomes a superhuman individual, the child's social existence begins. In the uroboric phase of the primal relationship, mother and child form a dual union within the unitary reality, but from this point on the normal development of the child depends on the ability of its Self and ego to break away, little by little, from the unity of the primal relationship. Now the child's auto-morphous development and specific predispositions come to the fore. The mother archetype remains dominant, which means that the child's development at this stage still depends on the mother-child relationship. But now the child emerges more and more from the maternal sphere to take root in a universally human world.

CHAPTER TWO

Primal Relationship and Development of the Ego-Self Relationship

Just as the general development of the child's body depends on nourishment by the mother, so the development of its psyche, of its ego-Self relationship depends on the psychic nourishment given by the mother figure. In this context, the primal relationship provides the child with four essential types of experience.

Where child and mother still form an undifferentiated identity, the primal relationship stands at once for the child's relations to its own body, to its Self, to the thou, and to the world. The primal relationship is the ontogenetic basis for being-in-one's-own-body, being-with-one Self, being-together, and being-in-the-world.

As we have seen, the undisturbed primal relationship of the postuterine embryo (in which the child's Self, externalized, is still with the mother), is characterized by the tensionless paradise-situation of the original unity between mother and child. The child is embedded in a soft containing vessel which represents mother, world, body and Self in one. Its natural existence is one of slumber and peace, almost as in the uterine phase. The symbolism connected with this phase is: satiety, warmth, security and total containment in the sheltering maternal vessel.

Ego-arousing disturbances — hunger, thirst, cold, wetness and pain — are regulated and compensated almost at once by the mother who represents the Self, so that the security and slumbering harmony and identity of world-thou and body-Self are always restored.

The relatedness or unrelatedness of the mother to the child's biopsychic unity is of crucial importance, not only for this unity but also for the child's earliest ego-formation, because the child's independent consciousness and the positive and negative forms of its ego reactions are closely bound up with its body experience. Tenderness, satiety and pleasure confer a feeling of security and of being wanted, which is the indispensable foundation for positive social behavior and a sense of security in the world, and for the earliest and most indispensable confirmation of the child's independent being. The instinct of self-preservation expressed in the drive to take food is the most fundamental of all drives; it is manifested of course through the body and is essentially an experience of the body. Among humankind it is inseparably bound up with the mother, and this constellates the inseparability of the automorphism and thou-relationship which is characteristic of the earliest human development.

It lies in the very nature of automorphism that from the very start large quantities of libido are directed toward the child's independent development. As the ego becomes independent, it is oriented toward this development, and this should not be regarded as an infantile, much less a pathological tendency. The equilibrium characteristic of the normal primal relationship, before the parts and nucleus of the ego have joined to form a conscious ego, already implicitly contains the productive tension out of which a healthy personality develops between the I and thou.

We have elsewhere[1] spoken of the importance of the body-Self and the metabolic symbolism of the uroboric phase for primitive psychology and for the mythology and rites of mankind, and have pointed out that this phylogenetic phase has its ontogenetic correspondence in earliest childhood. The body-Self, the totality of biopsychic unity, is a regulative authority which operates in the interest of wholeness and almost exclusively directs the child's biopsychic development, including its progression through archetypally conditioned phases. In the earliest stage, as we have seen, the mother as externalized Self, as relatedness-Self, complements the child's body-Self. In the unitary reality characteristic of the primal relationship, they are as yet undifferentiated.

One of the essential difficulties in child development is that the ego must gradually be located in the child's own unique, individual body. This process, which goes hand in hand with the development of the child ego, accounts for the extraordinary importance of all body experience in the first phase of childhood.

Hand in hand with this process goes the withdrawal of the Self from the mother to the person of the child, a development with whose completion the earliest form of child autonomy is achieved; it is with this formation of a unitary Self that the human child is truly born.[2] In the primal relationship the experience of the child-personality takes place largely, though not entirely, on the body level, through the bodies of both child and mother. Therefore the elementary body functions are the foci proper of experience: breathing, screaming, swallowing, urinating and defecating on the active side, and on the passive side being warmed, caressed, cleaned and bathed. The surface of the body with its erogenous zones is the principal scene of the child's experience both of itself and of others; that is, the infant still experiences everything in its own skin. The skin, where the infant comes into contact with the outside world, is the field of its world-experience, and the over-accented alimentary tract with its oral intake zone and its anal-urethral ejection zone, is the field of its inner experience. These border zones in which the exchange between inside and outside takes place are very active and the child becomes extremely conscious of them. Against the background of a generally pleasure-accented total body feeling and an alimentary pleasure which is co-ordinated with the alimentary drive and gives the whole body a sense of fulfillment amounting to alimentary orgasm (Rado), body zones gradually separate out as concentration points of experience.

Because the first phase of child development is dominated by the instinct of self-preservation and the drive to self-development, the accent is on nutritive symbolism for nourishment is not only the concrete substance from which the body is built, but at the same time signifies life, the joy of life and the intensification of life. Thus mother's milk is far more than concrete nourishment. It is the symbol of a friendly world and, what amounts to the same thing, of the archetype of the Great Good Mother. It symbolizes the essence of the positive dual union and is nourishment, appeasement of thirst, security, warmth, protection, pleasure, not-being-alone, relatedness, the overcoming of pain and discomfort, the possibility of rest and sleep, a sense of being at home in the world and in life as a whole.

In stressing the oral and anal zones, Freud recognized the importance of the alimentary tract, its entrance and exit. But confining his theory to erogenous zones and describing the constellation of drives connected with these zones as a preliminary phase of sexual development, proved quite inadequate. Only if the connection between the bio-psychic development specific to man and the corresponding symbolism is understood, can the connection between the archetypally conditioned phase on the one hand and the development of the ego and the Self on the other become clear.

"Milk" of course pertains to the oral sphere, but oral is here a symbol for all exchange with the world. The mouth has cosmic and later social implications that go far beyond the local, concrete and material significance of an erogenous mucous membrane zone. Like the whole body, but especially its accented zones, the mouth in this phase – and to a considerable extent later on as well – is a psychological unity. It is part of a symbolic world and of a symbolic apperception of the world. It is no accident that the kiss as expression of an inter-human situation is something other than a stimulation of the mucous membrane. The decisive factor of the kiss remains the fundamental symbolic experience of a coming to the outside, to the world, to the thou – and a connection with the thou.

Receiving and taking-in, or eating, is connected with the mouth as are breathing and speaking. Not only are sucking and licking oral, but babbling, speaking and singing as well. Hence when something is said to be oral, this is not, as the Psychoanalysts believe, the expression of an infantile stage of the libido, but marks the emergence of an archetypal symbol-world of fundamental importance. In the infant, of course, this world is just coming into being and is closely bound up with its existence; but in *all* human existence, it retains, in the spiritual as well as the psychic sphere, a crucial symbolic significance that cannot be reduced to the infantile.

When we speak of the alimentary uroboros, we mean that for the infant the totality of human experience is manifested at the basic level of the alimentary drive and of alimentary symbolism. It cannot be stressed enough that eating and food – as the symbolism of language, myth, dream and fairy tale show time and time again – signify a manner of interpreting the world and integrating oneself with it.

As we have seen, an infant deprived of the mother – of the primal relationship – falls ill. This illness is not primarily physical but psychic, reflected in the gradual cessation of its interest in life; it cannot be cured by material feeding but only by restoration of the primal relationship that feeds its totality. Accordingly, when we say that the "body" of the primal relationship is symbolic and world-embracing, we are merely attempting to formulate the real, original unity of inside and outside, which is both phylogenetically and ontogenetically the reality of early man. It is our polarizing consciousness which first attempts – often very inadequately – to break down this unitary reality into physical and psychic, concrete and abstract elements.

For the ego, which at first "awakens" only by fits and starts from the torpor of a pre-ego existence, in response to intense charges of libido, reality exists only in isolated fragments. These fragments of reality must be heavily charged as it is their charge which brings them to the perception of the ego. Among the foci of reality in this early phase are the erogenous zones discovered by Freud; they might equally well be termed *gnoseogenous*, for they communicate not only pleasure, but also the *knowledge* of reality[3]. It is only by considering these phenomena in the light of the human situation as a whole that we can arrive at an adequate understanding of child development. Also in myth, ritual and language – which has retained its symbolic character to this day – the earliest knowledge of the world is expressed through the symbolism of the body.* To apprehend is to "take in" and "to eat";

---

* *Editor's note:* In German the basic roots of the following terms are clearly the same.

to understand is "to take in hand," "to digest" or "to assimilate";
to negate is "to reject" or "to eliminate" – and innumerable
other examples might be adduced of the body symbolism governing man's pristine knowledge of the world.[4]

This earliest knowing of the world and ego development in and
through the body occur in the closest union with the mother, not
only with her body which gives nourishment, warmth and protection, but also with the child's whole unconscious love for its
mother and the mother's whole conscious and unconscious love for
the child and its body. Because in the early phase of human
development love and knowledge, ego development and thou-
relationship are intimately linked, the primal relationship with
the mother is fateful also in this respect. A radical disturbance of
the primal relationship may lead to idiocy in the child,[5] while a
positive relationship provides an essential foundation – not the
only foundation to be sure – for the openness to the world
indispensable to the child's subsequent intellectual development. This is one more reason why the "Great Mother" in her
positive aspect is not only she who confers life and love but, in
her highest form, is Sophia, the goddess of knowledge and of
wisdom.[6]

In this phase the entire psychophysical process is still drawn into
the positive primal relationship and furthered by the mother as
Self. Normally there is as yet no division into a positive head-pole
and a negative lower pole embracing all the anal, urethral and
later genital processes, which comes to be questioned or even
rejected. In this phase all the biopsychic processes, the pleasure-
giving sucking as well as a good bowel movement, are still "love";
the entire body-Self with all its erogenous and gnoseogenous
functions is productive, a living source of pleasure and development for the child.

In this uroboric phase the experience of the body has a com-
pleteness that is never again attained, because here receptivity
and productivity and passivity, masculinity and femininity are
experienced at both poles of the body and connected with the processes of systole and diastole, the movements of intake and output.
Here the oral pole – like the head – plays a leading part, though
to the child the anal pole is equal in importance. The unitary

reality is directed by respiration as a link between inside and outside, and as the first self-evident movement of introversion and extraversion, and by screaming as a preliminary form of speech, for it is through screaming that the ego experiences an environment that relieves discomfort. In sucking and swallowing the inner world – which however is never experienced as a separate world – is experienced as warm, pleasurable and satisfying, so that here again extraversion is connected with an introversion that may be called a fulfillment in the truest sense of the word.

As we have known since Freud, the contrary anal pole is also of the utmost significance. Here however tension and release are not experienced only as discomfort and pleasure. The first feeling of exertion, accomplishment and production is bound up with the act of defecation, which in our culture is heavily stressed by mothers and consequently provides a positive source of stimulation. Though it is only recently that mothers have attached so much importance to their babies' bowel movements – and our knowledge of the child's metabolism surely has a good deal to do with it – the tenderness connected with infant care and the resulting intensification of anal stimulation are unquestionably as old as man himself.

But the anal pole is also essentially creative. On the body level, "to express oneself" has always meant to give out something from oneself, to create something material, a bit of world. We shall speak below of the later connection between this expression and childbearing. The tie between the self-expressive producer and his product is just as present at this stage as later when the tie between expression and the totality of body is reflected on other levels.

Ernst Cassirer has shown how in primitive man the experience of space and time is gained through orientation by the body and has placed the development of language, both in mankind and in the child, in the same context, namely, dependency on the fundamental experience of the body; or what we term the body-Self. Cassirer writes:

"It would seem as though logical and ideal relations became accessible to the linguistic consciousness only when projected into space and there analogically 'reproduced.' ... In the very first babblings of children a sharp distinction is evident between sound groups of essentially (centripetal) and essentially (centrifugal) tendency. The *m* and *n* clearly reveal the inward direction, while the explosive sounds *p* and *b*, *t* and *d* reveal the opposite trend. In the one case the sound indicates a striving back to the subject; in the other, a relation to the 'outside world', a pointing or rejection. The one corresponds to the gestures of grasping, of attempting to draw close, the other to the gestures of showing or thrusting away. By this original distinction we can account for the astonishing similarity between the first 'words' of children all over the world. And the same phonetic groups are found in essentially identical or similar functions when we inquire into the origin and earliest phonetic form of the demonstrative particles and pronouns in different languages."[7] Similarly Piaget pointed out that the child's experience of the world begins with the body and the symbolism of the body.

The main reason why it is so hard for us to know the world of the child, and especially of the baby and infant, is that its primary unitary reality is so fundamentally different from our polarized world of consciousness. We have pointed out that the world of primitive man is experienced primarily as an equation of body and world,[8] and that at this stage the feminine body, the body of the mother, appears as world body. Being "in the world" is originally experienced as a being "in something"; this containing vessel is the Great Mother who, in the guise of what we call nature, still seems to contain us.

The primary unitary reality is not merely something that precedes our experience; it remains the foundation of our existence even after our consciousness, grown independent with the separation of the systems, has begun to elaborate its scientifically objective view of the world.

We have often stressed the necessity of the development of consciousness; but we have also pointed out that conscious experience, with its necessary polarization into subjective and objective, represents the experience of only a limited segment of total reality. In other words: our clear, conscious vision apprehends a smaller area of reality than that accessible to the psychic wholeness which experiences the unitary reality.[9] The so-called objectification of consciousness is necessarily bound up with a loss of emotion and libido, the consequence of which is that in the last analysis we apprehend only dead fragments detached from the living whole.[10]

But the child lives in the world of the unitary reality, which is not yet divided into the oppositions characteristic of consciousness. Even after it has been physically born and its Self has moved from the mother into its own body-Self, it experiences the world in and through the primal relationship. "The whole universe," says Piaget, "is felt to be 'in communion' with and obedient to the self."[11] The truly magical relation between the infant's Self and the world is one of identity, of *participation mystique*. The child's Self is manifested as a body-Self, as the child's biopsychic totality, and the world is experienced as one with the child.

For the child, as for primitive man, everything that our consciousness looks upon as a quality or function is a physical thing, a substance, an embodiment. Accordingly, Piaget says of the child: "Reality is impregnated with the self and a thought is understood as if it belonged to the category of physical matter." It is only when we understand this equation of body-world-nature in its full scope and in its natural connection with the primal relationship that a true, and not reductive, approach to the psyche of the child, and of primitive man as well, becomes possible.

Initially the world is always mother-world; at the very outset in fact it is mother-body-world. Concerning the child's world, Melanie Klein writes: "The manifold things have lain within the mother's body"; and concerning the child's relation to the inside of its mother's body: "This part becomes an epitome of the whole person as an object and symbolizes at once the outside world and reality."[12] Here she has hit upon the body-vessel-world-equation of which we are speaking.

The mistake, however, which falsifies many of her findings and conclusions, is that she takes a concretistic view of the symbolic-mythological world of the child and of early mankind. Of course the child thinks its world is real; nevertheless it *is* a symbolic world. For this reason a child's utterances must always be taken as symbolic, not interpreted rationalistically from the standpoint of adult consciousness.[13] When, for example, a child expresses the desire to have, to possess, to introject the objects of the world, as in a desire to eat them, this should not be interpreted as aggressive sadism. The child does not want to eat up its mother – even if it expresses itself in such terms – but wants to take in, to grasp, to understand the world, which in this phase is not yet differentiated from the mother, in other words, to "eat" it.[14]

The symbolism of the first world experience derives largely from the alimentary drive; it is presexual and pregenital. In this phase almost everything is expressed with the help of alimentary symbolism, in oral and anal terms.

We have said that the child psyche apprehends mythologically, that it apprehends the world in categories known to us from myth. The child-like and mythological views of the world are so similar as to be almost identical,[15] and this applies especially to their conceptions of creation, generation and birth, to the kinship between child-like theories of birth and creation mythology.

Later on, the symbolism of the alimentary drive is sexualized; here the opposite occurs. If disappearing into the body is translated as eating, coitus, observed or described, can be interpreted as an eating of the penis by the mother and a feeding of the mother by the father. Such equations, characteristic of the language of the alimentary uroboros and perfectly natural in this early phase, can carry over into neuroses and psychoses, such as the anxiety neurosis centered round the fear that one's penis will be bitten off by the vagina. To the same level of alimentary symbolism belong all child-like – and primitive – theories which look upon impregnation as eating and childbirth as defecation.

We shall have more to say of anal symbolism and its connection with death, and later on with sin. Emphasis on the close, positive connection between the anal and the earth and its fertility is an essential foundation of all the rebirth rituals and some of the fertility rituals of mankind. Here we encounter the basic law that in psychic development the personal is almost always derived from the transpersonal and understood in terms of its symbolism. "The earth does not imitate woman," says Plato; "it is woman who imitates the earth." And this applies to the primary relationship between feces and the earth. As Adolf Jensen has shown, it is an essential belief of certain matriarchally accented agricultural cults that the fertility of the plant world presupposes the death and self-sacrifice of a god.[16] The connection between life and death centers

Basic Law

around the symbolism of decay, of darkness, of the earth, of the lower regions as the source of life. In decaying, the body "becomes earth," and from this same earth springs the living vegetation that men live on. The most perfect symbol of this context, originally belonging to the feminine earth-precinct, is the corpse of the slain Osiris, the Green One, from which the grain grows. Later, especially in the patriarchal world, the accent shifts to the luminous significance of the life-giving bread in its connection with the sun and the golden wheat, but originally the moldering darkness of death, the realm of the fruitful earth and the mother, are the dark womb of the mysteries. In alchemy the fertility myth is again repeated in the transmutation of rot to green and gold. The human body is just such a numinosum; for primitive man and for the child as well, feces are connected with the fertility symbolism of darkness.

In the child psyche, provided the lower pole has incurred no negative evaluation, the upper and lower poles of the body are equally accented, and this is characteristic of the first phase of the primal relationship. In this phase the accent is on the chthonic-matriarchal symbols and mysteries and not yet on those of the celestial, patriarchal world corresponding to the accentuation and overaccentuation of consciousness, which will become dominant in a later phase.

Just as each of the senses is a world in itself, just as later the motor system reaches out beyond the individual to create the entire world of technology, which is essentially nothing more than a prolongation of the first implement, the stick that the ape uses to lengthen its arm, so the oral and anal worlds are among the concentration points of the total body-world of the earliest phase of development. The pleasure of this phase has been rightly termed "alimentary orgasm," because it is an inner pleasure attaching to the whole alimentary tract from mouth to anus. For this experience, satiety is fulfillment-as-such, hunger is longing-as-such, because here the relatedness to the mother archetype with its emotional, automorphous and social implications is always at work. When we speak of psychic or spiritual hunger, we are harking back to this early phase in which hunger is still a single whole, because body, soul and spirit are still one and all these realms of life, which will later become differentiated and unfold, are still *enfolded* within the bud of the alimentary symbol.

It is neither a wild exaggeration nor a materialistic concretization to say that the "milk" of the Great Mother encompasses the supreme symbol, the "milk of Sophia" which feeds the philosophers;[17] such a statement merely expresses and draws the implications of a symbolic reality, valid for all levels of life, namely, that all individual beings and things are nurtured by the Great Mother of Life, without whose flowing abundance all existence must languish. Since ingestion, digestion and excretion are the fundamental alchemical conditions of all child growth and every transformation, sucking and swallowing, at this pregenital stage, become conception, while defecating becomes childbearing. For this reason the symbolism of the alimentary uroboros extends linguistically to the highest levels of spiritual life. The notions of assimilation, digestion and rejection, of growth and giving birth are, like innumerable symbols of this zone, indispensable to any description of the process of creation and transformation.

This bodily function, which is essential to the primal relationship and to child development, goes through phases characteristic of the human species. In the earliest, uroboric-pregenital phase, the alimentary drive and its symbolism are dominant. In its beginnings the truly sexual and genital development is also assimilated to this alimentary symbolism. For this reason we do not classify this phase under the head of child sexuality, because in it a specifically different symbolism prevails, arising in the main from a different drive, the alimentary drive. This phase like every other is all-embracing; it expresses everything in terms of its own symbolism. When later the genital organs achieve primacy and the sexual drive becomes dominant, a sexual symbolism arises which in turn apprehends and interprets everything from its own standpoint, that is, sexualizes it.

The later phase cannot be derived from the earlier. Sexuality is not a later differentiation of the alimentary drive, nor is the alimentary drive a preliminary stage of sexuality. It is characteristic of transitional states that the later, here the sexual phase, is at first apprehended through the symbolism of the former, in this case the alimentary phase. Accordingly, it is inadmissible to interpret the earliest, oral phase as sadistic. A man who bites something off when eating is no more a sadist than an ethnological cannibal. And this remains true regardless of the fact that at the later, sexual-stage of child development the contents and functions of the alimentary stage are sexualized. Eating as incorporation has nothing to do with castration, and the image of the good or bad mother, or of the good or bad breasts, does not arise through projection of the child's positive or aggressive feelings toward the mother, but is the expression of an objective situation unrelated to infantile aggression or sadism; these are always *secondary* in origin, the functional expression of a distressed ego.

When Melanie Klein writes: "The mother's body is therefore a kind of store house which contains the gratification of all desires and the appeasement of all fears . . ."[18] she is describing a genuine objective element in the primal situation, not an infantile projection. Similarly the image of the negative mother is a secondary anxiety-image of a dangerous distress situation produced by an unsatisfactory primal relationship and not a projection of primary infantile aggressions.

Only if we understand the development of the various phases and learn to distinguish the symbolisms pertaining to them can we arrive at a sound interpretation of the normal and abnormal psychic manifestation of the child and the adult. In the unitary reality phase the infant already begins to distinguish between itself and what is outside, and to take elements of the cosmos back into itself; thus it is understandable that the earliest consciousness of distinct individuality should develop by way of the skin, the surface which delimits the body from the outside world. But here again not only the child's ties with its mother but its growing independence as well is fashioned by the primal relationship. Constantly recurring contact with the mother's body gradually brings home the existence of the body-Self to the experience and consciousness of the ego-complex.

In man the motor functions develop only gradually and only gradually does the head pole, the seat of most of the senses and hence also of the ego, assert its preeminence. Normally, apart from pain resulting from illness, there is less feeling in the trunk of the body – that is why small children paint creatures consisting only of head and feet – while the entrance and exit of the alimentary tract are from the outset feeling-accented.

The indispensable basis for the development of the child ego is the figure of the mother as an archetypal Great Mother, who confers not only pleasure but also compensation, security and shelter. The ego, at first largely somnolent, emerging only in isolated impulses which gradually become more frequent, more active and independent as the child is differentiated from the mother, is characterized by a process of integration which the mother makes possible and of which she sets an example.

The fundamental experience of this phase as characterized by the Great Mother is one of shelteredness in the continuity of existence. The ego has perfect confidence in the self. The first polarising experiences, of pleasure and discomfort, inside and outside, for example, are safeguarded by a process of compensation provided by the mother-Self. Thus even tensions that bring discomfort are endured and integrated thanks to a confidence, unconscious of course and not perceived by the ego, that they will be relieved. For only in rare cases is the archetypal mother not willing or able to appease the child's tension and distress.

All active and passive body functions are embedded in this situation of shelteredness characteristic of the primal relationship and subject to the benevolent supervision of the mother who approves them. Not only are they attended by the biopsychic pleasure of tension and release; they are also, at least in our culture, which will alone concern us here, accompanied by the tender emotions of the mother, who as world and Self confers inner and outer security, and so confirms them.

Not only is the dominant constellation of security and confidence manifested in the unquestioned pleasant body-feeling that is essential to the sound development of the total personality; but it also has other vital consequences, such as a normally tensionless and fearless transition from waking to sleeping, in which the ego, with the natural confidence which is the foundation of the ego-Self axis in child and adult alike, suspends itself and entrusts itself to the Self. Even in its states of not-being-an-ego, the ego must be suspended in the sheltering wholeness of the Self and, though of course the ego does not reflect on the matter, this is one of the essential conditions for its existence. For this reason, and not only in children, difficulty in sleeping is often the expression of a deep-seated anxiety springing from a disturbance in the relationship between ego and Self and lack of the unconscious sense of confidence which is one of the essential conditions of health.

The primal relationship with the mother, and the child's containment in the mother, are the foundation not only of the child's relation to its body, but also of its relation to others. In this phase the security of the primal relationship does not yet involve a thou since, in the unitary reality, the boundaries between mother and child are not yet drawn and the two emerge only gradually as two related poles from this togetherness in dual union. Therefore, this initial sense of security is the foundation for the emotional relatedness indispensable to all social contact.

The significance of the body in the primal relationship, as the basis of all future social relations, extends far beyond the human sphere. Adolf Portmann has pointed out[19] that the elementary functions of the animal body provide the foundation for its social relations. The breathing organs are transformed into vocal organs, the warming garment of hair or feathers – and at a still earlier stage the coloration of the fishes – becomes an expression of mood; urine, feces and the secretions of the sebaceous glands have an important "character of communication." This is not to mention the social organs proper, which serve to orient and reorient the group.

Shelteredness in the primal relationship with the mother is the child's first and most pregnant social context. This takes on a particular significance at the stage when, with the consolidation of the ego, the Self that has been externalized must gradually be taken back into the child. Now shelteredness in the mother is no longer, as it was in the beginning, a shelteredness in the Self; it is also the thou and society as represented by this thou. Confidence in the mother is identical with confidence in the society she represents. Society is here a maternally sheltering world, and adaptation to the mother, to her guidance, her order, her commands and prohibitions takes place in emotional attunement to her affection and to the security provided by her as containing vessel. This basic matriarchal situation is determinant, regardless of whether or not we assume with Briffault[20] that, phylogenetically speaking, man developed into a special creature (*Homo sapiens*) in the matriarchal family group of mother and child. (This hypothesis does not conflict with what we know of the primary family.)

More clearly than any subsequent development the human infant's embeddedness in the primal relationship show that man's very existence is dependent on society, because in the primal relationship the mother represents society. Concerning animals, Portmann writes: "The attraction to those of like species precedes any tendency to turn away from them; solitary existence is a late flight from a natural bond."[21] Assuredly this is also true of human development. A child is prepared for life in society by its fundamental capacity for erotic relations in the broadest sense; and this preparation in turn is rooted in the shelteredness of the primal relationship, which is the foundation of every feeling of being at home in a social group.

A child's later personal relationship to its mother, as the basis for every subsequent love relationship and indeed of every human relationship, stands or falls with the primal relationship. Only the unquestioned sense of security conferred by shelteredness in a mother's love, which enables the developing child to endure unpleasant tensions during the process of differentiation, can enable it to endure the curtailment of infantile automorphism inevitably imposed by the process of growing into the world and society. Only through the experience that discomfort is relieved by compensation and appeasement, by the intervention of the Good Mother, does the child acquire the ability, so necessary for man and so characteristic of man, to endure prolonged unpleasant tensions and to develop its ego in such a way that it can endure such tensions while accepting the demands of society. The instinctive reaction would generally be to avoid discomfort or abbreviate it as much as possible. Thus the foundation of man's development as a social being is not hate – as the Psychoanalysts who fail to recognise the positive character of the primal matriarchal relationship suppose – but security; not anxiety and the withdrawal of love, but the positive primal relationship with the mother, in which security, emotional concern and love are predominant.[22]

Freud

Only through the emotionally satisfying experience of confidence and security does the child acquire the ability to bear discomfort and to exchange comfort for discomfort when social relations require it – in other words, to make erotic-social sacrifices.

A negative primal relationship characterized by withdrawal of love and the accompanying anxiety gives rise to aggressions and is the worst possible foundation for sound social behavior. In such cases, to be sure, an overaccentuation of the conscience-anxiety can result in ethical conduct, but a deeper psychological analysis shows that any such development of social behavior through conscience is dangerous. The early experience of genuine love leads, on the contrary, to a psychic structure that is capable of love and therefore able to develop its relatedness components in dealings with society.

Not only the relation of the child to the thou, to society, but also its relation to itself is determined by the primal relationship. Precisely because in the uroboric phase the Self is externalized in the mother and the child is wholly dependent on her for better or worse, a positive life-situation is reflected in the child's unconscious, symbolic and mythological apperception by the love and acceptance of the Good Mother, while a negative life-situation is reflected by the rejection and condemnation of the Terrible Mother. We have already stressed this in connection with the mother's attitude toward the child's body. But precisely because the infant's body is identical with its body-Self, acceptance of the body, which in this phase is virtually the exclusive scene of the child's life, becomes acceptance as such.

If the experience of this phase is anywhere discernible, it is in the symbolic images of mythology, which always express the totality of the psyche rather than a partial aspect of consciousness. In the later phases of child development this symbolic reality is demonstrable; in this early phase in the development of mankind and of the individual, it can only be inferred from certain indications.

It is one of the basic facts of human development that self-affirmation, an affirmative attitude toward oneself and one's personality, is not innate – although here again constitutional factors both of a positive and of a negative nature seem to be at work –

but develops in the course of the primal relationship, which is in a very meaningful sense inter-personal.

In the older terminology, all positive feelings or attitudes oriented toward the individual – self-affirmation, self-confidence, etc. – hence all the automorphous attitudes that do not relate primarily to a thou or derive from an evaluation on the part of a thou, are said to be narcissistic. Despite all attempts to modify this impression, this term always includes overtones of self-mirroring and self-love. A true understanding of the specifically human form of existence is possible only if we grasp the lasting dialectical relationship between the thou-relationship and the automorphism that makes the individual a unique individual and enables him to experience the growth of his individuality as the true meaning of his existence. The importance of creative man for society as a whole shows that there is a meaningful dialectical connection between an individual's need to pursue his own automorphous development and his ability to play a fruitful role in the life of the collectivity.[23] On the other hand, the adaptation of the individual to the collective, in disregard of his own needs not only castrates the individual but also endangers the community, for such unreserved adaptation to the collective transforms men into the components of a mass and, as the history of mankind has repeatedly shown, makes them a prey to every conceivable mass psychosis.[24]

The foundation of automorphous Self-consciousness is a positive ego-Self axis, an initially unconscious experience of the harmony of the individual ego with the totality of its nature, with its constitutional make-up, or in the last analysis, with the Self. But in the primal relationship this experience takes the form of harmony with the mother. Self-confidence, the impairment of which is demonstrable in all neurotic and many psychotic disorders, depends almost entirely on the primal relationship with the mother – and here again we encounter the fundamental interwovenness of automorphism and thou-relationship.

A normally positive primal relationship results on the one hand in an attitude of confidence toward the human environment and one's own body, and on the other hand in unquestioning confidence in the Self. Such confidence is indispensable to the stability of the ego-Self axis, which is the spinal cord of individual auto-morphism and, later on, of a stable ego and ego-consciousness. A stable, secure ego, it should be stressed, must not be confused with a rigid ego – a phenomenon we shall deal with at length later on. A secure ego is able to entrust itself to the Self, for example, in sleep, in danger, or in the creative process. A rigid ego is, on the other hand, precisely an insecure ego that is impelled by anxiety to cling to itself.

The unfolding of the relations between ego and thou between ego and body, and between ego and Self, which in the primal relationship are inextricably bound together, is among the essential processes of child development; to a very great extent, the sickness or health of the individual and his success or failure in later life are dependent on this process. From the very outset, not only the development of the ego, but the over-all viability of the individual depend on the nature of the relations between ego and Self.

An undisturbed being-identical-with-one's Self goes hand in hand with a safe relationship to one's own body that is achieved in the earliest phase of psychic development, just as the insecurity manifested in experiences of alienation goes hand in hand with an insecure feeling of body and Self, often extending back to the earliest childhood experience. The ability to make contact, which is manifested in a positive ego-Self relationship and whose normal development is based on the Eros constellation of the primal relationship, relates to contact in the broadest sense and not only to contact with the human environment. The making of contacts begins with the identity between mother-world-body and the child's own body. Out of this unity, contact with the mother as a thou and contact with the child's own body are subsequently differentiated. Contact with society and with the world in general develops on the basis of the child's Eros-contact with its mother, while contact with its own body and body-Self is closely related to the development of a stable ego-Self axis.

Thus a securely grounded relationship enables the child personality to form a bond not only with the part of the Self that we term body-Self but also with the part of the Self originally experienced through the mother. As we have seen, the formation of a unified Self (the true "birth" of the child), is dependent on a positive experience of the primal relationship in the first year of life. This humanly normal, that is, archetypally grounded, development is sponsored by the Good Mother and by the confidence in her which gradually develops as the child breaks away from its original identity with her.

The development not only of a healthy ego, but also of a healthy unified Self, and of a healthy relationship between the ego and the Self, is dependent on the course taken by the primal relationship. Paradoxically, the Self is experienced by the ego both as its very own and as an alien thou, and this paradox develops through the relation of the ego to the body-Self and to the mother as Self.[25]

Not only the security of the ego and of its feeling of Self, but also the ability of the ego to make contact with the Self and the unconscious depends on the positive contact provided by the primal relationship. For the unconscious also confronts the ego and consciousness as a thou. Just as the secure contact acquired in the primal relationship makes possible a secure relation to the thou in every form (human thou, world, body, Self and unconscious), so an insecurity acquired in the primal relationship undermines contact with every thou, including the unconscious, which is at once the child's own and alien, at once other world and psychic opposite.

The line of psychic development does not, as the Psychoanalysts suppose, run from an objectless or narcissistic phase of self-love to love of an object as ultimate symptom of psychic maturity. We should rather say that in the progress from the primal relationship *Freud* to the mature capacity for love, automorphous processes of development, in which the accent is on the autonomous development of the individual personality, go hand in hand with the heteronomous relational development, in which dependency on the thou is dominant.

For this reason automorphous development must not be confused with the psychology of the ego. The ego-Self axis is the center of a complex of parallel and opposing processes which take place between the directing totality center on the one hand, and consciousness and the ego center on the other.

The failure of the Psychoanalysts to recognize the fundamental importance of the primal relationship is reflected in their failure to understand such central human phenomena as love or the creative spirit. They dispose of the child's secure, trusting relation to its mother, so fundamental to human development, with formulations such as: "narcissistic aids are expected from trusted sources"[26] or, in line with the same reductive misinterpretation: "external affects or rather narcissistic aids."[27]

The Psychoanalysts are unable to understand a phenomenon so crucial for the development of every human individual as love, because in this sphere any antithesis between identification and subject-object relationship or between "narcissistic and sexual needs" is inapplicable. Even when a Psychoanalyst rather grotesquely though with apparent modesty declares: "The nature of the identification on a higher level which constitutes love is still obscure,"[28] he continues to look upon love, especially in woman, from a reductive point of view.

Only when it is recognized that in the primal relationship the unity of relatedness, automorphous activity and pleasurable being-outside-oneself are one, can the experience of love in adults and its erroneous — though plausible — identification with the mother-relationship be understood. Precisely because the uroboric phase of child development is an identification which, with its diffuse, "oceanic" character does not yet know the boundaries between ego and non-ego, does it become the prototype of the love experience as such.

Thus the possibility of love between the sexes originates in the primal relationship, or to say the same thing in mythological terms, the Great Mother, the matriarchal archetype of the feminine, is the guardian and bestower of all human love.

Another common mistake in regard to this early phase of human development is to attribute a feeling of total power to the pre-ego of the dual union and to find in this feeling the foundation of the infantile ego's magical attitude toward the world. Actually the pre-ego phase is characterized by an absence of differentiation corresponding exactly to Szondi's "A-dualism";[29] under such circumstances one cannot legitimately speak of power. The concept and feeling of power relate always and exclusively to the ego-complex and its derivatives, never to a personality structure open to the experience of the unitary reality.

It is meaningful to speak of power only when an ego is present whose libido charge, or will, is strong enough to desire and exert power, and to empower itself of an object. None of this applies to the subjectless and objectless phase of the uroboric pre-ego. Once this phase was interpreted as auto-erotic in the sense of an objectless self-love, it seemed logical to characterize it as a period of primary narcissism. But actually its reality can be formulated only in a paradox, for precisely because it is a pre-ego constellation, it cannot be described in terms of a subject-object relationship. Accordingly, if we speak of an objectless self-love in this connection, we must at the same time speak of a subjectless universal love and of a subjectless and objectless universal being-loved. In the pleasurable state of diffusion preceding the birth of the ego, the child makes no distinction between world, mother and its own body; thus its total relatedness with all things is just as characteristic of its situation as is its being-only-itself.

We speak of the ego-Self axis because the psychic development and processes that take place between the systems of consciousness and the unconscious and between the corresponding centers of the ego and Self [30] are such that two centers and systems sometimes move away from, and sometimes toward each other. The ego-Self axis comes into being when the ego is established as a derivative of the Self, when it moves away from the Self. This moving away attains its culmination in the first half of life when the psyche separates into conscious and unconscious systems and the ego achieves an apparent autonomy. In the individuation process characteristic of the second half of life, the ego and the Self move back together again. But normally, quite apart from these age-conditioned shifts in the psychic center of gravity, the ego-Self axis is always in motion, for it is affected by every change in consciousness. Not only in sleep and in dreams, but in every psychic process the relations between consciousness and the unconscious and between the ego and the Self, are modified.

But in giving itself up to the Self, the ego does not cease to be; it is only suspended, it ceases temporarily to experience itself. This does not mean that the total personality ceases to be a subject of experience, but only that the subject of experience now becomes the total personality, the Self, and no longer its derivative, the ego.[31]

When we speak of the ego as a derivative of the Self, we imply that the Self exists earlier than, and independent of, the ego. The biopsychic totality's regulation of the personality exists before the ego and consciousness have developed and it is also operative when — as in sleep — they are suspended. But even after the ego has become independent and consciousness has been systematized and stabilized, they are neither constant nor absolutely necessary to the biopsychic totality. The child lives without them, and so does the sleeper or the man who is "absent" in psychic disorder or ecstasy. On its return to waking consciousness from such an absence, the ego is able — potentially — to bring back an experience from a state in which it was suspended, that is, seemingly non-existent.

When the ego returns from the unconscious state of the pre-ego constellation to a state of consciousness, it may be totally without memory, as after a seemingly dreamless sleep or under posthypnotic suggestion; it may possess or acquire relatively clear traces of memory, as when one suddenly or gradually remembers snatches of a dream; or it may have a gradual or relatively immediate total recollection, in which unconscious contents prove to be rememberable, that is, capable of being raised to consciousness.

In any event the essential bond between the ego and the Self expressed in the notion of the ego-Self axis enables the ego, through the Self, to gain knowledge of experiences which have set their imprint on the total personality in a situation where the ego is not yet — as in the child — or no longer — as in the adult — capable of experience.[32]

Every entrance into an archetypal field[33] leads to an *abaissement du niveau mental*, a diminution of consciousness, an intensification of the phenomena that may be described as *participation mystique*, in which the boundaries between subject and object available to consciousness are blurred and the unitary reality takes the place of the normal reality posited by our consciousness. With every shift of the ego in the direction of the Self, the unitary reality aspect becomes more prominent; with every shift in the direction of the ego, it recedes.

Not only the child's experience of the primal relationship, but also the religious experience of ecstasy – for the moment we shall leave the "Great Experience" of art out of account[34] – is an experience of the "unitary/reality." This phenomenon becomes most distinct where, as in Zen Buddhism,[35] there is no *unio mystica* with a God-image, but mystic experience opens the way to a transformed reality. Such individual and collective experience is characteristic not only of mystics, but also of the creative process, quite apart from the fact that nearly all the peoples of history have attempted to induce such experiences ritually with the help of intoxicants. The basis of this psychic constellation is a shift in the ego-Self axis: the ego is taken back into the Self and normal ego-centered consciousness is suspended.

Here it is a matter of crucial importance whether the ego-Self axis is normally developed and stable, whether or not the above-mentioned development of the unified Self has really been affected in childhood. If it has, the shift from the ego to the Self takes place within an integrated psyche, the ego and consciousness are – as occurs every night – taken back into what we call the unconscious, and released unimpaired. Despite their well-known formal similarity to psychosis, dreams are not pathological; they stand in a meaningful compensatory relation to the total personality and to consciousness, and make for psychic wholeness. But where a defective development has weakened or disturbed the ego-Self axis, as for example in the case of a defective development of the unified Self in childhood, the result is a disorder not only of the development of ego and consciousness, but also of the relationship between the ego and Self. An insecure primal relationship and the related instability of the ego-Self axis are expressed in a negative Self-figure and in an exaggerated defense mechanism of the ego. A displacement of the ego-Self axis in the direction of the Self can lead to a disintegration of the personality with all the destructive phenomena characteristic of psychosis. The inundation by the unconscious, which normally occurs where the ego is displaced in the direction of the Self, is here replaced by a rending of the personality which destroys the unity of the personality and is

expressed by the image of the Terrible Mother. Here the totality
function of the Self fails to exert its normal compensatory action.
One consequence of this situation is that dreams often lose their
compensatory, totality-oriented character.

We have said that the primal relationship is the ontogenetic
foundation for being-in-the-world. Only now does the full meaning of this statement become clear. The child's emotional relatedness with its mother, who, as we have seen, is initially not only its
thou and Self, but also the world, enables the developing
child personality to experience itself in an active and coherent
world.

As we know, every living creature has many environments,
different in kind and in scope; what we call "world structure" is
always dependent on the constellation of the psyche and in man
primarily on the constellation of the ego-Self axis. Accordingly as
the ego or the Self, the polarizing force of consciousness or the tendency of the Self toward unity predominates, different aspects of
reality occupy the foreground. But the very fact that an *ordered*
reality is apprehended – not a dead juxtaposition of unrelated
things, but a fabric in which the subjective and objective elements
of experience are in some way related, is contingent on the Eros-
character of the libido, which is first manifested in the primal
relationship.

Unlike Psychoanalysis, analytical psychology takes a monistic
view. Its theory of libido does not imply a speculative opposition
between Eros and Thanatos, but holds that an individual's libido
is originally a unity and that its polarization is a secondary
phenomenon; as "interest" this libido "invests" all objective and
subjective contents and binds them either to the totality of the
psyche or to the ego-center. Just as in the primal relationship of
infancy the positive love bond is experienced as something primary,
so the life-giving libido is the basis of every experience of life and
of every broadening of experience. Only where a disturbance of
the primal relationship results in a deficiency or loss of libido, do
we encounter such secondary phenomena as the experience of
anxiety and death, which in a positive primal relationship are
always held in check by the Self, the mother, and the child's
integral ego which follows her.

By equating libido with "psychic interest," Jung clarifies both its relatedness character and its connection with the primal relationship. It is the child's integration into the living archetypal field of the primal relationship that first enables it to develop a relatedness embracing its relations to its body, to itself, and to its human and extra-human environment. The specifically human growth of the child's interest in life, in itself, and in its environment are fed by its interest in its mother, whose love, tenderness and care are the psychic milk and libido on which depend not only its physical but also its psychic and spiritual existence. For this reason, a destruction of the primal relationship leads to the psychic and spiritual decline and destruction of the child. It is the libido flowing into the child from its mother that animates and activates the specifically human channels and predispositions through which a human child attains to human behavior in a humanely apprehended world.

Just as human experience begins with the unconscious total conception of the world as "Great Round," so ontogenetically the totality of the primal relationship and of the mother-world unity is the determining factor in the life of the child. To the child, as we have seen, the mother is not only the world but also the Self. Thus the child finds itself in an ordered world where it can live and develop. Its feeling of shelteredness and security is the expression of an existence in an ordered world. Unshelteredness and insecurity, on the other hand, are always symptoms of an experience for which an ordered world of this kind does not exist or has disintegrated. This order – as we shall see more fully below – is necessarily anthropocentric and in the truest sense of the word Self-centered; in other words, it is experienced as if the child were its center. The most peripheral factor in this order is the cultural fabric of the group which through the mediation of the mother strongly affects the child's life from the very start by its norms of behavior in matters of child care; feeding, sleeping hours, etc. But at the base of this all-important "world order" lies a world of libidinous interests and structures which, quite unbeknownst to mother and child alike, cause the child to experience the world as an ordered, integrated whole. The entire development of the child from the pre-ego to the ego stage, from inarticulateness to speech, from a passive, helpless, and utterly dependent infant to a child capable of moving in the world, is embedded in the living relatedness of mother to child, in her living interest which molds and determines the child's interest and directions of interest.

The "world-order" retains this libidinous character whether it is experienced by primitive or modern man, by a child or adult. Even a modern adult takes a largely anthropocentric view of the world. The experience of world-unity gained in the unitary reality of the primal relationship (whose Eros-character we have already stressed) presupposes a free flow of libido between child (the unconscious) and world (the mother). From the containment, coexistence and nascent differentiation characteristic of the child's primal relationship with its mother, there develops an analogous relatedness to the world as a whole. For all its anthropocentric accent this world of the integral child ego is open to the collectivity, because it is normally characterized by attitudes of relatedness which prevent the central position of the child from becoming solipsistic and narcissistic.

This connection between mother and world explains why in mythology the archetype of the Great Mother takes the form of the spinner who makes the web, (that is, the varied structure of the world and of life), and guards over it. The meaningful order of the world and a meaningful relatedness of the individual to the world depend on a libidinous-erotic world-interest that is molded by the primal relationship. Accordingly, the Great Mother of the beginning is not only the mother with her child, but also the mother of love and fertility, for it is through the mutual relatedness of the sexes that adult man experiences most clearly the universal Eros- and relatedness-character of the human and extra-human psyche.

When we speak of the order of this matriarchal stage, it must be understood that this order is not that of the later patriarchal logos principle, but pertains to an earlier matriarchal principle, namely the principle of Eros, an experience of order and meaning that is largely determined by feeling. In mythological terms, the sun as begettor is correlated with the patriarchal spirit of the logos, while the nocturnal light-world of the moon, representing a different spirit principle, is correlated with the matriarchal world of the beginning.[36]

In Greek myth the ancient god Eros as cosmogonic principle is seen to be the spirit-principle of the matriarchal stage. The following description of the beginning of things is taken from an early Greek writer: Night was "a bird with black wings. Ancient Night conceived of the Wind and laid her silver Egg in the gigantic lap of Darkness. From the Egg sprang the son of the rushing Wind, a god with golden wings. He is called Eros, the god of love, but this is only one name, the loveliest of all the names this god bore.

"The god's other names, such of them as we still know, sound very scholastic, but even they refer only to particular details of the old story. His name of Protogonos means only that he was the 'firstborn' of all gods. His name of Phanes exactly explains what he did when he was hatched from the Egg: he revealed and brought into the light everything that had previously lain hidden in the silver Egg – in other words, the whole world."[37]

The silver egg of night is the moon, to it corresponds the winged nocturnal spirit god, as later the phallus-sun would correspond to the spirit god of day. This moon spirit – Eros – originating in the feminine nocturnal aspect corresponds to the matriarchal consciousness.[38]

The matriarchal consciousness, not merely a precursor of our patriarchal consciousness but a form of consciousness closer to the unconscious, is emotion-toned; it is a "light-quality" springing from strong emotion, from essentially feeling-toned constellations of the unconscious. The changing, inconstant quality of this emotional light contrasts with the constant light-logos-brightness of the sun. The matriarchal consciousness is a relatedness-consciousness of nearness,[39] its highest form is a wisdom contrasting with the objective, abstract wisdom of the patriarchal logos which looks at things from a distance. It has been called "a wisdom of the unconscious and the instincts of life and relatedness." For this reason the highest form of the Great Mother is Sophia, whose maternal wisdom is bound up with all living things.

This Eros-character of unconscious, instinctive wisdom always applies to *relations* between living things. It determines the primal

relationship and normally presides as Good Spirit and Good
Mother over the earliest existence of the child, which in it and
through it becomes integrated with life and the world. This integration of the child presupposes an order, and the mother is the
great orderer of life who unconsciously and consciously determines
the directions of the child's libido and the connections into which
it will enter.

Although we interpret this mother-world-order as parallel to
the alimentary or body stage, it is experienced as a unified order,
as a first form of cosmic environment. We stress once again that
this cosmos is chthonic and bodily in accent; it is symbolic in its
concreteness; all spiritual and psychic elements are experienced as
bodily, substantial and tangible. At this stage, accordingly, the
spirit is not an abstraction—even an adult requires something
concrete to ab-stract from—but a living and life-giving reality.
Without such reality the spirit arouses anxiety; at this stage
nonsensuous spirit is a "spook."

Phylogenetically for early man, and ontogenetically for the
child, the matriarchal world is a symbolic world, which for the
matriarchal consciousness represents the truly spiritual world.
Outside reality has not yet split off from the inner reality of the
soul and spirit; both are still experienced as a unity, as something
that is not only present but also significant, that is, relevant to
something else. The symbolic experience of milk, for example, signifies that milk is experienced immediately as a unity of essential
relationships which go far beyond the meaning of milk as an
outward reality, as a foodstuff.

When in *The Origins and History of Consciousness* we spoke of the
mythological apperception of early man and the child, we were
referring to the same context. The experience of the world in symbols—e.g. the experience of the mother as Great Mother—is
mythological apperception. At this stage there is no objective
world, no abstract, unrelated outside world; rather, currents of
libido—or one might say lines of relatedness—flow from the
anthropocentric center, where the child is situated, to world
contents that are all meaningful symbols. Thus these contents are
at once really present and imbued with soul and spirit, numinous
parts of a world of interactions, or system of relatedness. The

correspondence between the animistic, magical world view of early man and the child's world is well known; here I wish only to stress that it too is based on the relatedness and Eros-character of matriarchal reality.

To say that existence at this stage is subject to the maternal order does not mean that the world is seen only in the image of the Good Mother. The Great Mother encompasses life and death; but the day rises from the darkness of night and this great matriarchal power is always trustworthy. Even where she frightens and kills, the Great Mother is the eternal genetrix who revives everything that has been killed and maintains the eternal cycle in an indestructible order.

Anxiety, pain, renunciation are embedded in the primal relationship and are outweighed by the good aspect of the maternal, so that despite these negative experiences the child does not lose the feeling of shelteredness and security that come of being integrated with a higher order.

This ordered world, capable of integrating negative factors, is characteristic of healthy human beings, adult and child alike. Its dependence on an undisturbed primal relationship is shown by what happens when such a relationship does not prevail. A disturbed or destroyed primal relationship seems to be one of the main causes of the psychosis known as schizophrenia. The inception of this disorder is often marked by a phenomenon which the patient interprets as the end of the world. In his visions and dreams, and later in his conscious experience, the unity of the world is shattered. The world ceases to be, disintegrating into dead, isolated things, or if a partial world remains, its degeneration is manifested by a struggle between hostile things and forces.

Normally the world consists of dynamic, ordered, living relations constituting a unity of life in which, as in optical perspective, things are seen side by side in front of or behind one another, that is, in relation to one another. They are subject to a hierarchical order. All these orders and relations presuppose a libidinous animation by the psyche which stands in an unconscious relation of identity with the world. But when, regardless of the causes, there is a breakdown in the primal relationship, the Terrible Mother is constellated for the child and there is a disturbance in the unfolding (so indispensable to normal development) of the child's relatedness to its body, its Self, and the thou in all its aspects.

It is this destruction of the world-thou that is manifested in schizophrenia with its regression to the world of the Terrible Mother. The symbolic unitary reality, which in schizophrenia is often regressively animated in visions and hallucinations, disintegrates, and the consequence is the end of the world, which is experienced either as chaos, that is, dissolution into the meaningless confusion of amorphous, unrelated fragments, or as the empty coercive order and rigidity of a dead system, comparable to a system of co-ordinates without the living contents it is supposed to co-ordinate.

The archetype of the Terrible Mother is connected with death, doom, drought, famine and barrenness; it presides over the world of schizophrenia wherever there is too radical a separation from the basic productive forces of the maternal or a hostility toward them. This disintegration of the world and the personality through a reversal of the Eros principle contrasts with the natural development of the child personality, in which the Eros principle is manifested as preponderance of the Good Mother over the Terrible Mother, as integration of all the relationships between the child as ego and the thou as body, Self, fellow man and world.

The normal child development, guaranteed by a secure primal relationship, culminates in the formation of an integral ego which emerges while the child is living in a situation of identity with the Good Mother and has the power to assimilate negative experience up to a certain point, or to abreact it. This gradually becomes the ego-pole of the Self-ego axis, the Self being the ground in which the psyche is rooted.

In general the human situation is so equilibrated and so compensated by the interplay of natural biopsychic behavior and the social reactions represented by the mother that the maturation process goes on as a matter of course — unless unusual circumstances disturb this constellation.

The development of the integral ego begins in the first uroboric phase of the primal relationship, but it is only in the second, strictly-speaking matriarchal phase dominated by the mother archetype, that the integral ego achieves its central position. In other words, it is only after the first year of the child's life, after its true birth, that its ego development, and with it the development of the integral ego and of the child's anthropocentric position, enters the foreground.

CHAPTER THREE

Disturbances of the Primal Relationship and their Consequences

A decisive step in the development of the child within the primal relationship is the formation of a *positive-integral ego*, an ego that is able to assimilate and integrate even the negative or unpleasant qualities of the outer and inner worlds, such as deprivations, pain, etc. The mother, as compensatory Self, sees to it – as far as the circumstances of her life permit – that the negative factors should not predominate and that they should be replaced and overshadowed as quickly as possible by positive factors. This compensation extends not only to objective factors such as cold, hunger and frustration, which are all experienced by the infant as world factors, but gradually also to all negative experiences that come to the child from within but are at first also experienced as pressing in from outside, such as fear, rage and pain. Through the maternal function of compensation and appeasement, the child invests in its ego the positive integral tendency which the mother exemplifies and which she embodies over and over again in her contact with the child. In this way there arises a positive-integral ego capable of integrating positive and negative factors in such a way that the unity of the personality is guaranteed and is not split into antagonistic parts. Thus – to use an abbreviated formulation – there arises a positive tolerance on the part of the ego which, on the basis of its attitude of security and confidence toward the mother, is capable of accepting the world and itself, because it has a constant experience of positive tolerance and acceptedness through the mother.

A normal primal relationship characterized by a secure confidence in the mother's love, by the development of a positive integral ego and of a stable ego-Self axis, gradually brings the child's anthropocentric experience to relative consciousness; that is, the child comes to see itself as the center not only of its world, but also of the world as such. This anthropocentricity, which has nothing to do with the magical omnipotence which makes its appearance at a later phase, is the indispensable foundation of all human development. It is an expression of automorphism with its accent on the importance of the individual for the development of mankind.

The anthropocentric accent is the hallmark of the specific attitude of man which distinguishes him from all other living species. Not only his mastery of the world but also his specific culture-creating capacity is based on this experience of Self, this feeling of having been made in God's image, which is an expression not of pathological narcissism but of the "filialization" of the Self, and represents the realization of the ego-Self axis that lies at the base of all psychic development.

Human existence is determined not by obedience to the world of instinct, but by its own self-posited interpretations, which are based on the anthropocentric accent on the human group and on the individual. Wherever a positive accent is set on the individual personality, we find a bond between a personal factor, the ego, and a transpersonal factor, the Self. This transpersonal Self is often experienced in projection as an ancestral or group Self, and here the bond between the ego and the group creates, through rites and initiations, an identity of the individual with the transpersonal Self. From the earliest human history down to the present this interwovenness of automorphism and thou-relationship has been reflected in the interwovenness of the individual with his group.

The child's anthropocentric situation should not be mistaken for egocentricity. In this phase of the growth of the individual and the Self, there is as yet no isolated ego confronting the thou of Self, world, fellow man, and unconscious. The anthropocentric constellation is embedded in the primal relationship, and even in

the later phase where the Self has moved back into the child from
the mother the ego remains essentially one with this Self. In this
phase, to be sure, ego and Self are no longer linked like mother
and child, but though the child already possesses its own roots,
Self and mother are the soil of these roots and the child cannot
distinguish between what is part of itself and what is not. With the
strengthening of the ego and the advancing integration of the child
personality, serious and lasting conflicts may arise between ego and
thou, and between child and mother without uprooting the child.
The phase of development in which the child personality becomes
relatively independent and the ego becomes continuous rather
than intermittent, is therefore of particular importance, because in
it for the first time the automorphism of the total personality is
experienced by the ego.

But the relative independence of the ego is at the same time the
basis for the child's increasing consciousness of its own independence, which now becomes a central problem affecting the child's
relations both to its mother and to the world.

The uroboric existence that encompassed both inside and outside
was paradisiacal and autarchic because, thanks to the child's
identity with mother and world, it had no experience of its own
dependency. This non-experience of dependency is the basis of
the situation that has been interpreted as a feeling of omnipotence;
but this is an Eros-like wholeness without ego or power. Precisely
this primordial harmony between the freedom of one's own being
with the determining and completely accepted Self of the primal
relationship is the constellation that the adult ego looks upon as
"being-in-Tao," but not as omnipotence.

Because of the primary attachment of the Self to the thou as
mother, she, as embodiment of that which confers security, is the
child's first model for the experience of its own Self. Thanks to the
integrating quality of the mother, the crises and difficulties of
child development are, under normal circumstances, compensated.
Even physical separation from the mother, the weaning necessi-
tated by the child's development as well as the psychic separation
from the mother involved in the consolidation of the child ego, are
compensated by the love and acceptance of the same mother who
is moving away from the child or from whom the child is moving

away. This separation merely enlarges, as it were, the area of love between mother and child and the tension to be endured in it; it is a necessary step that does not endanger the security of the love relationship.

A Hasidic text, in which the role of the mother is characteristically taken over by God and Father, interprets the old Testament words "Noah went with God" as follows:

"Noah was so devoted to God that every step he took seemed to him to be guided by God, as though God stood facing him and set his feet in place and led him like a father teaching his little boy to walk. And so when the Father went away from him Noah knew: 'It is in order that I may learn to walk'."[1] This passage does not, as it would first appear, describe merely a simple, childlike attitude of trusting faith. Then the wording would have had to be: "God went with Noah." The opposite order puts the accent on Noah's attitude and signifies that Noah's attachment to God was indissoluble. This is unquestionably so, for Noah's all-embracing faith allows for God's absence as well as His presence. Noah accepts even the moments of God-forsakenness when God is totally eclipsed. Noah goes alone, he is independent and has no need of tutelage, but to him even aloneness and forsakenness constitute guidance, and for this reason he is able to surmount the extreme darkness that comes of being forsaken by God. His Self, molded by its relationship with God, operates independently as a guiding light.

In another Hasidic tale: "A young rabbi complained to the Zaddik of Rizin: 'In the hours when I devote myself to study, I feel life and light, but when I stop studying, everything vanishes. What should I do?' The Zaddik replied: 'That is as when a man goes through a forest on a dark night. For a time another man, holding a lantern, accompanies him, but at the crossroads they separate and the first man must grope his way alone. But if a man carries his own light, he need fear no darkness'."[2]

The religious situation disclosed in this story is obviously the constellation of the primal relationship transferred to God. Noah's religious attitude is on a higher plane, that of the integral ego which in the security of the primal relationship has acquired a secure relation to its own Self. In keeping with the patriarchal

Jewish attitude and development, the mother figure who naturally teaches the child to walk is replaced by God.

The security acquired in a successful primal relationship enables the ego to integrate the crises originating in the natural phases of transpersonal development as well as the personal and individual disorders endangering its natural course of development. With greater or lesser fluctuations, this occurs regardless of whether the disturbances emanate from the child's or the mother's sphere of life or from impersonal events. In any case a positive primal relationship provides the greatest likelihood that the child will surmount such disturbances.

This brings us to the problem of spoiling children, which some students of child psychology believe to be as important as that of the anxieties that rise in the course of the primal relationship. Actually too much love on the mother's part is by no means as dangerous or harmful as a negative mother-child relationship and too little love.

In the course of the primal relationship an unloving mother, as Terrible Mother, can destroy or seriously impair the foundations of the child's existence. Spoiling, on the other hand, does not produce serious disorders until it becomes necessary for the child to relax its ties with the mother and this process is impeded or prevented by the fact that the mother has spoiled her child. This can give rise to any number of neurotic disorders caused by the child's inordinate attachment to its mother. But as a rule a positive primal relationship in the first phase of life makes for a healthy personality that has an excellent chance of surmounting this and other disorders. This healthy personality is synonymous with a normal ego-Self axis; it provides a guarantee that the compensatory relationship between consciousness and the unconscious, which in certain grave disorders is radically impaired, will continue to function to some extent.

Moreover, the notion of spoiling is largely culture-conditioned. A mother who, true to the mother-archetype, treats her child affectionately, is said in a puritanical environment to spoil it, and where the patriarchal tendency to harden the child at an early age by sadistic methods prevails, she is even accused of making him effeminate. The culture-conditioned deviations from the normal primal relationship are very considerable, and indeed one can speak of a normal primal relationship only as an ideal fiction. Consequently, when we speak of authentic spoiling, we mean a deviation not from any culture-conditioned standard, but from what we regard as a normal primal relationship.

The cause of authentic spoiling is very frequently to be sought in an individual constellation or situation of the mother. Thus, for example, the mother of an only child, a mother who is widowed, who does not love her husband or is not loved by him, or whose husband is too old for her, is often abnormal. Deprived of other outlets, she floods the child with her love; the consequence is the authentic spoiling that comes of an excessive attachment. Such spoiling can hamper or stop the development of the child, but does not necessarily do so. We find this constellation in not a few creative individuals, in whom excessive mother love, the feeling of being the favorite child, has led to a primary intensification of their life-feeling and sense of assurance. In later life – Goethe is a good example – this takes the form of a lasting feeling of being a "Sunday child" especially gifted by nature, and in an attitude of assurance toward oneself and the outside world in all its aspects, which leads to a general creative openness.

Even this authentic spoiling involves the danger of the mother holding fast to her child. Here the individual constellation of the mother and the maturity of her personality regardless of age are decisive. It depends on her personality whether she will be able to release her over-loved child, or will tend rather to "devour" it. It is generally supposed, sometimes rightly so, that a mother who deprives her child of nothing often makes it harder for the child, as it grows up, to endure the privations which life inevitably imposes, a weakness that can result in failure. But the danger of authentic spoiling has been very much exaggerated, because a positive primal relationship makes for an integral ego that is enabled by confidence in the mother-Self and later in the child's own Self, to accept privations.

The intensified automorphism resulting from a too positive primal relationship leads to a conflict with the thou of society, but in the end the creative individual's openness to the world becomes fruitful for the collectivity because with his creative achievement he brings to the collective something it lacked and had tried to exclude from itself.

But where a mother clings to her child, her spoiling conceals something else that disguises itself as spoiling. In mythological terms, this "false" spoiling is that of the witch-mother who lures the child into her candy house (spoiling with sweets) and once the child enters becomes the Terrible Mother who "eats it up." But in this case the motive is never an excess of love with no other outlet; it is a will to power which replaces real love and disguises itself as spoiling.

There are mothers whose genuine capacity for love is undeveloped, atrophied or poisoned and who, as compensation for their own negative fulfillment, fling themselves on their children, not in order to give away a super-abundant love, but in order to fill their own emptiness with the child. This is not a real spoiling but a pseudo-spoiling. Such a mother cannot release her "beloved" child, because if she did, she would be left not with an overflowing heart, as in the case of authentic spoiling, but with a hungry heart. Such a mother's possessive "love" is always making demands on the child. She represents her love as a gift and demands gratitude, her love requires a payment and becomes a means of pressure. Often she pushes her child in the direction of her own unfulfilled affects and desires, which the child is then expected to fulfill out of love. That such mothers with their pseudo-spoiling are in reality "terrible" mothers can best be seen from the fact that they impair the child's automorphism and render it not only uncreative but also impotent or frigid.

Where we encounter spoiled children who are incapable of loving, we can with virtual certainty infer a terrible mother, whose "terrible" character is manifested indirectly through pseudo-spoiling. This is only one more indication that, as we have said above and shall discuss at length later on, a child's relation to the "thou" is determined almost entirely, for better or worse, by the primal relationship.

When a child's automorphism is enhanced by spoiling, the shift of the Self from mother to child and the formation of the total Self will be successful; from a secure primal relationship with its mother the child will move on to a secure relationship with its own Self and to all the resulting potentialities and developments. But when its automorphism is impaired by spoiling, the child will retain a dependency that will impede its development. In such cases the mother may seem to spoil her child, but she is in fact clinging, devouring and "terrible."

Like some spoiling, the inhibitions that are inevitably imposed on a child in the course of the primal relationship are culture-conditioned; they are a part of life's discomforts which begin with the very earliest phase.

"A child," writes C. Menninger, "is – like every quadruped – born primitive, cannibalistic, asocial and uninhibited."[3] Though accepted by many psychologists, this view is one-sided and absolutely false. A human child is not a quadruped, nor cannibalistic, nor in any way asocial. It lives in the primal relationship which is an eminently social relationship. True, a child is in many ways "polyvalent"; it is capable, by predisposition, of learning any existing language or of becoming integrated with any conceivable human society. In direct contrast to the animal, the quadruped, with its total subservience to instinct, inherited reactions, and patterns of behavior, the child is receptive to any existing group behavior pattern. And Melanie Klein to the contrary and notwithstanding, the child is no more cannibalistic than primitive man. In the present state of our knowledge, all we can say of the cannibalistic practices of primitive man is that they were always rituals, that is, socially conditioned, and never resulted from an original predisposition of man. True, the child is primitive to the extent that it is both phylogenetically and ontogenetically prehistorical, in the sense that it has still to grow into the historical society of its group. It is also – and this is indeed an important point – uninhibited, since every inhibition that is imposed on the development of the child is conditioned by the group, that is, by the society to which its mother belongs. On the other hand, we may state with equal certainty that it is a specifically human predisposition to accept inhibitions, to develop them, and even to require them for one's development.

There is ample evidence to show that too little inhibition is just as disastrous for the child as too much. The tendency to impose and accept forms is fundamental to the human psyche. There is

no known human group in which inhibiting formal tendencies do
not play a decisive role in custom and ritual, as for example in
exogamy with its basic prohibition of incest. The ability and the
need to build a social culture is an essential human predisposition;
culture-building tendencies have been at work in every early
human group. Culture presupposes the accentuation or inhibition
of certain individual qualities. The fact that only borderline cases
are incapable of accepting the culture of a given group proves that
every human child is born with the specifically human predisposition to accept inhibitions and to develop into a full-fledged
member of the group. The inhibiting formal tendencies which
make it possible to set limits upon the individual and his automorphism constellate the relationship between the group culture
into which the child grows and its own individual predisposition.
These inhibiting tendencies largely determine the formation and
development of what we call the psyche. Through commandments and prohibitions the primitive collectivity, from the very
outset, assigns to the individual his place and position: so and so
is a man of such and such an age, a woman has such and such
functions, the relations between members of the group must take
such and such forms. Thanks to such regulations, an individual is
differentiated from his fellow men. Such differentiation is necessary
to the collectivity and occurs also among gregarious animals, for
example, the ants and the bees. In early man the inhibitions which
give form to the polyvalent human predisposition are to some
extent compensated by the fact that the life of early mankind was
far more multi-sided than that of the overdifferentiated and occu-
pationally specialized modern man. Early man was at once
warrior, artist, poet, singer, dancer, and member of the council.
His individuality had every opportunity to express itself within
the framework of the collectivity.

The inhibitions imposed by every cultural canon or influence
upon the individuality and polyvalence of the child normally
make themselves felt in the course of the primal relationship
and in the first years of the child's development. But it is a
question of the utmost importance whether the child is drawn
smoothly and easily into the cultural canon, so that it need take
no notice of the process of inhibition, or whether it is forced

into the canon with a brutality that may penetrate the child's consciousness.

Where there is a positive primal relationship and an integral ego has developed, a child is capable of enduring inhibitions of every kind without too much resistance, or in any case without incurring lasting wounds – capable, too, of adapting itself to the demands made on it. It would seem to be perfectly normal for the human species that certain psychic contents should remain unconscious so that they do not affect the development of the personality; in other words unconsciousness of certain contents does not in itself make a child or adult neurotic. Now that we are able to survey a wide variety of cultural possibilities and of needs for partial inhibition, we can say that the human child can endure certain inhibitions without harm and that they will not prevent it from leading a satisfactory life not only within its own group but even in a very different environment.

A good many of our ideas of what is neurotic are culture-conditioned. What we term a neurosis may consist in an over-accentuation or under-accentuation of traits and predispositions which in another culture may pass for normal or even confer a position of prominence. Even in our own culture attitudes fluctuate; the traits of character that are held to be desirable in wartime may be regarded as criminal in times of peace.

Our western culture seems to be distinguished by the frequency, if not by the very existence, of the psychic disorders which we call neuroses and psychoses. We shall not go into the question of whether such disorders have existed among early and primitive cultures, however it seems safe to say that in our culture the tension between consciousness and the unconscious is particularly pronounced and that all psychic disorders characteristic of our culture are attributable to inability to endure this psychic tension.

As we have shown, a child's ability to accept inhibitions with relative ease depends on an ability to integrate, to form an integral ego and a positive ego-Self axis. These developments are initiated in a positive primal relationship and then expanded; in other words, a good many inhibitions and repressions can be imposed in the course of a positive primal relationship without critically disturbing the child's psyche. But, on the other hand, where there is a negative primal relationship the best outward conditions cannot prevent psychic disorder. In the latter cases, culture-conditioned inhibitions may become dangerous mental disorders. At this point we must try to give some idea of when a disorder becomes mortally dangerous.

All cultural adaptation is an adaptation to a set of inner and outer demands which must necessarily come into conflict with certain individual tendencies. It is necessary to impose inhibitions only where an individual tendency does not fit in with the demands of the culture. From the very outset there is a tension between automorphism and cultural adaptation. If we say that imagination stands for inner reality and cultural requirements stands for outer reality, it becomes incumbent on the individual to recognize both realities and to learn to strike a balance between them. This applies equally to the extrovert with his orientation toward the outside world and the demands of his culture and the introvert with his orientation toward the subjective and objective *inner* aspect of the psyche.

The danger that the psyche will be flooded from inside or outside is forestalled by *centroversion*, the tendency to establish centers or authorities that make possible a differentiated personality. It serves the wholeness of the personality and is an essential component of automorphism. Centroversion is a universal tendency, present in every human psyche; it leads to the formation of the ego and of the ego-Self axis, to the accentuation of ego-centrality in the first half of life and to a reversal of this trend in the second half. By *automorphism*, on the other hand, we mean the specific and unique tendency of every individual to realize his potentialities. The sharper and more one-sided the cultural demand to which the child is submitted, the more inhibitions will be imposed on it and the greater will be the tension between its consciousness and unconscious. This tension undoubtedly favors cultural adaptation, but it can hardly be said to favor the creative achievement which will benefit a culture, for creative achievement always depends on recognition of the individual, on the automorphism which is endangered by excessive adaptation to the culture of the day.

Under normal conditions a child's upbringing gives rise to a conflict between its natural automorphism and the need for cultural adaptation. This conflict becomes dangerous, often critically so, when a negative primal relationship impairs the child's capacity for integration. The ability to react automorphously safeguards an individual's self-assurance in the face both of the demands of the world and of the strokes of fate to which man is inevitably exposed. On a small scale failures and disappointments, on a large scale unhappiness, sickness and death, are the trials that challenge not man's "thou-capacity" but his "Self-capacity," his ability to be himself, and to be a Self. Thus a man's ability to surmount these crucial situations of life presupposes unimpaired automorphism, the power to integrate, and a sound ego-Self axis.

The anthropocentric position of a child in the world is essentially bound up with the preponderance of the *integral* ego which prevents the negative ego (that part of the ego which – whether by nature or reactively – is affective, aggressive and destructive) from gaining the upper hand. Inhibitions imposed by a negative primal relationship become critically dangerous when the ego's relation to the Self and to the thou is fundamentally disturbed; then neither sociocultural adaptation nor a compensatory automorphous development is possible.

As we have seen, both the ego's relation to the Self and the development of its relation to the thou are largely dependent on the primary mother-child relationship. The anthropocentric accent on the individual, which is based on the relation of the ego to the Self as an inner-outer thou, is the foundation of a creative development of automorphism and also of any positive social behavior. Only an individual who takes himself seriously in his anthropocentric dignity and looks upon himself as one of the purposes of creation is capable of taking his fellow man's dignity seriously and of recognizing him to be a meaningful center of the world. The love-tolerance experienced in the primal relationship and the formation of an integral ego make possible the tolerance which enables a man to love himself, as well as his neighbor, with both his good and his bad qualities.

Thanks to the interwovenness of automorphism with a positive primal relationship, the integral ego is always an expression of a positive, free and creative ego-Self axis adequate to the child's disposition to orient himself creatively to the thou, to his Self and to the world.

This "confidence foundation" of the total personality, represented by the integral ego, makes possible an open psychic system in which there is no insurmountable tension between the world and the ego or between the unconscious and the ego. The ego is open on all sides, perceiving, observing, and expressing itself.[4] In this phase a "matriarchally perceiving" consciousness and the processes originating in the unconscious are predominant. The integral ego predominates, experiences of the ego are always at the same time experiences of the total personality, because the later separation of consciousness and unconscious into clearly defined systems has not yet come between the ego and the Self. For this reason the reactions of an un-impaired ego that has not yet been intimidated and negativized by outward interference are extremely vigorous.

The matriarchal consciousness of the child is most clearly revealed by the role of fantasy and its close relative, play. Fantasy is by no means identical with a wishful inner pleasure principle; rather, it is an inner sense organ that perceives and expresses inner worlds and laws as the outward sense organs perceive and express the outside world and its laws. The world of play is of extreme importance not only for children but also for the adults of all cultures; it is not a world to be transcended.[5] It is especially important for children. Only an individual embedded in this symbolic reality of play can become a complete human being. One of the main dangers implicit in this modern, occidental-patriarchal culture with its overaccentuation of rational consciousness and its one-sidedly extroverted adaptation to reality, is that it tends to damage, if not destroy, this pregnant and sustaining symbol-world of childhood. Total embeddedness in the magical-mythical symbol-world of fantasy and play is at least as significant an expression of the child personality's openness as is its power to assimilate impressions of the outside world and society. The two forms of openness go hand in hand and normally counterbalance one another. In the normal development of the adult the process of growing into the consciousness and experience of objective reality specific to one's culture is no more important than the process of growing into the religion, art, ritual and laws of the group, however these may vary from group to group.

Here we shall not try to determine under what conditions disturbances of development leave lasting scars and under what conditions they are mere passing accidents; suffice it to point out that the rooting of the child in society effected through the primal relationship always includes an influence by the cultural canon in which the child's mother and family live. Though this cultural influence comes to the child's consciousness only later when the ego is relatively developed, it demonstrably exerts a determining effect, from a very early age, on the primal relationship and on the formation of the ego and of the ego-Self axis.

It is of crucial importance, for example, whether in a given culture the child's sex is regarded as desirable or undesirable, as a dominant value or as a liability. The repression and devaluation of woman in the patriarchate can give a mother a fundamental sense of inferiority and a weakness of the ego-Self axis, which make her incapable of fulfilling her security-giving function in the primal relationship. Or she may be in a state of conscious or unconscious protest against this patriarchal devaluation. Each of these constellations is bound to affect the primal relationship and in particular to influence the mother's attitude toward the sex of her child from the outset. A mother whose self-esteem has been shaken by the patriarchate will react very differently to a son than to a daughter. She may prefer the son and reject the daughter: or conversely, by way of conscious or unconscious protest, she may accentuate her solidarity with her daughter and identify her son positively or negatively with the father. All these attitudes so crucial to the primal relationship take many forms, varying with the individual case.

But here again the personal situations are only varieties of constellations which are subject to general laws and which, because they are to a high degree typical of certain cultural situations, can be shown to be transpersonally conditioned. The fundamental distinction between patriarchal and matriarchal, conscious and unconscious orientations provides a basis not only for understanding the mother-child relationship but also for diagnosing our culture and devising a therapy.

The elucidation of the situation of women in relation to the cultural canon and its consequences for the primal relationship is of the utmost importance for the development of Western mankind. But before taking up the effect of the cultural canon on the development of the primal situation, we must attempt to outline the consequences of a disturbance in the primal relationship.

We have pointed out that in a positive, successful primal relationship the negative experiences inseparable from child development are compensated by the mother who represents the world and the Self. Since positive experience involves revulsion on the part of the ego, the attitudes of the ego corresponding to these experiences become habitual, that is, they develop into authentic part-structures of the ego. In a normal primal relationship, as we have seen, there develops a superordinate part of the ego, the integral ego, capable of accepting and synthesizing positive and negative experiences and attitudes.

Possibly such attitudes and structures are constitutional and not mere reactions; we are still unable to draw a clear dividing line between those that are constitutional and those that come into being in the course of individual development. Positive as well as negative reactions strike us as inordinate. One child's unusual ability to integrate experience, another's inability to assimilate even relatively minor injuries without harm to itself, lead us time and time again to speak of constitutional factors because we can think of no other explanation. But if we set aside such borderline cases which unquestionably exist, the influence of the primal relationship on the child's development and on its psychic weal or woe can hardly be overestimated.

Once we appreciate the positive significance of the child's total dependency on the primal relationship, we cannot be surprised by the catastrophic effects that ensue when that relationship is disturbed or destroyed. But a negative development of the primal relationship in the earliest and crucial phase of child development is by no means always identical with failure or guilt on the part of the personal mother. Here again the archetypal constellation of the uroboros phase, the determining role of the mother archetype, is evident.

A negative constellation of the primal relationship occurs not only where the mother's emotional attachment to her child is insufficient, but wherever the child "loses" its mother, the foundation of its existence. Such loss is usually constellated by the psychic inadequacy of the mother or by her physical elimination through death, sickness or separation, but also there can be an overwhelmingly negative experience on the part of the child, which may have nothing to do with the personal mother. Such experiences result from an alimentary deficiency or from other negative factors on the body plane, for which the personal mother cannot be held responsible. But since at the earliest stage not only the world and the thou, but also the child's own body and Self are localized in the mother and in the child's reactions to her, since they are experienced in her image, all these negative experiences create disturbances of the primal relationship. Thus what we call constitution or fate pertains, on the mythological plane, to the domain of the mother archetype.

A "good" personal mother can become for her child a "terrible" mother through the preponderance of negative transpersonal factors such as sickness or affliction. Similarly, both from the physical and the psychical angle, a stable, elastic constitution can be experienced as a positive fate, as a good mother and as a positive primal relationship, and can affect the child accordingly. For this reason an anamnesis restricted to personalistic factors is never adequate to the understanding of either a healthy or a disordered development. The crucial factors are always the child's archetypal experiences and never mere objective data, and herein lies the fundamental significance of the child's mythological apperception and of the archetypal interpretation characteristic of analytical psychology.

There is a permanent cleavage between the personal reality of the human environment and the world of archetypal determinants. Insofar as the human environment is guided archetypally by instinct, and functions normally, it fulfills its function. The archetypal components, apprehended in the images of the "good," the "great," or the "terrible" Mother, remain the superordinate reality. In the mythological apperception of this stage, the transpersonal powers are the true sources of weal of woe. However in their earthly incarnation the personal embodiment of their images, in the form of the child's mother, is identical with the superordinate deity.

In the situation of containment in the maternal vessel, the child is helpless, empty and dependent, a defenseless part-existence; the mother is life, nourishment, shelter, security, and comforting compensation for all negative experiences. Because in the child the total reaction outweighs the ego-reaction, its experience is – from our point of view – boundless. For this reason the predominance of positive factors constellates the image of the positive mother, while the predominance of negative factors constellates the image of the negative mother. The predominance of a negative experience inundates the ego nucleus, dissolves it or gives it a negative charge. The ego of a child thus marked by a negative primal relationship we call a distress-ego, because its experiences of the world, the thou, and the Self bears the imprint of distress or doom. Thus in the child's mythological apperception a positive primal relationship is reflected in the archetypal image of paradise, and a disturbed primal relationship of the distress-ego in that of hell.

A reversal of the paradise situation is characterized by the partial or total reversal of the natural situation of the primal relationship. It is attended by hunger, pain, emptiness, cold, helplessness, utter loneliness, loss of all security and shelteredness; it is a headlong fall into the forsakenness and fear of the bottomless void.

The central symbol of this state is hunger. In the symbolism of the alimentary stage, hunger and pain are therefore characterized as gnawing and devouring. When the primal relationship is in any way disturbed, helplessness and defenselessness constellate the terrible, negative mother, who in myth as well is endowed with all the symbols and attributes that appear in this situation of the child. She becomes a witch, the diabolical mother of suffering and pain. She rejects, condemns to solitude and sickness, and torments with hunger and thirst, heat and cold the unhappy creatures whom the good mother has abandoned to her. If this constellation sets in too early, it leads to egoless apathy and decline. If it sets in when the ego has achieved a certain stability, it leads, through a reinforcement of the negative ego, to a distressed and negativized ego.

Where this phase is negative, that is when no integral ego has formed, or the first beginnings of one have been stifled, the negative situation is intensified by the reduction of the child ego. Then aggressions make their appearance; they may take the form of self-defense or alarm where the child's well-being is disturbed by hunger, pain or fear, or of necessary reactions to the inception of new but predetermined phases of psychic development, such as the child's partial and gradually increasing detachment from the primal relationship or the conflict that arises in the phase where the child's sex is differentiated from the opposite sex and stabilized. When the child is integrated with the Great Mother, or later with its personal mother, it normally succeeds in integrating its own aggressions. In the feeling that its aggressions are accepted by its mother, but also limited and directed by her, it learns to accept, limit and direct its own aggressions in other words to subordinate them to the integral ego.

One of the essential factors in a child's integration is the absorption of infantile aggression into its total psychic structure, through which this aggression becomes a positive component in the child's psychodynamic unity. The affective abreaction of disturbances of every kind by screaming and flailing about is a normal expression of the child's personality and is accepted as such by any normal mother. Even when for some reason (i.e. educational principles) her response to these disturbances is not directly positive, her reaction as a rule is affectively positive in her sympathy and her attempts to soothe the child.

In certain cultures – primitive as well as modern – this normal attitude on the part of the mother is discouraged by the collectivity.[6] Here we find culture-conditioned deviations from the norm. The consequence is that people brought up in such cultures always show deviations, which remain deviations even if they are regarded as normal in the societies where they prevail. A thoroughgoing study of certain cultures and their determination of basic personality (that is, by the form they impose on the psychic structure of the child), is impossible unless we have the courage to measure such developments against an ideal type of human development. A mother who neglects her child to the point of provoking lifelong injury must be regarded as abnormal because she fails to fulfill her archetypal role of furthering the child's specifically human capacities for development, even if she is regarded as normal within her culture.

The particular phases and forms of the dynamic distribution of aggression among the integral ego, the superego, the shadow and the Self will concern us later on. The aggresssion available to the integral ego is necessary in so far as outwardly it makes possible the affirmation and assertion of the ego and inwardly expresses itself as self-criticism and self-control. The dynamic interplay of Self, superego and unconscious varies with every constellation. Thus aggression guided by the Self is as helpful for the development of automorphism, or the development of the individual in his opposition to environment and culture, as is the aggression available to the superego which, on the contrary, *limits* the individual in his adaptation to environment and culture.

In the natural process of the child's differentiation from the mother, in the conflict between the individual's automorphism and the primal relationship, hate and feelings of aggression make their appearance as necessary weapons in the incipient struggle for independence. These secondary negative reactions are normally compensated and integrated in the primal relationship. Only a disturbance of the primal relationship and the attendant more or less pronounced disturbance of automorphous development make for an abnormal development of the ego.

If a negative primal relationship has produced a negativized ego, the resulting aggressions can no longer be integrated, and then we have the phenomenon to which the term narcissism properly applies.

The child's impotence and rage, its alternation of helplessness and of meaningful alarm – reactions to a distress that endangers its very life – are characteristic of the infantile distress-ego. Where the infant does not become apathetic, its ego, at the mercy of the numinous power of the Terrible Mother, is alarmed, and this alarm releases compensatory reactions. The pathological situation of a child abandoned in its helplessness and dependency causes it to erupt into rage and aggression, or in terms of the symbolism of the alimentary stage, into a cannibalistic, sadistic desire to devour its mother.

Here, as so often, the errors of Psychoanalysis result from its pre-occupation with the mentally ill. It is not true that "hate precedes love,"[7] or that the infant is in any primary sense cannibalistc and sadistic. Similarly, distrust in a child[8] is not primary but is a reaction to distress. The positive, creative side of the unconscious and of normal human development (which analytical psychology sets in the foreground of psychic reality), is obscured by such misinterpretations. A patriarchal consequence of such neurotic thinking is a secret or avowed culture-pessimism.

When the ego becomes a distress-ego, whose experience of the world, the Self and the thou is marked and characterized by hunger, insecurity, and helplessness, the Good Mother becomes in like degree a negative and Terrible Mother. If the ego of this phase has already acquired a certain stability and independence, it becomes prematurely overaccentuated by way of compensation for this situation of distress and forsakenness. Normally the ego develops in the shelter of the primal situation and can rely confidently on the Good Mother and her care. Where the primal relationship is disturbed, the distress-ego is prematurely thrown back on itself; it is awakened too soon and *driven* to independence by the situation of anxiety, hunger and distress.

Understandably enough, a radically disturbed primal relationship such as we find in many neurotic disorders and psychoses is chiefly experienced as unlovedness. Consequently the feeling of not being loved is often accompanied by an almost insatiable longing (which often underlies neuroses) to repair and compensate for the lack of love in the primal relationship by intense love experiences.

The paradise of the primal relationship is by nature lacking in contours and cannot be apprehended in the categories of adult consciousness. For this reason its cosmic character can be mistaken for immoderation, its openness for aimlessness. But normal development leads to automorphism, to ego-formation, to sociability, to the integral ego and to adaptation to the environment. This development is not forced by a negative withdrawal of love, but is guided by a relationship of love and confidence. It is only the distress-ego, deprived of the experience of security – the foundation of all faith and trust – which, because of its anxiety and distrust,

is forced to develop a narcissism that is the expression of an ego
reduced to its own resources.

It is only the forsakenness of the negativized ego that leads to
an exacerbated ego — egoistic, egocentric and narcissistic. Though
reactively necessary and understandable, such an exacerbation of
the ego is pathological, because the contact of such an ego with
the thou, with the world, and with the Self is impaired and in
extreme cases virtually destroyed.

A disturbance of the primal relationship in an early phase, when
the ego is not yet consolidated and has not yet taken on its independent structure, leads to a weakening of the ego that makes
possible a direct inundation by the unconscious and a dissolution
of consciousness. However, the negativized ego is different. It is
the expression of a later disturbance in which a consolidated
ego and a systematized consciousness centered around this ego
become reactively rigid, defend themselves on all fronts, and
barricade themselves against the world and the Self. This tendency
of the negativized ego to shut itself off intensifies the child's situation of forsakenness and feeling of insecurity, and this is the beginning of a vicious circle in which ego-rigidity, aggression and
negativism alternate with feelings of forsakenness, inferiority and
unlovedness, each set of feelings intensifying the other. This is
one of the main causes of sadomasochistic reactions and of the
pathological narcissistic ego-rigidity that often accompanies them.

The negativized ego is narcissistic but not anthropocentric, for
the basis of anthropocentrism in both child and adult is the solidity
of the ego-Self axis and the resultant grounding of the personal
ego in a transpersonal element, namely, the Self, which is not only
merely individual but universally human. In contrast to narcissism, the anthropocentric attitude reflects a successful love relationship. It is precisely on the basis of the primal relationship
with its superhuman, transpersonal character that man develops
the anthropocentric sense of security which not only enables
him to perceive his life as meaningful but also to form a bond of
solidarity with his fellow men.

The ego-stability of normal development ultimately enables the
personality to identify itself with the ego-complex and center of
consciousness. It is a prolongation of the integral ego of child-

hood which is able to join positive and negative contents into a productive and progressive unity. The ego's task is to represent the total personality in its confrontation with the inner and outer world, to act – at least in the first half of life – as the executive organ of centroversion. It comprises two functions which would seem at first sight to be mutually exclusive. On the one hand, the ego must, by systematization and integration, create a unity of consciousness and preserve it by defense mechanisms. It must prevent the flooding and dissolution of consciousness. Because of its defenses against the unconscious and its strengthening of the ego, this function belongs to the phase of the patriarchate and of patriarchal ego development. But, on the other hand, the ego and consciousness have the function of remaining at all times open to the changing impressions and influences pouring in from the world and from the unconscious. Only such openness makes possible an awareness of the situation and the adaptation of the personality to it. This attitude of the ego corresponds to the matriarchal consciousness; and without a living, flexible interaction of the two attitudes the ego and consciousness cannot function effectively.[9]

This living functioning of the ego both without and within, in its patriarchal as well as its matriarchal aspect, is the indispensable foundation of a productive integration of consciousness and an open personality capable of progressive transformation and growth. Unlike this stable ego with its capacity for integration, the negativized ego develops a rigidity accompanied by excessive defense mechanisms. But since this rigidity of the ego disturbs and often impedes the progressive development of the personality, the excluded contents and drives of the unconscious accumulate and finally break through the barrier, erupting into consciousness and flooding it. Then the oscillating twofold orientation of the integral personality and integral ego is replaced by an alternation of rigidity and chaos, typical of certain psychic disorders.

Even in the average adult these contexts remain unconscious. Yet time and time again the analysis of sick and healthy alike reveals the essential ties between (1) a sound primal relationship and stability of the ego-Self axis, (2) openness toward the world and the unconscious, and (3) sociability. Analysis also reveals that a disturbance of the primal relationship endangers all these qualities, provoking an insecure, closed, unrelated and asocial personality.[10]

However, the diagnosis of a damaged primal relationship and of a hungry, forsaken, lonely, and despairing child is never a sufficient basis for a prognosis. It is also necessary to consider the extent of the damage, the time of its inception, its duration, the way in which it has been compensated by the environment, and last but not least the constitutional factors. If the damage did not occur too early, if the earliest phase of life was characterized by a positive primal relationship, a compensatory experience of the Good Mother as impersonal archetype of nature, or as tree, garden, forest, home or sky, is perfectly possible. Here it should be remembered that a child lives in a symbolic world of mythological apperception. His whole world, or in any case parts of it, are close to the unitary reality, and the garden in front of the house, the nearby woods, or some tree may represent a sheltering reality into which the child can withdraw. Here the primordial, archetypal experience of the world comes into its own, and forest, garden, or tree as symbol of the Great Mother becomes the Great Mother herself, ready to embrace the child in need of help.

Such mythological worlds are alive in every childhood. As centers of the child's fantasy and dream reality they are full of mystery. They are the hidden source of life; the child surrounds them with secret rites and usually conceals their significance from adults unless they too participate in this world as fellow players. The seemingly almost compulsive desire to hear stories repeated in the same words corresponds to the child's need for the ritual which enables it to enter into another world which it regards as the real world. That is why evening – bedtime – is the mother's time. With her stories, her songs, her sheltering tenderness she then becomes the Great Mother of the primal relationship. She confers a sense of security and shelteredness as Mother of the Night, and Goddess of the Inner World into which the child now enters. Here again, in our culture, the father God, and prayer to Him, later assume the role which at first belonged exclusively to the mother.

Sometimes an older child turns back to the mother archetype

as embodied in nature. This may be helpful, and in certain cases it may even save the child, but it is not wholly incompatible with a healthy development. When thou-relatedness cannot be experienced through a human mother figure but becomes dependent on the cosmic character of the mother archetype, the child's relatedness to the human thou can be impaired. (Of course this applies only where this experience of nature takes the place of the mother-relationship, not where the two exist side by side.)

An intense early activation of the mother archetype can also be made possible by a creative predisposition characterized by an active archetypal image world. Just as the world of childhood remains a creative possession — remembered as a symbol world and as experience of the unitary reality, so the inner image of the mother archetype occupies an essential place in the psychic world of the child and of the adult as well. Under unfavorable conditions, however, an activation of the collective unconscious compensating for the loss of the real mother can involve a danger of psychosis. This occurs, in particular, when no creative possibility for the expression of this world of inner images is present and none have been developed.

A child's negative distress-ego is the expression of a pathologically reinforced ego into which it has been forced and in which it must subsist on its own resources though not equipped by nature and its stage of development to do so. Behind such forced and violent self-assertion there is always anxiety, forsakenness and a lack of trust embracing the entire sphere of what is normally contained in the primal relationship, namely, the child's relation to the thou, the world, the Self, and the unconscious. The specific nature of this danger is that the compensatory action of the psyche, which normally (with the help of the ego-Self axis) creates a balance between the deviating tendencies of the ego and its power of adaptation, becomes more or less inoperative.

The negativized ego is an ego deprived of its foundations. Thus its despair is perfectly understandable. Its anxiety and fundamental insecurity in the world are the expression of an isolation which shakes the foundations of automorphous development, and shatters the ego's roots in the Self, i.e., in its own encompassing nature.

The fact that the total Self comes into being when the Self that has been externalized in the mother moves back into the child creating a tie between the nature-given and the social function which is already active in the primal relationship.

The consequences of a disturbed primal relationship demonstrate that an archetype, that of the Self for example, should not be looked upon as an organic mechanism that functions automatically. The psychic activation of archetypes, or at least of a certain group among them, namely such human archetypes as Mother, Father, Wise Old Man, presupposes a primary evocation of the archetype – adequate to the child's stage of development – through an experience in the world.

The evocation of the archetypes and the related release of latent psychic developments are not only intrapsychic processes; they take place in an archetypal field which embraces inside and outside, and which always includes and presupposes an outside stimulus – a world factor.

"Wolf children," the human children raised by she-wolves, do not develop in the manner specific to the human race; no mother archetype of the collective unconscious makes its appearance to compensate for the loss of the personal mother, as one would expect if compensation by the archetype were an automatic organic process. The absence of compensation by the unconscious observed in certain neuroses also requires an explanation. In any event it argues against the simplistic thesis that the unconscious, or the total personality, invariably exerts a compensatory action. Such cases of absence of compensation become genetically understandable, however, once we assume that in the crucial phases of psychic development the personal world factor of the archetype (the personal mother or father) must be adequately evoked and activated for normal development, but that in certain patients this personal evocative factor has been absent or inadequate, so that the archetypal structure of the psyche has been radically disturbed in its functioning.

When we say that the archetype has "two feet," we mean that an archetype implies not only an intrapsychic predisposition but a world factor as well. When we say that an archetype is switched on by evocation, we mean that the archetypal aptitude of the psyche must be released by a corresponding world factor.

We shall leave the question open as to whether this interpretation applies to all archetypes and will confine our discussion for the present to the archetypes in which a human figure stands at the centre of the archetypal symbol canon, as in the case of the mother and father archetypes, the old man, the old woman, the *puer aeternus*, the anima, the animus, and the child archetype. They are all present as *latent* images and the symbols relating to them. The world which appears in connection with the human archetypes is in every sense a human, social world. Yet this human, social element must not be confused with the personal and private; it too is transpersonal and archetypal. The primal relationship between mother and child, for example, is universally human; rooted in the collective unconscious. It is one of the essential conditions of human existence. True, for the post-natal embryonic being, the mother is the first inter-human, social tie, but as we have seen, this social inter-human element represented by the mother is at first manifested in archetypal anonymity. As the symbolism of the mother archetype shows, this archetype, in keeping with the cosmic character of the primal relationship, has at first a diffuse, cosmic character. Only gradually, as the child's ego and personality develop does the mother archetype assume universally human and then, still later, individual human features.

But precisely because it is characteristic of man that every infant effects its post-natal embryonic development with and through its mother (only in rare pathological cases is this condition not fulfilled), it is understandable and self-evident that the innate psychic image of the mother archetype must be released by the world factor of the personal mother.

The primal relationship is a relationship between two living beings whose instinctive tendency[11] impels them to seek fulfillment in each other and who, just as in the instinct-directed drive of man and woman to unite, are oriented toward one another. Biologists have found that in the animal world one instinct fits into another as a key fits into a lock. Though in a different way, this is also true of human life. What strikes us as important here is not only to stress the transpersonal, universally human character of this relationship but to recognize it for one of the foundations of archetypal reality.

It is in the primal relationship that an archetypal context transcending the psyche and the person is most clearly demonstrable. For this reason it is here perhaps that we can most readily learn something about the origin of archetypes.

We question neither the autonomy of the unconscious nor the spontaneous emergence of archetypal images. Nor – by way of averting a possible misunderstanding – do we believe that in an adult, i.e., in a fully developed psyche, does an archetype have to be released from without. But the spontaneity of the psyche, and the emergence of spontaneous archetypal images of the unconscious, tell us nothing about the archetype as such. It was originally interpreted by analytical psychology as a correspondence to an outward experience – such as night sea journey, or the course of the sun – or as a category of experience, a primordial image that makes experience in general possible.

Up until now analytical psychologists have largely contented themselves with speaking of the compensatory action of the archetype in the psyche.

Jung repeatedly – and rightly – pointed out that in certain distress situations the archetypal image of the helpful mother can emerge, inducing a reaction in the total personality and in the most favorable cases bringing about a new orientation. In other words, analytical psychologists spoke almost exclusively of archetypal images and of the primordial images of the psyche and the collective unconscious. At first we confined ourselves to the human archetypes and were far from supposing that we could solve this uncommonly difficult complex of problems but hoped at least that our contributions would provide a basis for discussion.

We have said that the archetype is world-related and has "two feet" – because every psychic image must have its world factors. This means that the archetype as such is a living, dynamic relatedness field in the unitary reality, from which what we call the psyche detaches itself and develops only much later. Whereas the archetypal *image* is the representative of this relationship and the releaser of the most divergent psychic reactions, the archetype *as such* is the relatedness itself.

This relatedness – in the primal relationship for example – is the archetypal field which is normally filled by mother and child with their physical as well as psychic behavior. This field is equally present in the mother's feeding and physical warmth, in the sucking instinct of the infant, and in the affective bond between mother and child. The mother's milk is as much a part of the archetype – if one may speak of parts in this connection – as are her smile and her loving relatedness. For the infant, milk equals mother. And between all the functions of maternity that our consciousness regards as physical or psychic there is a relationship of contamination and participation which the imagery and mythological apperception of the psyche later describe as the symbol canon of the archetype of the Great Mother.

It is this archetypal field, transcending the realm of the psyche which under normal conditions guarantees the almost paradoxical phenomenon of a living psychophysical symbiosis between two living beings who are joined together in this field as the survival and development of the species require. In this sense the archetypal field – and this is true of the human archetypes in general and not only of the primal relationship – is an expression of the fact that mankind is a psychosocial unity.[12] No human being can exist and develop his specifically human faculties in isolation. Human existence is possible only as a social existence. The human archetypes are therefore the expression of relations between human beings. This social factor is prepsychic; then the psyche, which becomes differentiated in the unitary reality, gradually forms images in which this prepsychic state of affairs is expressed and so becomes intelligible. Only when the unitary reality is represented in images does the psyche develop in differentiation from the body and then, as consciousness comes into being, proceed to break down the unitary reality into a polarized subject-object reality.

When two human beings are united by a powerful bond, their mutual appetency forms a bilateral connection between them, releasing corresponding archetypes in the psyches of each other. So it takes two individuals to effect or set in motion these transpersonal factors of archetypes. Moreover – they thus partake of a unitary reality which transcends not only the individual but also the *merely* psychic (I use "merely" psychic here because it is transcended by the extraneous reality of the archetypal appetency existing beyond physical and psychic limitations). Once we have grasped this interhuman reality and the "two-footedness" of the archetype, it will be clear to us that an archetype cannot be evoked by any spontaneous process within the psyche – otherwise the mother archetype would emerge in infants abandoned by their mothers and they would develop instead of dying or succumbing to idiocy.

A mother-child relationship is the perfect example of a symbiotic field situation which is necessary for the release of the archetypal image. Once an archetype has been evoked successfully and the first stages of the primal relationship concluded, the archetype can become autonomous and function like an independent organ. It is then manifested with all the transpersonal symbols and qualities characteristic of the archetype – not merely of the personal mother who releases it.

A central symptom of a disturbed primal relationship is the *primary feeling of guilt.* It is characteristic of the psychic disorders of Western man. Surprising as it may seem, the need to counteract the lack of love resulting from a disturbed primal relationship causes the child not to blame the world and man, but to feel guilty. This type of guilt feeling appears in an early phase and is archaic; and it should not be confused with, and above all not derived from, the later guilt feelings connected with the separation of the World Parents and manifested in the Oedipus complex. The primary guilt feeling, it goes without saying, is not a matter of conscious reflection in the child, but it leads to the conviction, which will play a determining role in the child's existence and development, that not-to-be-loved is identical with being abnormal, sick, "leprous," and above all "condemned."

The child's "mythological apperception," which is still unaccompanied by an ego-consciousness, does not experience the defection of the personal mother as injustice; rather, the experience of being forsaken by the mother is molded by her mythical character which constitutes the essence of the archetype. Since the mother is thou, world and Self in one, her defection transforms the world into chaos and nothingness, the thou disappears, leaving the child utterly lonely and forlorn, or becomes an enemy and persecutor, while the child's own Self is transformed into a representative of the Terrible Mother. In this mythological situation life, as the Great Mother, has turned away and nothing remains but death. Just as "absence" and "death" are identical in the child's experience, here the mother's nonexistence signifies the child's own death. The Great Mother Figure of the primal relationship is a goddess of fate who, by her favor or disfavor, decided over life and death, positive or negative development; and moreover, her attitude is the supreme judgment, so that her defection is identical with a nameless guilt on the part of the child.

The primary guilt feeling goes back to the pre-ego phase. Consequently it seems to the adult ego that it has been afflicted with this sense of guilt from the very start. A primary guilt feeling leads a child to associate the disturbance of the primal relationship with its own primordial guilt or original sin. Because the Self has not yet taken form, because there is still no independent ego-Self axis and the opposite that has turned away is so great and godlike that there is no appeal against her verdict, the condemnation is experienced as a higher judgment. In this phase the child lays its misfortune to only one cause: its own guilt. If, as is often the case, the subsequent development of the child's relationship with its father does not repair the damage, the guilt feeling becomes a complex undermining the personality throughout life, unless it is resolved later on by being raised to consciousness or assimilated.

The guilt feeling of the matriarchal phase, deriving from a disturbed primal relationship, follows the formula: "To be good is to be loved by one's own mother; you are bad because your mother does not love you." A negative primal relationship in the early phase of childhood causes not merely a partial, but a total disturbance; a child expelled from the primal relationship is expelled from the natural order of the world and comes to doubt the justification for its existence.

In primitive psychology sickness and misfortune must have a cause; this cause, however, is not what we should call natural, but is always magical and moral. Some evil – an evil magician, an evil spirit, or an ethical transgression – is to blame for it. Such a correlation of misfortune, suffering and guilt is not confined to the Book of Job; it reaches deep into the religious consciousness of man, ancient and modern alike. Later on, to be sure, the primary guilt feelings of the pre-ego phase is rationalized and related to the development of the negativized ego and still later to the Oedipus complex, but analysis shows that this guilt feeling, like an un-analysable nuclear element of the psyche, tends to resist all attempts to explain it or raise it to consciousness. It would seem that virtually the only way in which this primary guilt feeling and its consequences can be reduced and resolved in the first half of life is through a situation of transfer that reconstitutes the primal relationship and regenerates the damaged ego-Self axis. Where the structural damage is less serious, another possibility may be offered by an intrapsychic process in which the figure of the Great Good Mother emerges and overcomes the negative element result-ing from the disturbed primal relationship.[13] But as a rule this happens only in the second half of life.

Subsequent ego-developments or rationalizations are unable, or able only with great difficulty, to extinguish a primary guilt feeling. This is because the disturbance of the primal relationship has truly injured the personality and ushered in a pathological development which — for all the child's absence of objective guilt — leads to a negativized ego and involves an abnormally heightened affectivity, intense unintegrated aggressions, and egocentric, nar-cissistic, asocial attitudes of which the reflecting ego is aware. This ego that has not been formed by tolerance within the primal relationship and so become capable of integration is no more tolerant toward itself than toward anyone else and, where the superego develops normally, it develops moral aggression against itself in addition to all the other aggressions that beset it.

In attempting to achieve an understanding of the psychic structure and its inner dynamic from the standpoint of analytical psychology, we here encounter a problem that is at once structural and genetic. At this point we must attempt to elucidate the rela-tion of the ego to the Self on the one hand and to the superego on the other, for the problem of anxiety and guilt which are so often at the center of a disordered psychic life cannot be solved without an understanding of these contexts.

The superego comes into being and achieves its importance at the time when the child breaks away from the primal relationship, in other words from the matriarchal phase of psychic development, and enters into the patriarchal phase in which the father archetype is dominant. Whereas the matriarchal phase is largely governed by nature, the patriarchal phase brings with it the systematization of consciousness, the separation of consciousness and unconscious, and the dominant influence of the "Fathers," that is, of the prevailing cultural canon, which is the time-conditioned and culture-conditioned expression of the lawgiving father archetype.

We find two different layers of the guilt feeling corresponding to these two phases. Even in normal development the patriarchal guilt feeling makes itself felt at a relatively early stage. Nevertheless this guilt feeling, the child's reaction to the part played by the cultural canon in its upbringing, must be termed secondary; its causes and consequences are relatively easy to determine and it is easily counteracted. The primary guilt feeling that precedes it, however, is matriarchal; the irrationality it provokes in the early ego is difficult both to understand and to cure.

Freud speaks of a "negative therapeutic reaction" and of "a sense of guilt which is finding its satisfaction in the illness and refuses to give up the punishment of suffering." "The description we have given," he goes on, "applies to the most extreme instances of this state of affairs, but in a lesser measure this factor has to be reckoned with in very many cases, perhaps in all comparatively severe cases of neurosis."[14] Here he seems to have hit on the "primary" feeling of guilt.

Freud makes the mistake of deriving the superego from the Oedipus complex and chiefly from the father; he regards it as a late authority resulting from introjection. As often happens with Freud, a particular confusion arises because he wishes at the same time to give the superego a phylogenetic foundation which — as in his speculations on totem and parricide — presupposes the inheritance of repeated individual experiences. Moreover, Freud sees women in a strange light, for in his view they have, strictly speaking, nothing to do with the genesis of morality.[15] (We shall see below that Freud's discoveries take on a new meaning when they are not taken from a personalistic point of view.)

When we follow morality back to its origins, that is, to the matriarchal phase, we encounter not only the primary guilt feeling that comes of a disturbed primal relationship, but also a positive factor correlated with this negative development, namely, where the primary relationship is successful, the primary ethical experience of the matriarchate, corresponds to the phylogenetic ethical experience of mankind in the matriarchate. The experience of the Self through the mother in the primal relationship and the formation of the integral ego lead the child not only to the experience of its weakness, dependency and helplessness, but at the same time to a feeling of security and confidence in an ordered world. The fact that the Self, of which the ego is a product, is experienced through the mother in the unitary reality of trusting oneness with her, is the foundation of the individual's belief not only in the thou and in himself, but also in the ordered coherence of the world. Harmony with this naturally given world order is the primary ethical experience of the matriarchal epoch – and, characteristically, it proves to be the ethical standard also of adult woman.

The childlike formula: "As your mother loves you to be, so should you be, and" – in the case of a successful primal relationship – "so indeed you are" is the basis of an experience of the world in which the anthropocentric feeling of existence is not yet detached from its natural embeddedness in an encompassing reality. The inner law of instinctive order is the (unconsciously) directing morality. The automorphism of unconsciously directed self-formation, based on a successful primal relationship with its Eros-components of loving and being-loved, is in harmony with the inner and outward ethical law. To use Freud's formulation: Religion, morality and social feeling are still one and have their positive root in the primal relationship; on its success depends the development of these principal contents of man's higher life. Phylogenetically, the order and morality of the Great Mother are conditioned by the child's experience of the order of its own body and of the cosmic rhythm of day and night and of the seasons. This rhythm determines the life of the entire organic world and the main rituals of mankind are attuned to it; to be embedded in it means, at the matriarchal stage, to be, both in general and in particular, in order.

Under normal circumstances the same thing occurs ontogenetically in and through the child's relationship with its mother, provided she does not offend against the child's natural rhythm but adapts herself to it. Through the harmony between the child's own rhythm and that of the mother – who in the primal relationship is experienced by the child as identical with its own – the mother's image becomes the representative of both the inner and outward order. As long as the mother in her loving relatedness to the child knows what the child needs and acts accordingly, the child's innate order accords with the order implemented by its mother. The child's experience of a loving harmony with a higher order which at the same time corresponds to its own nature is the first foundation of a morality that does not do violence to the individual but allows him to develop in a process of slow growth. Here too we have the foundation of a world order encompassing inside and outside, to which the child belongs, in which indeed it is embedded as in the mother who contains it.

The root of the earliest and most basic matriarchal morality is then to be sought in a harmony between the still unsplit total personality of the child and the Self which is experienced through the mother. This fundamental experience of harmony with the Self is the foundation of automorphism. It reappears in the second half of life as the moral problem of individuation. To become and to be whole are possible only in a state of harmony with the order of the world, with what the Chinese call the Tao. The fact that this matriarchal morality is based not on the ego but on the total personality, distinguishes it – necessarily – from the secondary ego-morality of the patriarchal stage of consciousness.

This primary, matriarchal experience of order molds the child and is the positive basis of its social feeling, which Briffault was first to derive from the mother-child relationship as it has existed throughout history.[16] Here again Freud was led astray by his patriarchal prejudice and his overemphasis on the father archetype. "Even today," he wrote, "social feelings arise in the individual as a superstructure built upon impulses of jealous rivalry against brothers and sisters."[17]

It is true that the part of social conscience that is based on the repression and suppression of negative impulses originates in this way, but the "morality of conscience" which has nothing to do with social feeling but is an adaptation of the ego to the restrictive commandments of society, is a secondary development. It is preceded by the true social feeling which develops in a positive primal relationship and must be regarded as the basis of all individual relations with others. It corresponds to a primary experience of order and is not a superstructure.

Here it might be asked whether the experience of order in the matriarchal stage actually has anything to do with morality or whether it is not merely a naturally harmonious but in a sense extramoral or premoral feeling of existence. But since a reversal of the positive experience of order in the primal relationship gives rise to a primary guilt feeling, we must also speak positively of a moral experience.

In the development of consciousness leading from mother to father archetypes and from the unitary reality to the polarized reality of consciousness, the ego gradually achieves independence. It begins to lead an existence of its own, no longer sheltered by the embrace of the primal relationship and the Self. Whereas the first phase of existence still under the guardianship of the primal relationship leads to the transfer of the child's Self from mother to child and to the formation of the integral ego, there now begins a process of development leading gradually to the separation of systems and to an opposition between ego and Self.

As long as the ego is contained in the mother's Self, this Self as ordering principle is also the sole moral authority. It is only when conflicts arise between the ego and the Self in the process of differentiation, that a conflict also arises between different types of moral authorities within the personality. Such conflicts play a crucial role both in the normal and in the pathological development of the ego.

It has been shown in *The Origins and History of Consciousness* that the ego is not, as Freud supposed, merely a "representative of the outside world" which makes the outside world accessible to the unconscious and to the id with its blind orientation by the pleasure principle: – "The id experiences the outside world only through the ego."[18] In the view of analytical psychology, the total psychic system, of which the unconscious is a part, is not cut off from the outside world, but comes into being in contact with the world and develops in and through it. As in animals, the instinctive world of the unconscious with its reactions and regulations is "in the world." It does not carry on a solitary, segregated existence which must be adapted to reality by the ego and consciousness. This continuous adaptation of the instincts to the world is the precondition and foundation of human as well as animal development.

The role of ego-consciousness is to bring the collective reactions of the unconscious with their orientation toward the world into harmony with the divergent needs imposed by the unique objective and subjective situation of the individual. The collective consciousness of the cultural canon, that is, the body of values and demands imposed by the collectivity, must also be taken as part of the objective situation. If it is fully to perform its synthetic function, the ego as integral ego must achieve a balance between conflicting demands of the inside and outside, of the collectivity and the individual.

As it gradually assumes its role in the world, the ego is caught up in a conflict that will affect it profoundly during almost its entire existence. If it were merely the exponent of the ego-Self axis and the executive organ of automorphism, it would only come into conflict with nature. Its existence – at least its conscious existence – would, as in animals, serve no other purpose than that of self-preservation and self-assertion in the face of the environment. But the situation is significantly complicated and enriched by the human social constellation.

From the very outset the human ego grows in a human environment, and even the unconscious archetypal factors which in part condition it are from the outset human. When we speak of the collective unconscious and of archetypes that shape and predetermine human reactions, we are speaking very largely of factors which characterize the human species as such, that is, which set man apart from the animals. Man's ego must grow into the collective culture that determines it, and this in itself is a specifically human development. Certain prefigured dispositions must be actualized; the personal figures of the parents activate and help to shape the archetypal situation, but they do not create it. The very nature of the human species conditions an archetypally determined development in the first phase of which the natural mother archetype is dominant; in the second phase it is the cultural father type. This archetypal situation is usually incarnated and, as we have seen, in part shaped by the personal parents, but these phases of the child's development involve not only its family history but also go far beyond it to encompass the development of mankind from an existence in nature to an existence in nature *and* culture. Accordingly, the child emerging from the primal relationship and growing into a social context faces the task of accomplishing the psychic development corresponding to this phylogenetic development, of freeing itself from containment in the unconscious and entering into the twofold nature of the adult human psyche, which is unconscious and conscious in one.

CHAPTER FOUR

From Matriarchate to Patriarchate

In our culture the necessary development by which the child
emerges from the primal relationship to achieve greater independence corresponds to a transition from the psychological matriarchate in which the mother archetype is dominant to the
psychological patriarchate in which the father archetype is
dominant.

In *The Origins and History of Consciousness* we showed that this
transition is indispensable to the development of consciousness.
But there the accent was on the universally human and the symbolic. Here we shall attempt to indicate a few of the ontogenetic
processes in the child which correspond to this transition.

This development can be described as a whole because the progression from the matriarchate of the primal relationship to the
patriarchate applies both to boys and to girls. The male child's
release from his mother is described at length in *The Origins and
History of Consciousness*. The difference in the development of the
girl will at least be touched upon in a later section of this book,
since special importance must be attached to the mother-daughter
relationship as the first phase of the specifically feminine development.

In the uroboric phase of the primal relationship, the mother
reveals active and passive, begetting and conceiving attributes side
by side. These are precursors of what the child will later perceive
in its conflict between mother and father. Thus the flow from the
mother's breast to the child can be experienced as fatherly and
begetting, although her embrace manifests the motherly-contain-
ing. In the unitary reality of the uroboric phase the world parents

are still one, and the child's earliest experience of its mother would, if it could be raised to consciousness, be that of a bisexual primeval being. Not only the maternal and paternal, but also the feminine and masculine are contained in the uroboric Great Round of the mother; the child experiences them not only symbolically, in its unconscious mythological apperception, but also physically through the mother's actions.

Analytical psychology interprets man as a twofold being, in whom important psychic elements of the opposite sex are always present in both physiological sexes, the anima in man, the animus in woman.[1] This fundamental fact which applies also to the mother of the primal relationship – that is, the presence of a masculine principle, the animus, in her psyche – plays a crucial role not only in the primal relationship but also in the phase during which the child grows away from it.

The Patriarchal Uroboros and Woman

In *The Psychology of Transference*,[2] Jung showed that the relationship between two adults is characterized by the constellation of the Quaternio; in other words, their relatedness is fourfold. In the adult with his separate systems of consciousness and unconscious, the masculine consciousness and female unconscious of the man and the feminine consciousness and masculine unconscious of the woman are linked together and mutually fructify one another. This gives rise to a crossed-over, fourfold relationship. The child, in whom the antithetical structure of masculine and feminine, conscious and unconscious is not yet constellated, learns to differentiate between the opposites on the basis of the mother's antithetical male-female structure. In other words, the child in the *participation* of the primal relationship develops its own active and passive, masculine and feminine modes of reaction in and through its relation both to the feminine and masculine elements in the mother. Before it is confronted with the masculine principle as father, it experiences the masculine principle as an unconscious aspect of the mother. Whereas the conscious orientation of woman toward the world and man (insofar as it is not fully identified with the world of masculine values) is dominated largely by the Eros principle of relatedness, the unconscious masculine world in woman represents the principle of *logos* and *nomos* (law), spirit and morality, which in analytical psychology is termed the world of the "animi."

The animus aspect of woman consists in the unconscious convictions, attitudes, interpretations and opinions which (in so far as they do not belong to her unconscious structure by virtue of which her feminine spirit differs from that of man) stem from the culture in which she lives. In our culture, woman from earliest childhood unconsciously absorbs patriarchal values from her cultural environment. Consequently woman in her development faces the difficult task of throwing off the prejudices accruing to her through the values of the patriarchal culture and of overcoming the patriarchal animi sufficiently to make herself accessible to the spiritual aspect specific to woman's nature. This means not only that the mother's culture-conditioned consciousness, which shapes the child's ego and consciousness with its judgments, values and convictions, is shaped by the cultural canon in which the mother lives, but also that the uppermost layer of her unconscious with its unconscious evaluations and judgments is determined by the cultural canon, which in our case is patriarchal. These attitudes arise through a woman's personal experience, through introjected figures and conceptions of the masculine world about her.

Unbeknownst to her, father, brother, uncle, teacher, and husband shape her manner of reacting. In the guise of the mother's judgments and prejudices, all these masculine elements play a part in the care and upbringing of the child and so prepare it for adaptation to the prevailing culture.

But under this animus layer formed by the patriarchate there lies, even in modern woman, the world of matriarchal consciousness, in which on the one hand the masculine forces encompassed in the mother archetype and on the other hand the "patriarchal uroboros," a masculine spirit aspect specific to woman, are dominant. Here we discern a hierarchical order. Uppermost, at the level closest to consciousness lie the animi pertaining to the largely patriarchal cultural stratum. The "Old Man," the archetype of meaning, cannot be counted among the animi of the feminine,

because he is a universally human archetype. Nevertheless, the
meaning he represents is not meaning as such, but meaning in its
masculine form. The "Old Woman" is also a universally human
archetype of meaning, active both in man and woman, but here
the accent is feminine. The figure of the Old Man is close to the
masculine Self and the Old Woman is close to the feminine Self.
The spiritual forces of the Old Woman, who incarnates the human
stage of matriarchally determined existence, are likewise masculine; that is, they are animi of the matriarchal stratum; they
belong to the spiritual aspect of the feminine and like it are
largely overlaid and repressed by patriarchal animi. Characteristically, these matriarchal animi appear as companions of the
Old Woman, often taking the form of wisely speaking animals
endowed with magical powers, or of dwarfs, goblins, devils and
demons — symbols of the feminine wisdom rooted in nature and
instinct.

The figure of the patriarchal uroboros borders on the formless.
It belongs to the deepest archetypal stratum of the masculine
forces at work in woman and is closely bound up with nature. But
this nature-spirit takes on cosmic dimensions. In its lower aspect it
can assume the form of an animal — snake, bird, bull or ram. However, as a demonic or divine spirit which bursts in upon woman
and inwardly fertilises her, it usually takes wind and storm, rain,
thunder and lightning as its symbols. In its highest form it is
manifested as a supernatural music that brings intoxication,
ecstasy and fulfillment of the senses, as the enchantment of a
supreme clarity and harmony, a *conjunction* with existence by
which woman is overpowered. In such terms as fulfilled, overpowered, or ecstatic annihilation, language still preserves the
powerful imagery of the sexual symbolism pertaining to the irruption of the patriarchal uroboros into woman. But despite this
masculine-patriarchal aspect, the symbolism of the patriarchal
uroboros transcends the polarity of sexual symbolism and encompasses the opposites in a single totality, just as music encompasses
the feminine minor and the masculine major scales.

The Great Mother is related to this transpersonal masculine
principle, this master and fructifier as to a spirit by which she is
overpowered and which speaks within her. This patriarchal uro-

boros as moon spirit is a lower chthonian masculine principle, mythologically speaking a phallic lord of sexuality, of drives, of growth and fertility, and at the same time an upper spiritual principle which in the form of ecstasy and vision fulfills the seeress and muse, the prophetess and the woman possessed. Like all mythological powers, this moon spirit is also at work in modern man. It is a fundamental psychic constellation in woman, in children, and in these deeper strata of the male psyche that are dominated by the basic forces of the feminine.

If, as in the primal situation, this masculine principle is still inextricably bound up with a feminine principle and is not projected outward upon a bearer of spirit, woman is experienced as parthenogenic, as the "mother of her own father," as genetrix of man, whom she precedes.

As long as the feminine is still the Great Mother, the masculine as a formless spiritual principle is her equal, but as a figure is usually subordinated to her. Thus, invisibly as wind or visibly as a beam of light, the masculine can fructify not only physically but also spiritually. But later on the Great Goddess who encompasses life and death has male companions, the phallus-bearing generative masculine as god of life, the weapon-bearing, death-dealing masculine as god of death. The moon is the most frequent figure combining all these masculine aspects. As symbol of the patriarchal uroboros, it is at once that which is born of woman and the spiritual principle which begets upon women. It is the phallic bull and the hero's crescent-shaped sword, but it is also the overpowering spirit of the Pythia and the spirit of madness as companion to the destructive, madness-bringing Great Mother, who makes those she has seized moonstruck and lunatic.

Woman experiences this moon spirit of the patriarchal uroboros as something masculine which penetrates and overpowers, something to which the receptive, passive feminine psyche is open, and by which as by an unknown, unconscious force it is wholly captivated and filled. This unconscious force is manifested in woman as a drive which compels and directs her personality, but at the same time it is a spiritual content, a spiritual instinct which as image and intuition, as inspiring feeling and mood, or as a pressing need, guides and fructifies her.

The intuitively knowing, instinct-directed, feeling-toned and emotional, natural and unconscious qualities which are so often attributed to woman, are by no means mere projections upon the woman of the feminine side of the man; they spring from a fundamental constellation, namely, the greater closeness of woman to her unconscious and in particular to a spiritual aspect. This closeness, this relatively greater openness to the incursion of the unconscious, is the basis for the greater irrationality of woman. Unless controlled by consciousness it presents the disadvantage of being open to everything. Woman is generally held to be more superstitious, impressionable, and uncritical than man; this is the necessary shadow side of her superior sensibility, inner receptiveness and intuition.

These inner spiritual influences of the unconscious are manifested in woman as attitudes of faith and knowledge, as conceptions and values which often determine her life and existence independently of, if not in opposition to, her conscious beliefs. As a masculine spirit to which the feminine ego is attuned, they spring from a deeper stratum than do the spiritual attitudes which as animi of the patriarchal world dominate the consciousness of woman. The animus figures of both strata appear in dreams and fantasies as complexes that take possession of woman's unconscious. Here they assume masculine form because one of their essential characteristics is their quality of insistence and penetration which overpowers the feminine personality and consciousness.

For this reason women in all cultures and at all times have been frequent victims of "possession," and in every case the spirit that possesses them is looked upon as masculine. This was the case with the priestess or seeress of the gods or ancestral spirits, with the shamaness, with the hysterical woman possessed by the Tsar or by a *dibbuk*, with the witch possessed by the Devil, and with the female saint or medium. Characteristically, even where possession expresses purely spiritual or psychic contents, it often presents a sexual symbolism with the accent on "penetration," "receiving" and "conceiving." But at the same time the patriarchal uroboros carried revelations of a higher spiritual order and of a higher meaning which assert themselves in opposition to the woman's resistance and fear. But this insight conveyed by the patriarchal uroboros is a supreme revelation which becomes clear only very gradually after the woman surrenders to the principle incarnated in the man and begins to follow its instructions.

But this instruction does not take the form of logical knowledge; rather, it is a wisdom of Eros, which woman in her relatedness follows. In going the ways of Eros, she may be said not so much to fulfill herself as to realize the feminine spirit which is the secret revealed by the patriarchal uroboros. Thus side by side with this Eros aspect, the patriarchal uroboros is at the same time a creative form of the logos which, true to its masculine symbolism, begets upon the feminine principle in woman – and in man – and so becomes fruitful.

Thus the patriarchal uroboros is for woman a first emerging image of a compelling orientation rising up from the unconscious, an orientation which imposes itself against other instinctive tendencies but also against the resistance of consciousness where such resistance is present. It is characterized not only by the spontaneous assault of the unconscious content and the overpowering emotion that accompanies it, but also by the fact that with its active and determining power of orientation it is an unconsciously ordering spiritual principle. Every early culture is based, first unconsciously, then consciously, on such an order, which finds its deposit in ritual and custom. Since this order also delimits the sacred from the profane, the permitted from the forbidden, the good from the bad, it is a precursor of what at a more advanced stage is manifested as masculine logos principle, consciousness and masculine spirit.

In a patriarchal culture of consciousness the influence of this unconscious spiritual aspect in woman, oriented primarily toward nature and toward the universal, recurrent constellations of life, gradually dwindles. Men are concerned more with the unique, changing factors of existence and with the development of abstract consciousness culminating in science and technology. In a patriarchal culture, accordingly, the accent is on the development of consciousness and on the active magic that went hand in hand with it in early times. In the primal relationship, however, the matriarchal "life-accent" is preserved, for in man as in all mammals the rearing of the young necessary to the survival of the

species requires the mother to be open to unconscious orientation
by the spiritual side of the instincts. This orientation is dependent
on the development of the Eros or relatedness principle whereby the ego participates both in the environment and the world
of the unconscious. This participation and the openness that
is almost identical with it are indispensable if the spiritual
aspect of the instincts is to come to the fore and exert its directing
influence.

In the animal world and among human beings whose lives are
predominantly unconscious, this unconscious spiritual principle
makes itself felt in instinctive guidance, in sudden moods or inspirations that show the way. Rudimentary forms of this orientating
attunement are also to be found among animals, whose behavior
in courtship and in the rearing of their young depends on occurrence or nonoccurrence of certain moods. In the animal world,
where the male is not, as in man, specialized in the development
of consciousness, the unconscious spirit prevails equally in both
sexes, just as in primitive man the matriarchal psychic situation
directed by the unconscious is dominant.

The Child and the Masculine in the Matriarchal Phase

In the earliest phase of the primal relationship, a typical
matriarchal situation prevails, for the psychobiological situation of
the child depends on the presence and continuous vitality of a sustaining Eros relationship. Feeling tone and mood are the atmosphere in which the child lives and in which ego and consciousness
take form and develop. Within this sustaining Eros-tone of the
primal relationship, the child continually experiences "interventions," which express themselves in positive and negative stimuli
by which the child is directed. In her Eros-quality the Great
Mother appears symbolically as the feminine-maternal, but in her
function of intervention and stimulation she is manifested as the
masculine part of her totality, as patriarchal uroboros and as
animus. Conscious attitudes of the mother as well as contents of
the personal and collective unconscious play a part in these interventions and incursions into the child's existence. Conceptions and
attitudes of the logos-aspect and of morality, as well as unconscious

inspirations and evaluating animi of the mother are communicated to the child and direct it. Since all these emotionally charged interventions, regardless of the stratum in which they originate, are manifested in the symbolism of the masculine, the child's problem is whether and to what degree it is open and receptive to these interventions and incursions or closed and unreceptive.

To the infant the animus aspect of the mother, standing for order, for the *nomos*-principle, partakes at first of the Terrible Mother insofar as it disturbs the child's well-being and is associated with an intervention in, and assault on, its existence. For as Freud noted — rightly as far as this phase is concerned — to a being that has not yet achieved its full psychic development every limitation and restriction can appear as a denial and withdrawal of love. But in resisting this intervention, the child comes into conflict with the principle of social adaptation of which the mother is the representative.

Later on, the child acquires a positive along with the negative experience of this masculine aspect of the Great Mother, which now, concurrently or successively, confers both pleasure and pain or discomfort. Unconsciously and consciously the child attributes the pleasant to the "good" Mother and the unpleasant to the "terrible" Mother.

In human development the opposition between masculine and feminine is preceded by the more general opposition between active and passive, stimulating and stimulated, that which provokes suffering and that which suffers. Everything that troubles the initial repose of the child psyche — privations from outside or pain within, sudden waking from sleep or an affect provoked by whatever causes, the discomfort of hunger, but also the pleasure of movement, of eating and evacuating — all these amount to disturbances which upset the child's general well-being and overpower its still feeble ego. To the child, well-being means a protected but fluid balance between itself and its environment and between its ego and unconscious. Thus in the earliest phase the child's body represents both a part of the ego's environment and an incarnation of what we call the unconscious. It is precisely this intermediate position of the body which causes all psychic factors as well as the child's relation to world and environment to be experienced in the symbolism of the alimentary and metabolic uroboros, which is the dynamic symbol of the body.

In the earliest phase, when the ego still possesses little libido, the overpowering of the ego may be manifested in the tiredness preceding sleep; such tiredness expresses exhaustion of the child's ego and consciousness.

At first, disturbances appear to the child under two aspects: the positive stimulation which can lead to a pleasant overpowering of the ego, and the negative stimulation which leads to affects and to an anxious overpowering of the ego. Thus even in the matriarchal phase of the primal relationship, before the principle of opposition experienced in the symbols of masculine and feminine has emerged, early forms of what is later experienced in the image of the terrifying masculine make their appearance.

When the child's consciousness is sufficiently differentiated that a disturbing factor is reflected not only by symptoms but also by psychic images it becomes evident that the child psyche interprets all disturbances of its state of equilibrium, regardless of kind, as emanating from the masculine. In the dreams of children – as of grownups – the negative stimulant is often symbolized by terrifying animals or of robbers or burglars. Whether or not they are accompanied by corresponding psychic images, a considerable share of infantile anxieties are connected with this phenomenon of masculine incursion, the earliest form of which may be the disturbance of the child's equilibrium, of its state of physical repose, to which the smallest infant reacts with fear. This equilibrium, of course, is differently constellated according to the child's phase of development; the more highly developed and differentiated the psyche, the more oppositions it is capable of compensating and integrating. In the archaic psyche that expresses itself in images, these disturbances are experienced as if they emanated from a person, a masculine archetype or a complex-figure.

Though every child experiences such irrupting disturbances in the course of its development, not only the intensity of the irruption but also the intensity of the psychic reaction to it vary in the extreme. Constitutional factors as well as practical circumstances may abnormally enhance this experience of the "irruptive-masculine" or attenuate it, for it is an experience that combines elements originating in the child itself with others rooted in outward events and circumstances.

A constitutionally lively unconscious, a constitutional proneness to affects that assail the child from within, or an underdeveloped ego regardless of its causes will intensify the irruptive factor. The same goes for all intense disturbances in the child's development such as disturbances of the primal relationship, of the environment, physical deficiencies, hunger, sickness, or animus-attitudes on the part of the mother (who, for example, may let her child cry from hunger "as a matter of principle"). The child experiences all these as one and the same thing: as a hostile, compelling, interfering, overpowering force, hence a transpersonal masculine factor pertaining to the uroboric Mother.

In the primal relationship all these stimuli and disturbances are experienced as coming directly from the mother whether they are actually caused by the mother or by some factor in the unconscious or the environment. In the dual union of the primal relationship, in which inside and outside, mine and thine are still undifferentiated, not only a stimulus within the child, be it pain or hunger or pleasure, but also such outside disturbances as light or darkness, voices or sounds, are included in the all-encompassing world of the Great Mother. And conversely an inner stimulus from the mother, her tenderness and affects, her positive or negative moods are experienced by the child as a disturbance of its balance, which is secured by the maternal world-unity in which the child lives.

Independently of its content, every irruptive factor is experienced emotionally. In the relatedness-character of the primal relationship, this emotional component is so strongly stressed that all understanding and orientation depend on it. And even a somewhat older child experiences the mother's intentions as emotional expressions of affection or rejection, of positive or negative feeling. The Eros-component of relatedness is primary: consciousness and its logos-aspect come later and develop under its direction.

This formative power of the primal relationship not only guides the development of the child's consciousness, but also determines its whole attitude toward the environment. And not last, it instills the spiritual and religious values laid down by the cultural milieu in the child, who thus comes to take them for granted. Under normal conditions, these values remain unquestioned, the child participates in them unconsciously. Thus it is in earliest childhood, in the course of the primal relationship that the powers and demons of feast and rite, God and Devil, but also the child's village, city or native land – in short everything that constitutes the spiritual world of the group – take their place in the child psyche. And only under special conditions are these elements subjected to the critique of consciousness.

And the *nomos* – the moral component – is from the very outset involved in the primal relationship with the Great Mother. For it is through its mother, who is Self, society, and world in one, that the child first experiences order, limitation, affirmation and negation. This *nomos*-component, this "no" or "enough" which confronts the child as the supreme law, is also an intervention, a disturbance, to which the child naturally reacts with agitation, indeed with affects, but through which it learns to regulate its behavior and adapt it to the law of its environment.

The orders and limits which the mother represents for the child do not, however, spring from her conscious world, but from the world of her animi, her unconscious masculine-spiritual and feminine-spiritual background. Thus, far more than the attitudes that the mother consciously communicates, those of her animi that are closest to consciousness convey to the child the demands of the cultural environment, the restrictions, prohibitions, disciplines, and also the value-judgments and habits which take on their importance when the child develops beyond the physiological plane of the vital functions. Wherever ritual and custom affect the physiological life of an infant – in matters of feeding, cleanliness, etc. – they represent an intervention of society in the life of the child. But these "orders" reach down into deeper levels of the human psyche, for the formative principle of the maternal animi is a continuation of the formative principle that already makes itself felt in the instinctive behavior of the animal world, for example, in the orderly way in which animals care for their young.

But whereas the relatedness-principle of the Eros as experienced through the mother is associated with the feminine in the child psyche, the formative principle that is active in her is associated with the world of the masculine. It is symbolically masculine because it intervenes actively, directs, determines, guides and violates, but also because it tries consciously to establish the order indispensable to a rational, spiritual world. It possesses attributes which later on – after the primal relationship – pertain essentially to the Fathers and the male group. Where the woman as Great Mother still possesses these attributes, they are manifested as her masculine qualities and constitute the bisexual-uroboric character of the Great Feminine.

The mother of the primal relationship represents both the collective and the individual, the demands both of the unconscious and of the ego as it develops in society. This position, numinous in its superiority and ambivalence, enables her to integrate oppositions,[3] and for this reason (as we have explained) she is at first the child's relatedness-Self, in whose image the integrating function of the child's ego develops.

Thus the child psyche is sustained by the predominance of its experience of the Good Mother. In also accepting discomfort, the suffering and the limitations imposed by the Terrible Mother, it develops into a totality, capable of integrating the good and the bad, the pleasant and the unpleasant. Thus the child psyche unconsciously contains within itself the experience of the Great Mother, of the world and of itself in an ordered and meaningful whole.

For in its relation of identity with the Great Mother, the child is joined to the meaningful order of psychic life as a whole, as a coherent hierarchy of psychic powers and authorities. The fact that the mother is the child's Self is a fundamental ordering experience for the child's unconscious structure. In the spiritual order that is manifested in the mother as Self, consciousness and unconscious, body and psyche, inside and outside, world and man are joined in a compensatory totality. This ordered structure of which the child is a part evokes its innate archetypal aptitude for order. And here again an archetypal process is released in the child by its experience of its personal mother, who is connected with the archetypes.

The later conflict between individual and cultural canon is

fore-shadowed at this stage by the conflict between the child's
affects and drives on the one hand and on the other hand the
mother's animus-world which evokes and sets in motion the inner
order innate in the child. The conflict between order and that-
which-is-to-be-ordered, between mother and child, also takes
place in the child's psyche as a conflict between its drives and
own ordering authorities.

What in the primal relationship acts upon the child as the
mother's unconscious spiritual aspect is still an undifferentiated,
universal factor that does not attach to any specific quality or
action on the part of the mother. Because of the child's undifferentiated psychic situation it can at first experience the animus world
of the Great Mother only as an undifferentiated whole, which is
irruptive, alarming, disturbing and hostile. Here we encounter a
paradox that is not at all unusual in the human psyche; a higher
ordering principle is experienced as an overpowering assault by
the psyche, which reacts with fear, but this fear is precisely the
fear of chaos and disorder.

Where the primal relationship is positive, a child can withstand
and accept this assault because its experience of the security of the
primal relationship has been so fundamental that, mythologically
speaking, the child can "die" in the certainty of being reborn by
the mother, just as it can go to sleep in the certainty of rewaking.
This surrender to the patriarchal uroboros of the Great Mother is
for the child, regardless of its sex, a preliminary form of the
"marriage of death" in which thanks to the predominance of the
Eros-principle, the psyche – despite its fear – is open to a negative
overpowering.

This ability to surrender itself to the intervention of a superior
power is an essential consequence of a successful primal relationship. It is of fundamental importance for the individual's subsequent development and specifically for his sense of security and
his relation to the world, the thou, and the unconscious.

Obviously, though this development takes place in a phase and
on a level where there is still no awareness of sex and sexual differences, it is of even more far-reaching importance for a girl than
for a boy. In any case, it has much to do with the possibility of
being open toward the world and one's own psyche. Regardless of

its sex, the child takes at first an essentially passive-receptive attitude. Even in this early phase, it already has its own spontaneous
activity toward the mother-world, but this too is integrated into
a successful primal relationship and is not manifested as an attitude of defense or defiance, much less as aggressive anti-relatedness.
But where the primal relationship is unsuccessful, the distressed
ego,[4] to which the instinct of self-preservation has prematurely
given rise, substitutes its defensive activity and aggression for
the security that a negative relationship with the mother has
denied it.

The Growing Independence of the Ego and the Appearance of Conflicts

In the early uroboric phase of the primal relationship it is
hardly possible to speak of an activity of the ego. But with the
"birth" of the Self and the ego at the end of the first year of life
the independence of the child personality begins to produce conflicts with the mother of the primal relationship. In the second
phase of the primal relationship the dominance of the mother as
mother archetype is still overpowering; but at this stage, what is
known in mythological terms as the "separation of the World
Parents," namely, the polarization of the world into opposites,
makes itself felt in the child psyche. The oppositions between I and
thou, Self and world, male and female make their appearance as
do those between opening and closing oneself, accepting and rejecting. True, the psychic functions of opposition were present at
an earlier stage, but in the phase of the separation of the World
Parents they begin to play a particularly active part in the child's
ego-development. Up to this point, the opposites are so mingled
that just as one can speak of a uroboric Great Mother one can
speak of uroboric behavior in the child. Boy and girl react both in
a feminine, passive-receptive manner and in an active, masculine
manner, and it is just as natural for a girl child to behave in a
masculine way toward her mother as for a boy to react in a passive-
feminine way toward his mother's animus-aspect.

The development of the child personality brings with it an increased ambivalence that prepares the way for the necessary beginning of a conflict between mother and child. By splitting the

image of the Great Mother into images of the Good and of the Terrible Mother, the child psyche gives rise to a polarization of the world, to a separation of the World Parents within the maternal "Great Round." In gradually achieving independence, the child comes to experience the mother as turning-away and rejecting no less often than as accepting and containing. At the same time, still under the dominance of the mother-archetype, the oppositions between good and bad, friendly and unfriendly, pleasant and unpleasant, between the ego and not-ego, consciousness and the unconscious make their appearance as do the mythological oppositions between night and day, heaven and earth, light and dark. This differentiation occurs in the maternal sphere and within the primal relationship as the sheltering home of child existence.

But increasing independence always means defenselessness and every even apparent departure from the child's position of security is experienced as loneliness. But although the child at this stage of development turns away from its mother and toward the world, and then experiences its mother as bad and rejecting, this does not fundamentally endanger the child's central feeling of security once the positive foundation of the primal relationship has been laid.

Now the original identity is differentiated more and more, and the figures of personal mother, world-mother, mother as world, and of night-mother, mother as unconscious, slowly separate, conflict with one another and alternate. Normally the feeling of confidence acquired in the primal relationship carries over from the start to the child's attitude toward the night-mother of the unconscious; a child sheltered in the primal relationship entrusts itself without anxiety to the sleep that obliterates consciousness; it falls asleep with a sense of security which continues into the life of the adult, though the same adult reacts with anxiety to other extinctions of his ego-consciousness. Such a positive relation to the personal mother and the night-mother also expresses itself in the child's attitude toward the world, which it views as world-mother and confronts with a primary confidence.

This world-mother which satisfies the child's spreading curiosity and the pleasurable tendency of its ego to expand, is good. She becomes bad when the child is tired or disappointed in its demands on the world. Then, when the world-mother has become dark and hostile, the child turns as a matter of course to its personal mother or returns to the good mother of sleep and night, who is related to the personal mother. But conversely, when a child's personal mother is "bad," it tends toward the world and its pleasures, upon which it looks with the same confidence as upon its personal mother.

Thus in this phase of its development the child moves into the maternal area between the personal mother, who is associated with a part of the outside world and has become mother-of-the-bed, of the room, of the home, as well as the world-mother of the outside world. Alternately the child is attracted and repelled by these two poles, and through both experiences the "yes" and "no," the good and the bad, in other words, the opposites.

This ambivalence is the first appearance of those human attitudes toward inside and outside which are necessary to the experience of the world as a whole and which later become habitual as introverted and extroverted attitudes. In the first phase of a normal primal relationship the mother integrated the necessary denials or rejections by the predominance of her positive existence. Now with the development of the child ego, the mother's "terrible" attitudes are progressively intensified even when in reality, that is, objectively, the mother remains a positive, integrating authority. Only in this way can the child develop the necessary opposition to its mother, which ultimately ends in its turning away from her and the matriarchal world. This is the mythological "matricide" which makes possible the transition to the father archetype.

In the phase of the primal relationship in which the alimentary drive and the symbolism of the metabolic uroboros are dominant, the child's attachment to its mother is largely localized in its body. The child's total body and the mother as Self are the poles of the unitary field in which the primal relationship is at first realized. The child's unitary body-feeling is the determinant for its vegetative existence; its skin and its oral zone – later the anal zone as well – are accented fields of a total experience, whose multiple facets are still undeveloped. But this unitary body-feeling is by nature polyvalent, for it contains bodily, psychic and spiritual, individual, automorphous and social factors.

At this stage the Great Mother appears predominantly as "Mistress of the Plants," as the goddess of growth and nourishment. The world and the time allotted to it are determined by hunger and its appeasement, and the opposition between pleasant and unpleasant which underlies so many later polarities is experienced primarily on the basis of the alimentary urge. The alimentary rhythm also determines waking and sleeping, and at first this alimentary order even overshadows that of day and night, which impresses itself on the child only gradually. As far as we know, the dark phase of the intra-uterine embryonic period is interrupted by no consciousness or waking. This polarity sets in with birth when, under the pressure of hunger, consciousness makes its first sporadic appearances.

The child connects the experiences of satiety, warmth, awakeness, consciousness and light with the mother, and this connection is the basis for the feeling of security that the child acquires in the primal relationship. In this phase mother, warmth, satiety, pleasure, and the feeling of being one with itself are closely linked with the experience of light and awakedness. But at first the Great Mother of nourishment as light is mythologically and symbolically related to the moon, the light of night. For when it emerges from the darkness of the intra-uterine embryonic period, the child does not immediately enter into the polarity of a day-and-night world, but dozes in a world of continuous twilight, interrupted only by the rhythm in which the mother – as the light which brings nourishment, security and warmth – interrupts the child's sleep. The child who sleeps all night and is almost always asleep in the daytime has not yet entered into the diurnal order of the adult world. It is the alimentary drive that disturbs this twilight sleep and impels the child to grow into a polarized world.

For in waking and disturbing the child, hunger is its first stimulus to consciousness. Waking and consciousness are the first experiences of polarity to which the child is exposed; consequently, they are connected with discomfort. Whereas in the intra-uterine embryonic period being-nourished, sleeping, shelteredness in the darkness of the unconscious were identical, this changes with the child's entrance into the world, and even within the unitary field of the primal relationship the principle of opposition begins to exert its differentiating influence. The initially unavoidable co-incidence of waking, consciousness, and discomfort-hunger is modified by the mother. It is she who first enables the child to make the association, so characteristic for man, between pleasure and consciousness, for it is through her that the experience of waking, light and consciousness is linked with that of satiety, pleasure, warmth and security, which far outweighs the discomfort of waking and of hunger.

The feeling of security and shelteredness in the darkness of the unconscious is a primary pre-human and human experience; when a child slips back into sleep, it is returning to the primary state of containment in the uroboric darkness. To formulate it in a different way, the problem is not that an infant should sleep without anxiety, but that it should be able to wake up without anxiety. Because the moon-light-mother of the primal relationship is the vehicle of consciousness, of light amid darkness, because it is also she who brings satiety and security, an early disturbance of the primal relationship always brings with it a disturbance in the development of consciousness. For in a normal development, consciousness brings the child fulfillment and is not a disturbance of the original containing darkness of the unconscious. For this reason the good mother of the primal relationship is also the guardian of consciousness and its development; she is Sophia, whereas the "bad mother" is always hostile to the development of consciousness because she intensifies the tendency to remain in, or return to the darkness of the unconscious. For this reason, conversely, fear of the terrible mother usually tends to strengthen consciousness and often plays a positive role in the development of consciousness in the first half of life.

Thus under the supervision of the mother of the primal relationship the child gradually enters into the human world of day and night and the rhythmic correlation of waking, consciousness and day on the one hand, and of the unconscious, darkness and night on the other. From this point on, the world order determined by the course of the sun orders human existence. But under normal circumstances this world also remains at first within the matriarchal order and no coercion violates either the child's body rhythm or the mother who is joined with the child into a world unity. In this sense as well, the good mother of the primal relationship is the "Mistress of the Plants"; she is attuned to the natural growth of her child and to his "times," which like the tides are determined by an – unconscious – lunar rhythm.

The ritual and rhythm of life which accent, preserve and raise to consciousness the natural divisions of the day and night determined by the child's body-Self are governed by the bond of Eros, by the mother's bond with her child. The child's – and mother's – natural ritual behavior in regard to food and the satisfaction of needs, to play and exchanges of tenderness, to sleep and later on to the beginning of the learning process, is always colored by the Eros-character of the primal relationship. It is subject to a matriarchal ordering principle contrasting with the rationality of the logos principle. It is dominated by symbols and by a rhythmic repetition closely related to the body rhythm – the child's rhythmic body movements, sucking and thrashing about, crowing and mumbling, and the mother's humming and singing, rocking and caressing.

But under normal conditions the intervention of the patriarchal principle of order represented by the mother's consciousness and her animi also remains embedded in the matriarchal constellation of the primal relationship – and only then does it give rise to no disturbance. Even the conflict between the natural matriarchal order directed by the body-Self and the rational patriarchal order imposed by consciousness and culture is at first bridged over by the mother. Where the mother's love has led the child to trust, it will be imperceptibly and easily integrated into the rational daily order of the group.

Weaning

The development from the matriarchal to the patriarchal is symbolized by "weaning," a concept which should not be restricted to the weaning of the infant from its mother's breast, although the cessation of this closest bodily contact with the mother obviously represents a critical point in the child's development.

Within the primal relationship, weaning, removal from the mother's breast, means that physically the child is no longer quite so close to its mother. But normally the mother compensates for this loss by her tenderness. Where this is not the case or where the mother feels that with the end of nursing her duties to her child are also at an end and hands it over to helpers, weaning can come as a great shock. But just as breast-feeding by no means excludes a disturbed primal relationship, breast feeding can in a normal primal relationship be discontinued without the slightest disturbance. Weaning and the transition from the early to the late phase of the primal relationship and from the matriarchal to the patriarchal world are normal processes for the human child. In a normal development, the transition from one phase to the next under the mother's guidance is adapted to the child and its inner rhythm of growth. For this reason the mother is the "Mistress of Growth." In the unitary field between mother and child they both adapt themselves to the inner, transpersonal law of growth whose guardian is the mother.

Thus under normal circumstances weaning is not a catastrophe, since it augments the child's natural tendency toward autonomy, which expresses itself also in the increasing pleasure it takes in its own body and its functions, so that the negative element of loss is compensated by a gain. Because release from the dual union with the mother is one of the preconditions for the necessary development of the child's ego and Self, weaning involves harm to the child only when it is accompanied by an abrupt break in the primal relationship. In this case it represents a loss of paradise, which is the archetypal background of the castration complex (not only physical, but psychological and symbolical) in which man experiences his isolation, his exclusion from the world and from life as despair and loneliness. The continuous contact between the child and the mother's warm, life-giving body, characteristic of man's primitive situation, is reduced more and more. Because in the civilized world mother and child both wear clothes, the contact which at first extended to the child's whole body is reduced to its oral zone which comes into contact with the mother's breast only at feeding time, and even then a bottle may be substituted. A further complication arises if the original nature-attuned feeding in response to the child's hunger is replaced by the logos-like regularity of fixed feeding hours. Unquestionably this culture-conditioned development will have negative results for it puts an affective emphasis on feeding hours, restricts the pleasure of the whole body's feeling, and so overstresses the oral, anal and genital erogenous zones.

The mother compensates in part for this culture-conditioned reduction of bodily contact by kissing and caressing her child and carrying it about. But beyond a doubt the loss of the infantile "feeling" and "seeing" through which the children of primitive peoples came to take the body of the opposite sex for granted, is a flaw in the development of Western man, without which public voyeurism – in advertising, films, strip-tease shows, etc. – would not play so exaggerated a role.

In general, a part of the orientation characteristic of modern man, his nostalgia for the "good" lost past and his feeling of loneliness and insecurity in a cold world, go back to these fundamental deficiencies of childhood. At the same time, this lack of bodily contact in childhood leads to the oversexualization of modern man, whose yearning for contact with the body of another human being can be fulfilled only by sex. Why today's average male is so oversexed – a fact demonstrated by the pictures of naked and half-naked women that assail us at every turn – can only be understood through a study of the specific development of the male in our culture and in particular the circumstances attending his release from the primal relationship. On the other hand, it must also be asked whether the childhood deficiencies and neuroses so characteristic of Western man are not in part responsible for the development of his specific culture and in particular of his scientific culture. His exacerbated, reoriented curiosity is guided into other channels and allegedly sublimated. His loss of nature is compensated by an increase in the artificial fare of culture.

Not only is weaning a crucial step in the process of release from the maternal sphere; but it is also the child's first step into the culture of the group, into its environment. For the mothers of primitive cultures who often breast-feed their children for years, weaning does not represent a particular turning-point or break. But in modern Western society a mother has her field of activity not only in the home and immediate vicinity, as is still the case among peasants, but often goes out to work; thus weaning is necessarily a turning-point. Regular feeding times may be substituted too soon for the satisfaction of the child's alimentary rhythm; the weaning itself may be premature; or the child may be turned over to a stranger or to an institution that substitutes for the family.

But in any of these cases the child necessarily enters into the culture of its group and into the fundamental attitudes it prescribes; it is exposed – usually too soon – to the culturation process that will determine its whole future life. A mother's influence on the child's development depends in high degree on whether she herself has been molded into a healthy or a sick personality by her group, and whether her conscious and unconscious animus attitudes run counter to the nature of child development and especially to the needs of the primal relationship.

Cleanliness, Erect Posture and the Problem of Evil

Numerous as are the possibilities of infantile disorders connected with the mother-relationship, there is no doubt that in our culture training in anal cleanliness represents an important turning-point in child development. In the first phase of child development the anal zone is integrated with existence as a whole; its stimulations are in no way distinct from the body totality. Excrement is experienced as a part of the body-Self. In accordance with the *pars-pro-toto* law of the primitive world, each part of the body and all its excretions or waste-products – nails, hair, remnants of food, etc. – are held, among primitive peoples, to be identical with the whole of the body and of the individual, i.e., with the body-Self. This identity is the basis of a large number of magical actions, which make use of these parts of the body. In the phase of the body-Self, in which the archetype of wholeness as the "alimentary uroboros" – a living totality realized in ingestion and excretion on all bodily levels – is the dominant symbol, every function of this body is alive and sacral. To modern man this concept is perhaps most clearly illustrated by the symbolism of "breath," which in language and art – the breath of life or the breath of God, for example – is still a meaningful symbol for the substance of life and the soul.

In the same sense we find that in the phase when the Self is manifested predominantly as the body-Self, all bodily substances, not only those which we look upon as waste, such as hair, nails, urine, feces, menstrual blood, but also saliva, sweat, sperm and blood, are charged with mana, with soul and magic power, and closely related to the life of the individual. For this reason the significance of these "soul substances" has been preserved to this day in superstition and popular medicine.

Analogous to this phylogenetic condition, we find ontogenetically that for the child feces in particular are not only an essential part of himself, but moreover represent something which he has creatively made and which is connected with him. This creative quality of the anal is illustrated by the fact that in many languages "to make" is a popular term for to defecate. In a positive primal relationship this creative unity is preserved; defecation is at once a positive achievement and a gift embedded in the emotional atmosphere of the bond between mother and child.

The connection between oral and anal as a living field of ingestion and excretion – whose two poles are interdependent and of equal value – is archetypal. In many myths for this reason excrement, connected with the earthy, is the starting point for a creative life. Not only can food and of course specifically the tuberous plants be thought to originate in excrement, as is the case in many regions of the earth, but gods as well, a belief that is met with in Japan.[5]

Earth-colored excrement buried in the earth gives rise to growth, and from stinking putrid matter rises new, reborn life; and conversely, fragrant-smelling food turns to feces, which are given back to the earth and the life cycle of which man is an integral part. Thus in many cultures the connection between excrement as a living, organic part of the body and the living, organic earth in which it is buried is taken for granted. Even where it has little or no economic importance as a fertilizer, dung is regarded as a magical and significant substance. Even where it is looked upon as unclean, it retains a magic significance. At the matriarchal, pregenital level, oral and anal merge with one another as life and death; the one is indissolubly bound up with the other.

In the vegetatively accented world view – over which presides the Great Goddess as mistress of all plant life – death, rot, foul-smelling corruption are not felt to be hostile to life. Because life, death and rebirth are looked upon as a continuous process and the importance of the individual is not yet over-emphasized, death is not seen as an end or even as a dangerous crisis.[6]

Even in our modern Western civilization these same conditions apply to the first phase of the primal relationship. In all its functions, in all the parts and manifestations of its body, the child is an integral whole and its body-Self is still undivided. The mother's love – in so far as it is normal – knows no disgust toward the child's body or bodily functions; the mother accepts the child's natural needs as self-evident and does not intervene to regulate them.

Not only in Western culture, however, but also in a large number of so-called primitive cultures, the aversion to the anal seems to have occurred very early. Where this is the case, the anal training of the child has become a critical turning-point. Normally this training should not begin until the child can comply without difficulty. But often, as a result of culturally or individually neurotic attitudes, toilet training is begun too early. Such interference with the child's growth and development is unnatural and can have disastrous consequences.

A crucial stage in child development begins when a part of the motor nervous system that had not hitherto functioned matures and can be subordinated to the will of the ego. But this point in the development of the ego, which has its most visible manifestation in sitting, standing and later in walking has significant preliminary stages, for the motor system matures gradually and all its parts do not mature at the same time.

Thus the power to close the anal sphincter results from a process of growth which like grasping, talking, biting, standing and walking has its own natural timing. Although these times of development are biologically embedded in the life of the species, there are individual variations. One child talks, stands and walks sooner than another without being in the least abnormal, and cleanliness is likewise subject to individual variations.

There is an essential connection between the maturation of the motor nervous system, the first beginnings of an independent ego, and the assumption of the erect position. Motor maturation means that significant parts of the body are connected with the ego and gradually subordinated to it. But from the standpoint of the body-image, this commanding and acting ego is a head-ego, for in man the head is in high degree the vehicle of sensory orientation in the world. The extraordinary size of the head in comparison with the rest of the body in childhood corresponds to the role of the active ego, which reaches out and later steps out into the world, and the head is experienced as the central symbol of human-ego activity, as the cephalopods in children's drawings make clear.

At the beginning of the infant's life, the oral pole is chiefly passive and receptive and expresses its active or antagonistic aspect only in sucking. As the first teeth emerge, oral activity, manifested especially in preliminary forms of speech, is very much intensified. Yet this intensification is not strictly speaking aggressive: rather, it points to a new stage in the child's mastery of the world. In keeping with the alimentary symbolism that is dominant at this phase, eating, biting, and chewing are an essential form of world-assimilation.

At this point we must distinguish between the specifically human, socially recognized aggression (which hardly deserves the name of aggression), and the pathological aggression which exceeds the normal aggression accepted or even encouraged by society. The presence of teeth, for example, goes hand in hand with the chewing of food, which is normal human behavior and is not strictly speaking aggressive. But the same equipment can serve aggressive purposes, for example, when one human being bites another. On the other hand, when a carnivorous animal bites and eats another living creature, this cannot be called pathological aggression because it is the normal conduct of the species. When we call a dog "snappy" or "vicious," we mean that it is true to the behavior of its species and does not respond to domestication. Similarly – whether rightly or wrongly – we regard the human warrior who behaves aggressively in a way that is recognized and encouraged by society, as normally human and not pathological.

In this sense, the normal development of the child's dentition and its functions is specifically human and not pathologically aggressive. Perhaps we should term this normal behavior "aggressive activity" in order to distinguish it from genuine aggression, such as that of a child who bites its mother.

But where the development is normal, the mouth not only performs the function of receiving food, but is also an organ of sense and knowledge, and here again it engages in aggressive activity. Through the mouth the child learns to know and assimilate the world by tasting and eating it. For the infant, whose world was at first identical with the mother as breast and as nourishment, the mouth is one of the essential sources of experience; and this tends to be true also of the small child who puts everything in its mouth.

Thus the connection between the knowledge-drive and the aggressive activity of the oral zone is from the start embedded in the life of the human species; but here it must be said that the cognitive impulse is an essentially human form of world-mastery which cannot be developed from other drives, but which — as Jung pointed out — essentially determines the development of the child. The consciousness characteristic of man is far less a passive organ of play, into which the image of the world falls, than an organ and instrument of active formation which apprehends and grasps the world. Not only is the motif of mastery over nature that culminates in modern technology present in this "grasping" as in the magical phase; but even in the specific patriarchal form of the development of consciousness, it does not lose this accent which has its primal pattern in the mythological combat of the hero.

For this reason the symbols of aggressive activity are specific symbols of consciousness and especially of thought, to which language applies an abundance of military symbols. The patriarchal consciousness relates in principle to a sector of reality, and knowledge is always an operation, which detaches, isolates and delimits. Similarly the fact that we employ oral symbolism in referring to a form of world-assimilation typical of man, points to the role played by the aggressive activity of the teeth. It also finds expression in the activity of analytical reduction that precedes knowledge; and later the mouth takes on the antagonistic and compensatory function of reception and ingestion corresponding to the act of gaining knowledge. The arms stand for the apprehending and grasping of the world, quite apart from the function of world-refashioning that is connected with them. The hand is the specifically human organ in which active and receptive experience and grasp of the world are intimately combined.

Mouth and arms are essentially cognitive organs of the world-mastering head-pole; there is always a certain tone of aggressiveness in their striving for mastery, but we cannot for that reason speak of pathological aggression in the sense of sadism. For sadism, unlike aggression, necessarily implies the conscious infliction of pain, and this is utterly lacking in the naïve aggressive activity connected with the human drive to knowledge and mastery of the world.

At almost the same time as the appearance of the first teeth the child begins to sit up; this is an expression of the fact that the child's activity of reaching out and mastering the world has attained a new stage, encompassing a larger area of the world. This specifically human development goes hand in hand with a new orientation toward the body and the world. Still within the matriarchal world, a decisive step is taken toward polarization, a step that is the precursor of the later, definitive polarization of the world.

Among the quadruped mammals head and tail pole are equally accented; among the baboons, for example, the tail-genital-anal pole is accented by color. Similarly the recumbent infant, despite the accentuation of the head, the accent is on the body as a whole, and no particular zone is privileged; the experience of the lower body-pole is integrated with the experience of the whole body. At this stage the child's body-Self as center of the unconsciously directed body-psyche occupies the foreground. In the primal relationship the body-world — which with its drives, its pain and its pleasures, confronts the ego as something other — is almost entirely merged with the mother's thou-world. The child has no body of its own distinct from the mother and has not yet integrated the discomfort originating in its own body as something that belongs to itself. But as the ego is consolidated and its relation to the body and its functions develops, the body comes to be experienced as a whole. The child's own body and the body-Self, in other words, the child's experience of its body as a Self and as a whole, now becomes the basis for the independence of the ego and for its mastery of more and more bodily functions.

When the human child begins to sit up, the accent shifts to the head-pole. This corresponds to the development of the child's orientation in the world through the sensory organs situated in the head and the accelerated development of its brain. Now gradually the ego-head pole is emancipated as center of the personality, and this center gives rise to a new orientation based on the criteria of above and below, front and back.

In the course of this process the child psyche turns away from the earth and toward the sky. And this new development, this turn away from the lower body pole, is accompanied by a change in the aspect of the Great Mother. As Mistress of the Plants she was hitherto the highest authority of the laws of growth – largely unconscious and more or less conflictless – governing the child's development, in which the ego was still subordinate and the mother's Self played the leading role. Now, as Mistress of the Animals, she becomes the goddess of a more highly polarized and more complex existence, in which the child's ego and consciousness find themselves in conflict with drives and tendencies that are rejected by the superego representing the cultural canon of the group.

On the psychic plane the human figure of the Great Goddess who rules over the animals signifies that the Self incarnated in the mother (i.e. the body-Self which determines the totality of the body) overcomes the conflict between the different tendencies within the personality and as embodiment of the world-mother transcends and integrates the antagonisms between the child's personality and the community.

Where the primal relationship is positive, there is a positive balance between the ego and the "thou" of the child's own drives and also between the ego and the "thou" of society; one is not repressed at the expense of the other. A normally developing ego does not become the exponent of the unconscious, of drives and instincts in opposition to society, nor does it become the exponent of society in opposition to the unconscious, which it represses and inhibits. On the basis of a positive primal relationship, man develops a psychic system centered around a self and an ego joined in the "ego-Self axis." This axis is the basis for the tendency to compensation and balance between the ego and the unconscious and also between the world and the individual.

But the polarization of the world characteristic of this stage in human development goes hand in hand with the separation between psychic systems of consciousness and the unconscious. This is the most evident form of the opposition between ego and non-ego. The correlation between this separation and the child's body gives rise to the following schemata characteristic of the archaic world orientation: on the one hand, head-ego-above-sky, and on the other hand lower body-drives-darkness-earth. For this reason the conflicting situation even of the child corresponds to the polarization of the psyche into head system, will, consciousness on the one hand and on the other hand the conflicting world of the unconscious and the drives.

In this development the anal pole as first representative of the chthonian aspect plays a crucial role, for whereas the lower body pole is later represented symbolically by the genital system, now, in the preceding phase, namely, the phase of alimentary symbolism, it is represented by the anal zone. In a large number of mammals orientation by smell is confined to the earth and the body secretions attaching to it. The smells of sweat, urine, feces and sexual substances are here an essential basis for orientation in the social area and in the world. When the child sits up, this earth-related guidance by smell recedes and is overlaid by a visual orientation, which is directed toward the east, the sunrise, and bound up with the symbolism of light and consciousness.

By this it is not meant that visual orientation is limited to man; it is far more highly developed among the birds. Nor can olfactory orientation be said to disappear in man. But the upper, visual orientation enters at this phase into conflict with the lower orientation by smell. Here again a polarization sets in which is not yet present in the earliest stage of infancy. Now anal smells are rejected as disgusting, and indeed everything situated behind and below comes to be regarded as an embodiment of the disgusting, ugly, evil and sinful, an identification for which any number of examples might be cited from language, religion and custom. Especially in a patriarchal culture, this polarization is illustrated by the association between devil's stench, refuse and excrement, just as the body and sexual odor which is later on rejected, at least officially, by culture, is symbolized by the association between devil and he-goat.

This does not mean that the chthonian orientation by smell disappears. But it survives chiefly in the realm of superstition to which the patriarchal canon of values has not penetrated, in other words in vestiges of so-called paganism and primitivism. Thus we know that magic makes considerable use of the symbolic connection between smell, air and spirit; and the connection between the smell of sweat, menstrual blood and excrement on the one hand and the body-personality on the other is often the basis of magic, especially of love magic. The decline of this world resulted largely from repression at the hands of the Judeo-Christian and patriarchal "upper-spirit-world"; this is evident from the fact among others that even this upper sphere is still connected with the lower, earthly world of smell. The gods, too, love the smell of burnt offerings, incense, and perfumes, which, as we know, contain chemical substances also present in the disgusting rejected smells. But although fragrance plays an important role in the primitive world as well as in our own civilization, many persons today would hesitate to remark on someone's pleasant or unpleasant smell, though no one is ashamed to speak of a person's attractive or unattractive appearance. Yet the fact remains that "not to be able to smell someone" (*nicht riechen können*) is the expression of a profound and often instinctive revulsion.

The rejection of the anal pole posited by society goes so far that – as Malinowski tells us – the natives of the Trobriand Islands cite the fact that parents, and especially the father, have cleaned a child and removed its excrement as a special sign of parental love, for which the child owes them a debt of gratitude.[7]

Still, our art and fashions show that even in our culture the posterior region of the body is regarded – at least unofficially – as a zone of erotic attraction. As we have known since Freud, neither the smells nor substances connected with the anal zone are disgusting in any primary sense; this disgust is cultivated, quite consistently to be sure, by the patriarchal world which stresses everything "upper," spiritual and nonsensuous and rejects everything that is "lower," bodily and earthy.

Thus in the first phase of the primal relationship the anal pole is positively integrated, but later on it becomes the object of a moral devaluation and exclusion stemming from the symbolic hostility of the sky-heaven world to the earthly world. The connections between the anal pole and the plastic arts, sculpture as well as painting, were first discovered by Psychoanalysis, which however misinterpreted them reductively. In reality artistic creation is not under normal circumstances a sublimation of a repressed anal stage, but one among many creative continuations of an anal stage that has been preserved and integrated with the individual's development as a whole. The natural pleasure in plastic substances which a child experiences first with feces, later with mud and clay is an unconscious, universally human prerequisite for plastic expression and the use of plastic materials in the adult. It is no accident that body painting, mural painting and ceramics are among the earliest arts of mankind. In all of them the anal element of smearing, kneading, and the use of excremental colors plays a decisive role.

With the polarization of the two opposite body zones the child's self-evaluation is also polarized. At first its lower body pole and excrement were "loved" by its mother; they were a creative part of the child's total personality, and the child was able to deliver these valuable parts of its body-totality, with which it archaically identified itself, to its mother. Now a rejection of the lower body pole and its creative achievement sets in. If this re-evaluation is effected in the child's own time, if it takes place when the child is assuming the erect posture, developing its head-pole, achieving mastery over its motor nervous system, and learning to exercise its will, the conversion will be free from affects or disturbances and fit in with the child's natural social development; as toilet training, it will take place under the protection of a positive primal relationship. Cleanliness and regular bowel movements are at first love-gifts to the mother and achievements that fill the child with pride but recede into the background when other developments become accented. The initially positive evaluation of the anal pole is overlaid by a new evaluation of the head-pole, but the child does not develop an exaggerated disgust with its body that endangers its self-evaluation. The polarization into above and below, clean and unclean, head-pole and anal-pole occurs normally and the child does not develop a neurotic attitude toward its natural bodily functions.

This polarization which implies a re-evaluation of the world as well as of the body and its functions is the basis of the first phase of the super-ego, that is, of the development of a moral authority in the psyche which can enter into conflict with the other part of the psyche – the chthonian-anal part bound up with the lower body pole.

The first phases of this superego formation occur within the positive primal relationship in which the mother's Self and the child Self that follows it are integral. Consequently the evaluating authority of the superego does not come into conflict with the child's Self or body-Self. In the primal relationship integration by the mother this leads without difficulty to the child's acceptance of the first cultural values. For cleanliness, and the related polarization of both body and world into good and bad, form an essential foundation of all culture. For this reason, language applies the same terms to the body as to the ethical-religious sphere, namely, clean and unclean, though different cultures may regard very different things as clean or unclean, permitted or forbidden. And the purification rites and ablutions of all religions were at first purifications not of the soul but of the body.

Just as the anal pole plays a significant role in magic and in the symbolism of evil, anal cleanliness is for the child – and for the psychotic adult – not merely the practical performance of a bodily function, but also a ritual. Whereas a child identifies the ingestion of food with the pleasure of growing consciousness, the anal order becomes its first association with evil. At first the giving-off of feces was an approved creative process; now gradually the principle of adaptation to an order of consciousness becomes incarnated in it. Just as meal time becomes a ritual of positive assimilation, so the anal time becomes a ritual devoted to the rejection of the negative element, an unconscious rite by which evil is removed. Among primitive peoples, excrement is expelled from the body, banished from the human settlement and, for magical, hygienic and esthetic reasons "done away with," often secretly, because it is dangerous, disgusting, embarrassing, and unworthy of man. The basic phenomenon, which is of decisive importance both bodily and symbolically, is the function of expulsion of the feces, which now comes into conflict with the original matriarchal significance of feces as something "born."

This specifically human development of anal rejection provides one of the foundations of scapegoat psychology, of the notion of expelling one's own evil as something alien. Among primitive people as in the Old Testament, the negative element is carried away to a place outside the camp, village, city or community and so removed, alienated, and expelled. And this is the same phenomenon as the projection of one's guilt, of the negative part of oneself, in scapegoat psychology.

Thus the experience of original sin, of one's own inferiority, characteristic of patriarchal Judeo-Christian culture, is related to the negatively evaluated animal element in man's own nature to the fact that man is unclean, born *intre urinas et faeces*. To have a body means to possess a lower negative body pole belonging to the earth, whereas such heavenly spiritual beings as the angels have only an upper body and a head-pole.

The erect posture and the related rejection of the lower body poles are a contribution to the formation of the superego; this contribution has a strongly magical coloration because the formation of the super-ego stands at the beginning of phylogenetic and ontogenetic development. Since this development is specifically human and normal, a super-ego that has come into being in this way and is anchored in society corresponds to the child's constitution and inner development. The sense of being unclean is intensified, however, when the cultural canon and its ideal of cleanliness provoke a feeling of guilt, of sinfulness and uncleanness, so that the anal pole becomes identified with obligatory magical rituals for the elimination of evil.

It is only when this motif of elimination of evil makes its appearance that the destructive aspect of the psyche becomes amalgamated with the anal sphere. When cleansing becomes identified with the destruction of evil, the ethical motif takes on a dangerous admixture of destruction. The destruction of evil as enemy of the good becomes an expression of the widespread moral ideology which is responsible for the fact that ethics, to reverse Goethe's words, always wills the good and always creates evil. The rejection, repression and inhibition of the lower sphere gives rise not only to a polarization of good and evil, but far more to a struggle of the good against the allegedly evil, in which the combatant unconsciously develops a new form of evil in himself. This evil now becomes a part of the super-ego itself, which sets itself up as the advocate of the good and as the authority which conducts the struggle of the good against evil.

The connection between the destructive drive and the super-ego expresses itself in the psyche chiefly in the form of compulsion, a matter with which we shall deal at length later on. With its help, the super-ego and its representatives makes use of the child as well as the adult ego to reject and repress the lower elements.

Compulsion means not that something dead is rejected and expelled as in the natural anal process – this is sheer necessity and requires no compulsion – but that a resisting living thing is forcibly removed. Here compulsion, that is, violence, is required because this living thing defends itself. Where compulsion sets in, an individual is not following his own natural process of development; rather, something unnatural is forced on him from outside. It is no accident that the factor to be repressed is something natural, that is, the individual's pleasure-toned participation in the anal process, which is not only a natural process but is moreover experienced by the child as a creative giving. What is not natural or implicit in the development of the species is the coercive authority which, as culture, as spirit, as an accentuated conception of the beautiful or of human dignity, imposes itself on nature.

Here for the first time the fundamental conflict between Self and superego makes its appearance; it is the central problem of the patriarchal crisis of child development. Except in the case of pathological, constitutionally deviate beings, the natural development of the child never conflicts with the child Self as the agent of its unique biopsychic wholeness. The superego, however, is an

authority of the group, of the environment, a historically and culturally conditioned outside factor, whose demands must always
come into conflict with the individualities of those who make up
the group.

The formation of the super-ego as lawgiving authority is normally human; but what is not always normally human is its
changing contents. Be that as it may, the authority of the super-ego
is transpersonal for the individual growing up in his group, and
the success or failure of every individual development depends in
high degree on that individual's confrontation with the super-ego.

Whereas the primary guilt feeling growing from an early negative primal relationship is still the inarticulated basis for a subsequent negative super-ego, the child's confrontation with its mother's
animus in the anal crisis leads to a far more differentiated and
more easily demonstrable, but also more easily remedied, impairment of the child personality. When the crisis in anal development
takes a negative course, we speak (for reasons that will be set forth
below) of "anal castration."

The disturbance in the first phase of the primal relationship
which causes the primary guilt feeling is constellated by the identity of the child with the negative Great Mother who rejects the
child and so denies it the right and opportunity to live. Such a
disturbance is fundamental because it penetrates to the development of the total Self which, within the child's relation to its
mother, is formed from the child's world- and relatedness-Self. A
disturbance in the anal phase accompanied by the first beginnings
of a negative super-ego also leads to an intensified guilt feeling in
the child. But whereas the primary guilt feeling endangers the
foundations of the child's self-esteem and very existence, the guilt
feeling stemming from anal castration is a disorder which, though
it affects the development of the ego-Self axis, does not impair the
basis of the ego-Self axis, that is, the Self. In the phase of the anal
crisis, an ego has already come into being. Thus the guilt feeling
connected with this phase is not accompanied by the feeling that
all life in the world is impossible, but carries a social accent. Just
as this guilt feeling is socially conditioned by the intervention
of the moral cultural canon of the group or the mother, so also
the individual's attempt to overcome this guilt feeling takes

the form of an intensified and convulsive socialization, that is, a strengthening of the superego as a coercive and destructive authority.

The tension between super-ego and Self is implicit in the development of man. As long as the moral aspect of anal development corresponds to the child's natural predisposition, it is subordinated to the Self represented by the mother, which effects a positive synthesis and integration of the tensions. The Self which safeguards the automorphous development of the individual also provides for this adaptation to the world and society. The socially, heteronomously grounded morality of the super-ego can also be based on the normal instinctive trends laid down by the collective unconscious, within which it merely sets its evaluating accents. The normal super-ego is not fundamentally negative, it does not make excessive demands or violate the individual; nor is the individual's Self narcissistic and blind to the world. True, it finds itself in a permanent conflict, but this conflict leads to ever new progressions and syntheses.

Through its ego development a child enters into a conflict between dependency and freedom, heteronomy and autonomy. The problem of the development and consolidation of the ego becomes a social, impersonal problem which must be solved between ego and "thou," which means primarily but by no means exclusively between mother and child. But, on the other hand, ego development is in equal measure an individual, intrapersonal process enacted between the ego and the Self.

Only in the first phase of the primal relationship is the "thou" of the Self represented by the mother; as the child achieves greater independence, the Self becomes the totality of its own individual being, which drives the ego to new confrontations with society and with the super-ego representing the cultural canon of the community.

The interplay between freedom and dependency which from this point on determines human life is manifested in the growth of an independent personality possessed of an ego-consciousness endowed with free will and also in the dependency of this ego on a superordinate environment and a superordinate Self. The creative reciprocal bond between the ego and the Self, which secures the personality and sustains automorphous self-consciousness, plays a decisive role in the success or failure of this confrontation.

But where the cultural canon is in conflict with the natural predisposition of man, when it one-sidedly and unnaturally restricts natural drives and lines of development by compulsion and repression, the consequence is a violent form of the super-ego that enters into conflict with the Self, which, to be sure, as natural center of totality, presides over the polarization of spirit and nature within the psyche, but never countenances the one-sided suppression of one pole by the other.

That is why we speak of "anal castration" when the child's wholeness as represented by the Self—here the body-Self—is impaired through the imposition of anal cleanliness by coercion and devaluation. Where there is a negative primal relationship and a neurotic, disgusted, puritanical mother who has succumbed to the patriarchal animi of her cultural canon and for this reason cannot shelter her child's development in a positive relationship, the consequence is anal castration; the child feels that in losing its excrement it has lost part of its own body. If toilet training is begun not in the child's own time but prematurely, in a phase when normally the child's evaluation of its body-totality is positive, the child experiences this loss as an anxiety-inducing impairment of its body-totality. Because of the mother's disgust, which may be either neurotic or merely out of keeping with her child's phase of development, the child takes a negative view of the potty chair and experiences the regulated bowel movement as a violent deprivation.

Initially the child experiences the warmth of its urine and feces positively as part of its own body. Nevertheless it accepts the regulated bowel movement as perfectly natural if training is begun at the right stage of development, but receives it as a shock if it is begun too soon. Anal castration is more than an impairment of the body-totality; for negative self-evaluation induced by the mother constellates the formation of a negative super-ego. The super-ego becomes the representative of a morally devaluating outside intervention that is superimposed on the natural development of the child. Consequently, this negative super-ego enters into an unnatural conflict with the child's body-Self and Self, and a dangerous split in the personality sets in.

The compulsion that destroys the child's autonomous rhythm violates the child personality, thus causing a loss of security and an impairment of ego development. The Self, which confers security, is replaced by a violently over-exigent super-ego, which induces not only uncertainty but also guilt because the child cannot live up to its demands. In attempting to fulfill these exaggerated demands, the child actively takes the compulsion upon itself, identifies with it and so becomes compulsive.

The ego, which is dependent on guidance by the Self, cuts itself off in opposition to the Self, which as totality-Self and body-Self encompasses also the rejected lower aspect of the body and world, and, by introjecting the negatively evaluating group conscience, bases itself on the super-ego representing the cultural canon. The means by which it thus cuts itself off from and opposes itself to the Self—and thereby to its own nature—are the same as those employed by the group for this purpose—compulsion, suppression and repression. This split of the personality gives rise to aggressions which either are projected outward in a destructive, moralistic effort to destroy evil in others (scapegoat psychology) or else—when this is not entirely successful—lead to an intensification of the guilt feelings which continue to nourish the circular process of taboo and self-defense.

The anxiety arising in anal castration is manifested chiefly in the fear of being infected by evil and of being unable to eliminate the evil in one's own nature. Infection, sickness, devil and death are a coherent group of symbols standing for the lower, anal world which threatens and permanently endangers the upper existence of the head and ego. The loss of excrement and of the repressed lower body pole is experienced as being cut-off and killed; hence the term anal castration. No longer, as in the matriarchal world, are death and earth on the one hand, life and heaven on the other, joined into a superordinate unity; rather, earth-death-hell and lower world are hostile to the upper world. They are devouring powers wreaking a destruction from which there is no rebirth. The Christian conception of an eternal hell is a theological expression of the demand for the elimination of the lower

side of life, which is so completely split off that it can no longer
enter into a higher unity with the upper, celestial aspect. We have
already referred to the connection between devil and excrement
and stench. This anal aspect or "sink of hell" is only one of its
characteristics. But it is no accident that hell bears an anal stigma
in another respect as well. I am referring to the sadistic character
of the elimination of evil, which is so typical of the patriarchal hell
of all religions. The Christian, for example, who imputes to the
saints so nauseating a pleasure in the sufferings of their fellow men
is obviously avenging himself on the saints for repressing his own
chthonian aspect. For in the life of the psyche the tormented, the
tormentors and the onlookers belong together, and each party
plays all three roles at once. The sinner has tormented the saints
with his sin, he torments himself in self-punishment, and suffers
torment. But at the same time the saint is the tormentor of the
sinner who he himself is because he has tormented the chthonian-
earthly aspect in which he now suffers. But the devils are also
saints as representatives of heaven, who make people suffer and
must likewise endure the sufferings they themselves have imposed
on themselves, but at the same time they stand aside as saints and
observe the process. One of the most striking examples of the
connection between hell and the anal world is provided by the
hell of Hieronymus Bosch, who portrayed this anal aspect in a
manner unique in the art of the world. The connection between
devils and demons and the anal is also evident in folklore – Jewish
law and custom, for instance, offers innumerable examples of it.

In normal development, where there has been no disturbance of
the primal relationship in connection with the natural turning
away from the lower body pole, the head-ego pole develops in the
same way in the male and female infant, and the polarization of
the personality and the world is effected predominantly on the
basis of the opposition between active and passive rather than that
between masculine and feminine. At this phase, it is true, there
begins the "separation of the World Parents," which culminates
in awareness of the opposition between masculine and feminine.
But the Great Mother's character of containing the opposites
expresses itself also in the fact that the child connected with her
does not become sexually uncertain but is still unaware of sex, for

the development common to both sexes is still more pronounced than the aspect of sexual difference.

It is only after the anal accent and the concomitant anal crisis have been overcome that the process of shifting the accent upward (which will ultimately culminate in the domination of the upper head-ego as a "solar" ego), can proceed undisturbed. But this overcoming is also the precondition for a shift of accent within the lower body pole from back to front, for the differentiation of the anal-rear and the genital-front, which is often accompanied by a stimulation of the genital zone. This shift is also connected with the specifically human change-over to the erect posture whereby the genital zone, which is hidden in the quadruped mammals, is laid bare to the gaze and also to the child's grasping hands. This openness of the genital zone in its connection with the front is something specifically human, for it is only in man that sexual union takes place in a confrontation of front to front which, in contrast to the animal world, extends from the lower to the upper body pole, that is, embraces the whole body and with it the whole personality. But from the standpoint of body symbolism front means within the field of vision of the head-ego, whereas the anal, as behind, is outside this field of vision and therefore, like everything situated behind, partakes of the symbolism of the unconscious.

CHAPTER FIVE

The Stages in the Child's Ego-Development

Though up to this point we have concerned ourselves with the matriarchal phase of child development and the beginning of the child's release from it, we have constantly borne in mind the development of the ego. But this ego development was so much under the domination of the mother that our chief concern has been the relation, not of the ego but of the child's total Self to body, mother, and mother as representative of the world. That is why the erogenous zones of the child's body discovered by Freud have played so important a role in our discussion, although the significance of these zones has been placed in a different context than in Freud and importance has been attached not so much to their erogenous, pleasure-accented aspect as to their gnoso-genous aspect of experience. But both the infant's attachment to its body and its attachment to its mother are an expression of the fact that at this stage the body-totality, the body-Self, is of greater importance than the ego, which is configured only gradually.

We now turn to the progressive ego phases of child development, though we shall still have to turn back time and time again, to the early phases of child development that have concerned us up to now. Thus the following will be not only a continuation of what has proceeded, but also a recapitulation. The situation, however, will be considered in a new light. Now the ego will be the decisive factor, for from now on, as center of consciousness, it will be the pivotal point of human experience.

The development of the child personality from the matriarchate to the patriarchate is mirrored in the development of the ego. Our attempt to distinguish different phases of ego-development stems not from a systematizing tendency on the part of the author, but from a symbolism of the psyche which is apparent in the psychology of the child and adult alike and an understanding of which is important for an understanding of the normal development as well as the disorders of the ego.

By a number of stages the ego develops from the matriarchate to confrontation with the father archetype and then on to achieve its highest degree of independence in the patriarchate. Accordingly, we distinguish the lower stages in ego development which will belong to the primal relationship and to the matriarchate from the higher solar stages, in which the ego has already entered into connection with the masculine Self and the father archetype, which is manifested symbolically as the daytime sky and its center, the sun.

In discussing the development of the active ego, which at first is common to both sexes, we shall speak of "phallic stages of the ego." This term requires an explanation. In spite of the word "phallic" this term refers not to a sexually accented ego, but to ego activities that depend largely on the totality of the body, on the accentuation and experience of the body. It is no accident that in Latin the phallus is the *fascinum,* that which fascinates. In an early phase of human history the phallus became the *fascinum* for both sexes, while at a still earlier phase the *fascinum* was women's fertility and menstruation. For a personality not centered in a stable ego-consciousness the phallus is the symbol of the autonomy of the unconscious and of the body. In the phallus the creatively generative and overpowering autonomy of the body becomes for the ego the authentic, fascinating experience of a higher power which is here manifested as the body-Self.

The *fascinum* of the phallus is not experienced by the male of this stage as a part of himself, much less as a part of his body, but as something transpersonal. In the same sense we still speak of a "drive" as of something to which we – as ego – are subjected, by which we are driven. We too experience this driving force not as a part of ourselves of which we can dispose, but as something transpersonal, of which we are more or less at the mercy. For this reason the drives are later apprehended in the form of gods and worshipped as such, sexuality for example as Aphrodite and the aggressive drive as Mars.

Thus the phallic is something superior and transpersonal in the world of early man, and in the same way the phallic ego, in its independent development, is experienced by a human being who is not yet identified with the ego as a transpersonal power possessing an activity of its own.

In this phase of personality development the psyche has not yet been fully polarized into conscious and unconscious and, more specifically, the self-evident hierarchy of psychic authorities in which we identify ourselves with the ego as the center of consciousness has not yet developed. The ego is still an autonomous complex, one complex among many, and the identity of the personality with itself is not yet based on its identity with the ego. Thus we may equally well say that the Self-identity of the child is not yet developed or at least is not reflected upon as an adult reflects upon himself as an ego; or we may say that the child has, as it were, a free-floating, unlocalized consciousness and Self-consciousness.

This state of not being localized in the ego is connected with the predominance of the body-Self over the ego and with the fact that the opposition between ego and Self is not yet fully developed. That the child as a rule still speaks of himself as a "he" or "she," and that an adult as well, in many situations of guilt and alienation, has the feeling that not "he" but another part of him has acted, are expressions of this constellation.

This autonomy of the ego complex is experienced as something impersonal, especially when, as in the matriarchal phase, the personality is largely unconscious and directed by its own totality as by something superior and transpersonal. When in the later psychological development of Western man the individual gains direct experience of himself, something similar happens. In the Self-experience of the analytical process, the analysant often notes with amazement: "So this is I." Whereas initially the child's not-yet-ego experiences itself in amazement as an ego, in the late development of the individuation process man experiences himself as no-longer-an-ego and as a "nonego."

We speak of the nonego of the early phase because in this phase man's existence is to a very great extent collectively determined. He lives as part of a group, not as a separate individual. Only with the progressive development of the ego does automorphism become evident as a tendency of the psyche to let the individual develop in his uniqueness. It is expressed in centroversion, which sets ego-development in motion within the psyche and thrusts the ego complex and consciousness into the foreground. This development is reflected in the archetype of the hero, who embodies the proto-type of the ego in its opposition to the nonego. The instinctive formative activity of the ego in this phase has a masculine character in both sexes and enters into opposition to the Great Mother, the dominant figure of the matriarchal world, since the ego's war of liberation is directed against her.

The earliest forms of the ego in the process of gaining independence are phallic, but still matriarchal. The first phase in ego-development that we distinguish is the "phallic-chthonian" stage. Its vegetative and animal form is still in high degree passive and directed. It has not yet freed itself from the dominance of the matriarchal power of nature and the unconscious. By contrast, the ego in the following magical stages, the "magic-phallic" and the "magic-warlike" stage, already has a considerable activity of its own. It is the magic-warlike ego that first overcomes its dependence on the matriarchate, so much so that it effects the transition to the patriarchate with which the ensuing "solar ego" is correlated. In the solar-warlike phase, the ego identifies itself with the father archetype. It is followed by the solar-rational stage of the adult patriarchal ego, whose independence culminates in relative freedom of the will, and by the likewise relatively free cognitive-ego, which are characteristic of the modern Western development. We distinguish:

The phallic-chthonian stage of the ego   0-12/14m
b a) vegetative 2/3 - 6/7m   a) uroboric 0-2/3m
c b) animal 6/7 - 12/14m
The magic-phallic stage of the ego 16m - 4y
The magic-warlike stage of the ego 4-6/7y
The solar-warlike stage of the ego 7-12y
The solar-rational stage of the ego 12 - adolescents

The Phallic-chthonian and Phallic-magic Stages of the Ego

The phallic-chthonian stage of the ego is still matriarchal; it is correlated with the Great Mother as the Self. At this phase the Self becomes visible as body-Self and as determining unconscious, the world as social and cosmic environment. The child is so bound up with the Great Mother of the primal relationship that its ego is not yet independent but as in mythology appears as a satellite of the Great Mother, as something that belongs to her and is directed by her.

The childhood world of which modern psychology speaks is similar to that of primitive man which, like that of the child, we designate as matriarchal as long as the ego is small and the mother archetype is dominant. The matriarchal world of early man is not identical with the earth-accented agricultural period in which the figure of the Great Mother was worshipped in cult as a center and the sociological matriarchate prevailed. The people of the ice age already worshipped the figure of the Great Mother.

The psychological matriarchate is the period in which the unconscious is dominant, in which consciousness has not yet gained independence. We might speak phylogenetically of a primal-relationship phase of mankind, for the earliest human history – and not only the life of the individual – knew a long period in which the unconscious with its world of drives and forms, its instincts and urges as well as its rites, determined human existence and directed the development of the group and its consciousness. This period has left its mark. In this phase a man not yet centered in ego-consciousness lived like an infant in the unitary reality. The human world was determined by the containing Great Round; the encompassing world-vessel that sheltered all living things within it. In both cases there prevails a unity, a *participation mystique*, still far removed from the polarity of subject and object, I and thou, man and world, that is constellated by a developed ego-consciousness. This is most evident in the earliest phase of ego-development, the vegetative phase of the chthonian-phallic ego. Just as the autonomous activity of a plant is embedded in the chthonian element, that is, the environing earth, so the infantile ego is dependent on the transpersonal universally human laws governing its growth, which in turn are guided by the mother as Great Mother.

The vegetative ego of the phallic-chthonian stage is passive and receptive toward the directing activity of the Great Mother. Her uroboric character is manifested in the fact that toward the child she is also masculine, an active giver. The ego of this stage is determined by the body-Self projected upon the mother, and by the activity of the mother as world-Self. Since the child of this phase lives in the unitary reality, its ego still knows no isolated activity or passivity; rather it is a moon-ego, a reflection of the Self that animates the inner and outer world. The telepathic and teleactive experiences of this *participation mystique* are correlated not to an acting and suffering ego, but to the total child personality which has not yet detached itself from the mother.

Here we might speak symbolically of a belly stage of the ego, directed by the unconscious processes which take place inwardly and outwardly, in the mother, in the environment, and also in the child's biopsyche. At the later stage of the phallic-chthonian ego, when the Great Mother ceases to be the Mistress of the Plants and becomes the Mistress of the Animals, the child ego already seems to possess more autonomous activity, but even then the Self and not the ego remains the truly determining power.

Just as in the anal crisis ego development is directed upward by the transpersonal, universally human process of sitting or standing up, so the "animal" activities of the phallic-chthonian ego are guided largely by powers exterior to the ego.[1]

Depth psychology has taught us that even the actions of the fully developed adult ego which the individual looks upon as "free" are largely dependent on unconscious constellations and that creative actions, slips and neurotic symptoms are largely determined by factors outside the ego. If this heteronomous determination of the ego is still evident in a highly developed personality, how much more pronounced it must be in a phylogenetically and ontogenetically earlier phase, when the ego is still in process of formation, consciousness and the unconscious are only gradually separating into different systems, and the ego has not yet assumed its central position in consciousness. Thus actions which later seem to emanate from an intentional, "willing" ego are at this stage still governed by unconscious biopsychic constellations. A baby's "screaming ego," for example, is the executor of an unconscious general constellation determined by the body-Self. Even later when seemingly willing and pre-willing actions occur, they take the form of rage, spite, stubbornness etc. and have an affective character. Such actions are in a sense explosions in which the will is subordinated not to the ego but to the distressed or desirous total personality

Nevertheless this ego is entirely vegetative and passively impelled like a seed sprouting from the earth; it already possesses a spontaneous activity which we term "animal" because it has not yet achieved the relation to consciousness characteristic of the human species. One mythological expression for this relation of the ego to the Self is the animal companions of the Great Mother, whose spontaneous activity is always subject to her rule. These animals have a phallic character because, though nature-bound, they nevertheless embody an element of fecundating spontaneous activity which accounts in part for our terminology: we speak of a phallic ego whose chthonian, earth-bound and body-bound character corresponds to this mythological stage.

In progressing from the passive-vegetative stage to a more active animal stage the child begins to master the world with activity of increasing scope and in its expansive drive no longer clings entirely to its mother as the plant clings to the earth, but enlarges its sphere of experience and finally becomes free-moving as an animal and begins to walk.

In the phallic-chthonian phase of the ego the child still lives largely in the unitary reality characteristic of the *participation mystique* of the primal relationship. The magical reality of this stage of dual union is also postulated by Psychoanalysis.[2] It is embodied in the empathy prevailing between mother and child, in active and passive parapsychological telephenomena, and in the child's unconscious world-image. But this world-image is not reflected in a consciousness, nor is the magic directed by an active ego as in the next stage of development. The ego-Self identity leads, to be sure, to an unlimited feeling of existence in the infant but the non-existence of a differentiated ego makes it impossible for the child to have a feeling of omnipotence in the sense of a wielding of power.

When we reflect on the infant's uroboric existence and its un-limitedness — in so far as we are able to do so on the basis of similar adult experiences that transcend the limits of conscious-ness — we come to understand why the Psychoanalysts impute a magical-hallucinatory situation of omnipotence to the infant. The infant's world is unlimited because it is not restricted by the principle of reality correlated with our consciousness. But this unlimitedness is at once power and impotence, for in this phase of the primal relationship possession and helplessness are identical.

From the standpoint of later consciousness, for which the separa-tion of consciousness and the unconscious, of person and world, has been effected, such identification of a personal factor, the ego, with a transpersonal element, the Self, is something negative. It is an inflation which dangerously negates the limitation of the personal sphere. By contrast to consciousness, the magical ego which is just beginning to achieve independence and is not yet differentiated from the Self is necessarily inflationary, for it exceeds the objective limits of experience and action, which do not yet exist for it.

The magical situation of the child is fed by several sources which must be distinguished. First of all there is an omnipotence of feeling, not of thought, which is connected with the already described cosmic character of its still unlimited existence. But this is not so much a feeling of omnipotence as one of cosmic all-encompassing extendedness; it is a paradisiacal state of fulfillment without opposition; neither is it centered in an ego nor has it the character of power in the sense of possession.

The paradisiacal state of the child in the womb has nothing whatever to do with omnipotence and certainly nothing to do with the omnipotence of fulfilled desires, for if we can in any way conceive of this state, it corresponds rather to an absence of wishes and desires. Here, as so often, the concept of omnipotence is confused with that of autarchy. The fulfilled self-sufficiency of the embryonic state, in which there is as yet no problematic and questioning ego-consciousness, is, as an archetypal image of ful-filled peace, affective also for later development; but this state is unrelated to power since in it there is as yet no unfulfilled desire, that is, there is no desire at all.

Here again Psychoanalysis has been led astray by its experience of pathological states, which may indeed be marked by regression to the primal relationship and a flight from reality into this paradise and dream reality. This tendency to flight, as symptom of a disorder in which reality seems intolerable, leads to a regression in which the omnipotence of the ego or the paradise of egolessness emerges as a wish-image.

Possibly an experience of omnipotence may be correlated with a later stage of the ego, the head-ego which gains mastery over the world and the child's own body. At this stage the child encounters a phenomenon which every adult takes for granted but which is nonetheless baffling when first encountered, namely, the way in which the body blindly obeys the will of the ego and thought is immediately transposed into motor activity. This phenomenon is unquestionably one of the main sources of magical thinking, especially at this stage, because there is still no dividing line between inside and outside, between psyche and outward reality. What we call fantasy has not lost its bond with reality, and the world has not yet become objective.

But the human fantasy is not a regressively wishful function; rather, it is an anticipatory and preparatory form of adaptation to life. It is the source of everything that characterizes man as man. The fantasy of a transformed world is the first stage in its real transformation and must not be confused with the regressive wishful thinking which characterizes neurotic flight from the world. The world of art, the world of culture and civilization with all its inventions including the invention of science spring from man's creative fantasy. What determines whether a man is sick or healthy is not the intensity of his fantasy but his ability or inability to transform it into reality.

Like play which is closely related to it, fantasy is of vital importance to man. Reality does not consist solely of outside experience, and the function of reality is not solely adaptation to the outside world. The first reality to which a man must adapt is the unitary reality, an inseparable unity of inside and outside. Later, after the patriarchal development of consciousness, this one reality becomes a polarity of world-outside and psyche-inside. A deficient adaptation to the inner world of the psyche is just as unrealistic and neurotic as a deficient adaptation to the outside world.

But because the direction of development is from containment in the unitary reality to adaptation to a polarized world, the emphasis for early man and for the child as well is upon adaptation to the outside world; ordinarily the psychic element remains unconscious, and is brought to consciousness only when there is a disturbance of the unconscious system.

As ethnology has taught us, early man's functions were just as highly developed as those of modern man and, though different from ours, the state of his psyche must not be regarded as primitive. His magical thinking, for example, must not be interpreted as a kind of childlike delusion which made him behave like the allegedly hallucinated, power-hungry infant of the Psychoanalysts, instead of concerning himself with the real world. It seems obvious enough that if magical early man had really behaved in this wishful manner he would not have survived for long. The infant whose wishes are allegedly fulfilled in its hallucinations is fed by its mother, hallucinations or not, but early man was obliged to gain his sustenance under difficult conditions. It is unthinkable that a hallucinatory magical activity without practical utility, serving only the imaginary satisfaction of wishes and bearing no relation to experience or the mastery of reality, should have endured for tens or hundreds of thousands of years. Moreover, this magical activity recurs in ontogenesis and also plays a decisive role in the psyche of modern man, both sick and sound.

Another argument against the notion that magical man suffers from hallucinations is that at the magical stage the cognitive function of the ego is already developed. The magical attitude and the exact observation of nature are by no means mutually exclusive but may perfectly well go hand in hand, as the art of the Ice Age shows. But the objective knowledge of nature is subordinated to an unconscious experience that speaks in images. This archaic, irrational, and largely intuitive form of knowledge in which the unconscious outweighs consciousness is by no means identical with hallucinatory wish images subordinated to the pleasure principle as opposed to the reality principle. Quite aside from its importance in modern man, the unconscious, instinct-guided archaic experience of animals, of early man and children is world-experience and not wishful hallucination. The empathy between child and mother is authentic orientation, even though it is effected through the perception of the unconscious, and *participation mystique* as the foundation of life in the unitary reality is an authentic irrational bond with reality and an orientation in reality; it is not demented illusion independent of reality. The negative factor in this extended experience is its lack of clarity, but on the other hand the solar consciousness has had to pay for its greater clarity with a curtailment and loss of essential elements.

To simplify: Psychoanalysis starts from the notion that a child is born in a state akin to madness in which it follows only the pleasure principle and adapts itself to reality and the principle of reality only under pressure of the unpleasantness coming to it from the environment. This psychoanalytic conception of the development of the sense of reality should be replaced by another more in keeping with the facts of ethnology. No more than the animal does the child enter the world as a *tabula rasa*; rather, it has at its disposal a system of unconscious, instinctive and archetypal modes of reaction which are released by its environment and are attuned to it. Its unconscious modes of reaction have a world-content and, as we know, the instinctive behavior of the entire organic world always involves a specific adaptation to the average, normal reality in which the organism lives.

The child psyche is so constituted as to assimilate instinctively the unpleasant factors of existence. The mechanisms of this assimilation or adaptation are embedded in the psyche from the start, merely waiting to be released as life provides the corresponding stimuli. In the successive stages of the ego we encounter not only an increasing independence of the ego but also a steadily changing relation of this ego to reality. Not only the ego's relation to the world and the unconscious, but its relation to the Self as well is subject to continuous transformations. But these transformations, or at least their fundamental structures are a matter of universally human predisposition. Whereas the dependence of the phallic-chthonian ego on the body-Self and on the unconscious processes connected with the biopsyche is accompanied by a continued fluctuation of the ego and of the not yet fixated consciousness, the magic-active ego is already centered in a consciousness that is beginning to be systematized.

The magical activity of the ego, as well as the magical view of the world, correspond to a stage in which a personality which is becoming differentiated and taking on a stronger automorphism and a more independent consciousness exists in a reality that is not yet objectified or independent. It is in this constellation that the dividing line between person and world is first drawn, and at this stage the Self which our consciousness correlates with the psyche has not yet lost the cosmic extendedness characteristic of the unitary reality. The basis of the magical ego stage is that the Self in its comprehensive totality is experienced as belonging to the ego which exerts its magical authority. This relation of the Self to the ego is experience as analogous to the relationship of the body to the limbs which stand under the command of the ego.

This ego, gradually achieving independence, must consolidate itself both by assembling and systematizing the contents of consciousness and by experiencing itself as the center of a consciousness which gradually learns to delimit itself from the world and the unconscious.

The child's ritual, its need to experience the world as an ordered system in which times of day, people, activities and story-telling have their set places forms the necessary basis of an ego that must feel itself to be the stable center of an ordered world. Just as in painting, a child progresses steadily from disordered scribbling to the circular figure (the mandala) so the ego concentrates itself, that is, defines itself over against the psychic fluctuation of which it was a part, to become a world center representing the personality and connected with consciousness. This magical anthropocentric attitude is symptomatic for the growing independence of an ego which, no longer subordinated to the unconscious and to the world, begins to reach out and to master the world.

The circle, the mandala which plays so prominent a role in the earliest drawings of children, appears phylogenetically in magic as a magic circle in which the ego sets itself apart from the world and concentrates itself. This concentration is the precondition for the activity of the ego which in adults becomes the activity of the directing will. The earliest rituals are therefore rituals of ego-concentration, circle-mandala forms of ritual, whose probable earliest form, common to all early mankind, is the round dance, in which the human group sets itself apart from the world and gathers into a community. In the mandala of the psyche the Self forms the center, whereas the ego is the center of the mandala of consciousness. In both cases the circle is a defense and fortress of the psychic content. But the two circles belong together, for the lower is the basis for the upper, the Self is the root of the ego and the link between the two centers is the ego-Self axis. But by this same token the ego-Self axis is established as the axis of the personality which in achieving its independence sets itself apart from the unitary reality.

Psychoanalysis interprets this process as a withdrawal of the primary object-bound libido into a secondary narcissism which later becomes the starting point for the development of objective experience. In contrast to this theory, which presupposes an incomprehensible progression and regression of libido, we assume that the magical ego is a natural and progressive stage in a development leading from uroboric, subjectless and objectless unitary reality to the magical world characterized by an ego that gradually achieves independence and then further to a patriarchal solar ego which for the first time stands as a subject confronting an objective world.

The magical ego experiences the omnipotence of power over the body. In so doing, it dominates the world which in the unitary reality was one with it and so experiences itself as the center of the world.

This ego concentration is a self-inauguration of the ego, a consolidation of acts of the ego which were hitherto isolated and dispersed. Whereas the phallic-chthonian ego revolved like a satellite around the mother, now, in the phallic-magic stage, the ego achieves greater independence of the body-Self and the thou. Grounded in the Self, the ego comes into its own. However, the polarization of the ego-Self axis, the interrelatedness of the ego and the Self which becomes evident at this stage, also presupposes the beginnings of an independence of the ego from the Self. But this independence is definitely achieved only by the solar-patriarchal ego. The phallic-magic ego already possesses an autonomous activity with which it confronts the world, but it still lives in a matriarchal world determined by *participation mystique*.

Whether this ego is encompassed by the unitary reality or by the magical world of the matriarchy, its independence and consciousness are not yet secure. The ego is still subordinated to drives and emotions within and to the events of the world without. The magical activity of the ego still lacks the continuity of the lateral patriarchal-solar ego; it is fragmentary, existing only at moments set aside for the ritual of concentration.

In the early world, accordingly, every action must be prepared by libido-harnessing rituals, since the libido of the will is not yet available at all times as in the more mature ego. Just as a child must learn painstakingly to act willfully, to carry through its intention, to think consequently, to objectify itself and to become independent, directing system in its confrontation with the world, so the conscious activity of the magical ego is an exceptional, trying state which, because it is determined by accidental factors in the world, is time and time again reabsorbed into the matriarchal world of the unconscious, of the body and the world.

At the magic-phallic stage of the ego there is still a partial identity of the ego with the body-Self. The magical ego still operates partly as an exponent of the biopsyche. This ego is irrational and its activity in no way resembles that of the solar-rational ego. For this reason the intentions and ritual action of the magical ego are still in part unconscious and emotion-toned. The concentration of the magical ego both in the group and in the individual almost always begins with dance and exciting music. This means that this ego must take on an intense emotional charge in order to acquire the magical ego-capacity related to identification with the body-Self. Its activity, to be sure, is already world-conquering, but this conquest starts from the world-context of the matriarchate in which the factors that our consciousness separates into "symbolic image within" and "object without" are indissolubly bound together. For this reason magic is often based on images and the ritual "killing" of a portrayed animal is magically identical with the killing of the real animal. To a more highly developed consciousness the magical rite seems at most a preparation for the hunt; psychologically, it can be understood as a harnessing and concentration of the ego-will necessary for the hunt. But undoubtedly no such succession exists for the magical ego. On the contrary, the magical killing is the essential, the real killing is accessory. At this stage the two are actually identical, for the magical killing occurs in the world of unitary reality, which is here not the background of the world but the world itself.

This whole process takes place in the numinous twilight of archetypal images and of spiritual reality rather than in material reality. One indication of this is the fact that the object of the magical hunting group — the animal, which is given form in the magical image in order that it may be overpowered and killed in the magical act — is always taken as the entire species and never as an individual animal.

We term this magical activity phallic because it is a fecundating and transformative activity which confronts the world and the unconscious as receptive. As a vehicle of phallic-magic activity, the ego is fecundating in a supra-sexual and supra-personal sense.

The fecundation of this stage relates in high degree to the world of food which is closely connected with procreation. Man lives by the abundance of the wild herds, and the magic-phallic ego revolves around food and its acquisition, not yet around myth and tradition, and certainly not around the knowledge and law of a later spiritual-solar existence.[3] And insofar as tradition and myth begin to arise from ritual even at this early stage, they too revolve around the life contents of the Great Mother as bestower of food, as Mistress of the Plants and Animals, mastery over which is the main concern at this stage.

We have characterized the ego-stages of the matriarchal phase in which the ego is still guided by the unconscious as companion of the Great Mother, who is the goddess not only of vegetative and animal life but of human life as well. Thus the human ego first appears in the symbol of the child correlated with the mother; but the magic-phallic ego with its increased activity and independence corresponds mythologically to the Great Mother's youthful lover. He is the son she has borne, but then as dying youth he is killed by her; nevertheless he is a fecundating principle within her, which fecundates and transforms her with his phallic activity.

The mythological overpowering of the youthful lover by the Great Mother as Terrible Mother of Death means that the ego is weaker and more dependent than the matriarchal world of the unconscious from which it rises and by which it is extinguished. Just as the phallus is itself only in the act of fecundation, before and after which it is only a limp part of the whole, so the magic-phallic ego is itself only in action, after which it is "slain" by the Great Mother and returns to a state of childhood.[4] But the youthful ego is nevertheless fecundating, for, through its activity toward the body and the unconscious, drives and emotions can be harnessed and utilized in the concentration of magical activity. By consciously pursuing its aims and intentions — as opposed to those of the body and the unconscious — the ego brings about a change in the unconscious and the world and a new relation between them and the ego.

For both world and environment are transformed by the intervention of the magical youthful ego. With the magical ego begins the world of *homo faber* who no longer lives from a world that nourishes him matriarchally but changes that world by a productive process. Thus the magical youthful ego is productive, active, procreative and phallic. It confronts the world not with passive wishes but with active intervention, although this world is still predominantly the matriarchal unitary reality and now the objective world of the solar-rational consciousness. For this reason the fecundating act of the youthful lover always ends in his death at the hands of the Great Mother. For the ego, not only in its chthonian, earth-bound plant and animal stage, but in its magic-phallic stage as well, is still at the mercy of the Great Mother's superiority. Its independent activity succumbs to the superior power of the matriarchal as unconscious and as world, because its independent activity is too feeble. For it is not yet connected with an archetypal power which enables it to form a counterweight to the mother archetype.

The progressive strengthening of the magical ego is identical with its progressive independence. The ego of the youthful lover is still an ego that clings to the Great Mother, but as it gains in strength the ego shows its independence by beginning to assume its anthropocentric position at the center of the world. The human personality begins to identify itself with the ego as the center of consciousness and to relate the world to it. This anthropocentric position is the natural foundation of human existence in the world. It finds its first form in the attitude of the magical ego, which still exists in a thoroughly matriarchal world but experiences itself as its center to which the world as a whole is related.

But the magical ego does not consciously comprehend the world in the same degree as does the solar ego of modern man: its experience of the world is emotional, and it is through this charge of feeling and emotion that the world becomes significant. In a sense only that which is striking or appealing, in short, significant, is experienced, and this world of experience is ordered on the basis of what is significant for man. This fluid world of emotions which fills existence with what it finds striking, appealing and significant, is dominated by the symbolic life of mythological apperception, in which the categories of experience are not concepts of consciousness but symbols and archetypes. This non-objective, undivided world becomes a symbolic figure and is so experienced. Here we have not yet a world of things among which man moves and which he deals with, but an image world which stirs and moves him from both without and within, which directs him and which he circumambulates in ritual.

From the standpoint of consciousness this symbolic experience is an unconscious view of the world, in which the world or a segment of the world is apperceived (from an ethnological standpoint one might speak here of animism or preanimism) as a unitary, thoroughly animated world. This experience is oriented toward a unitary context which is evident to man, which he cannot escape, and in the center of which he finds himself.

At this stage both symbol and archetype prove to be at once a deposit of experience and a category of expression. The symbolic figure rising up from the unconscious originates in man's universal unconscious relatedness to the world, and for that very reason it has an objective and by no means purely subjective character. The containing and the contained, the nourishing and the

nourished are objectively present in the world, and in the mythological apperception of the psyche are reflected as the archetype
of the Great Mother. This image is indeed archetypal, that is,
universally human, and it is a category of human experience, for
man gains experience with the help of this image in the psyche.
But this image corresponds to something that exists objectively in
the world; the image is adequate to the world. A psychic image of
something in the world is both a deposit of experience and an organ
of the psyche which through this image experiences and later
interprets the world.

In the unitary world experienced by the magical ego there is a
universal relatedness; everything is connected with everything else
and one thing can and must stand for the rest. The notion of unconscious identity, of *participation mystique*, stems from this world,
as does the notion, valid for the early world, of the identity of the
part with the whole. This latter notion, operative only before
consciousness in elaborating reality, has drawn dividing lines
between the things and contents of the world. This binding unitary
context between man and world is the basis of early man's conduct, especially of his rites. In return for everything that he takes
for himself from nature as a whole, for everything he uses and so
withdraws from the totality of being, he always restores a representative as a sacrifice, in order that the totality of being may be
preserved. This emotional bond with existence determines the
actions of man in the world just as the symbolic image determines
the form of his world-experience. Both are consequences of the
anthropocentric world-relatedness of early man and the child,
which is a part of their magical world orientation.

Once man has assumed this anthropocentric position, man as
the body-Self becomes the center to which events in the world,
in space and time, are related.[5] Man's images of space and time
are ordered around this anthropocentric position; the directions,
for example, the quarters of the heavens and the earth, the colors,
and things themselves are seen in relation to parts of man's body,
and his orientation in time, his notions of before and after stem
from this central position he occupies. This correlation of directions and parts of the world with the body schema signifies not
only that man is dependent on the world, but also that the world

is dependent on the body whose dominant focal point is the magical ego localized in the head. In other words, the dynamic expression of the anthropocentric accent, crucial for man's position in the world, is the conception that man is responsible for the existence of the world. Among many peoples we find rites that must be performed before sunrise in order that the sun may rise, and in the Mexican high culture an abundance of human sacrifices were needed to enable the sun to complete its course. This magical activity cannot be adequately explained as a fear reaction. It is of equal importance that man occupies a central position in the world and that his magical-ritual relation to the powers helps to guarantee the survival of the world.

But this being-at-the-center does not signify a domination over nature comparable to the violation of nature by Western man, divorced as he is from nature. For this central position of man is perfectly compatible with a view which assigns to animals or to particular animals a rank superior to that of man. The bear, for example, was so revered by early man. And even later – as in the Bible – when this position of man had become conscious, it is the expression not so much of a will to dominate the world as of a mission of mastery which for that very reason imposes the greatest obligations on man.

The magical thinking of the magical ego makes possible the establishment of an ego-center at the core of consciousness and the liberation of ego-consciousness from the total domination of the unconscious within and the world without. Man's relative freedom resides in his active ego and in his consciousness which sets itself apart from and confronts the world and the psyche. These presuppose release on the one hand from the direction of the unconscious and the instincts and on the other hand from the domination of the environment. Not omnipotence but power – with all its problematic consequences – is now the necessary goal of an ego development in which, after formation of the ego-Self axis, the conscious ego rather than the Self becomes the executor of the vital will of the personality.

Power and mastery over nature without and the unconscious within, in other words self-mastery, is one of the first aims of ego-consciousness; it is carried out in the patriarchal phase with the help of an abundance of psychic dynamisms, of repression and inhibition, identification and projection. Another aim is the development of the individual in the face of the community and the outside world.

The anthropocentric accent, the accent on the fact that man is the measure of all things, that, created in God's image, he names the animals and knows orders, and forms the world centered around himself, is the basis of the development of man, who believes himself destined to dominate the world of nature and the psyche. Man's feeling that he was created in the image of the creative God is the leading symbol of this central position of man within a world ordered around him and for him. As far as we know, from the very beginning magical action was always an action of a group which through magic set itself apart from that nature with which it had originally been united. The magical rites of the hunt which we find in the painting of the Ice Age – probably the first rites that ever existed – are a first spiritual confrontation with the animal as something "other" which it is necessary to kill. This magic operated with identifications. In ritual dance man represented the animals, but also the hunting and killing of the animal, thereby configuring not only his identification with the animal but also his otherness from it and superiority to it. In the ritual slaying of the animal by the slaying of its image, attested by the many arrow marks in the paintings of the Ice Age, man set himself apart from animals and established his domination over them.

This psychic act of magical ritual is the expression not of a desire, but of the establishment of the human ego which as group-ego and individual ego set itself at the center of a world that was to be dominated. Originally magic was always group magic, and anthropocentrism refers to the central position of the human group of which the individual was only a part. Similarly, hunting was at first almost always a common action of the group with which the individual with his independent activity was integrated. The magical security of the individual ego, on which the success of the group action was largely dependent, was based on the evocation of the group-Self, on an actualization of the higher unity of the group, which embraced and directed the individual and operated as a kind of "outside Self" incarnated in the leader of the group — be he medicine man or chief — who was traditionally related to a transpersonal being, an ancestor or spirit.

This incarnation of an authority which was not yet an inner psychic reality in the individual but could be experienced by him only outside, through a particular man, a Great Individual, is of the utmost importance for the structuring of the human psyche. For in this development the authority of the Self as mana-personality takes form as a power-wielding center, emerges from anonymity and becomes the leader of the group. And at the same time it gives a clearer configuration to the ego, determined by the Self of each individual group member.

The earliest group known to us is the male group of hunters; it is the precursor of all male groups. To judge by everything we know of it, it was here that the magical ego developed. This group reaches back to the earliest times of human development when the magical fertility ritual was still in the hands of women, the supreme authority in all domains such as nourishment and fertility which were subject to the Great Mother Goddess.

The activities of the male group were subservient to this matriarchal world. The magic of the male group related to the possibility of gaining power over edible game and of killing it. Accordingly, in the paintings of the Ice Age, the earliest known documents of human magic, the pregnant animal plays the central role. But at the matriarchal stage the beast of prey was looked upon as the terrible aspect of the Great Mother in her terrible masculine aspect. She herself, or her terrible aspect, is often represented as tiger, lion, panther or leopard.

In the matriarchal phase the male group identified itself ritually with this killing aspect of the Great Mother. The hunting male group represents the death-aspect of the Terrible Mother, who as Great Mother is the ruler not only over life but also over death. For this reason the rites of hunting and killing are those of men; rites of life, procreation and rebirth are those of the female group. In the identification of the male group with the terrible aspect of the Great Mother, the male becomes identical with the killing symbol of the weapon as the destructive phallus. This symbol is introjected by the male group. And as "terrible Masculine" this introjection strengthens the man, especially accentuating his activity and aggression, which are archetypal masculine traits.

This strengthening and accentuation of the masculine principle plays a special role in the establishment of the patriarchate through men's societies. Just as the Terrible Masculine is a preliminary phase of the "Terrible Father," who plays so important a role in the formation of the super-ego in patriarchal culture, so the warlike-killing, magical-warlike ego of the hunting male group is the preliminary form of the solar ego which later frees itself definitely from the domination of the mother archetype.

The Transcending of the Matriarchate by the Magical-warlike Ego and the Solar Ego

Within the magical phase of the ego we have distinguished the magic-phallic stage, in which the ego is still essentially determined by the mother archetype, from the magical-warlike stage, in which the ego not only begins to oppose the mother archetype but gains consciousness of the masculinity which will culminate in the solar stage of the patriarchate.

Already at the phallic stage the ego begins to experience itself as specifically masculine over against woman, the Great Mother and the matriarchate. The strengthening of the male ego begins with a strengthening of its resistance to the feminine principle. This tendency toward resistance is intensified by men's support of each other within male groups and men's societies which always take on extreme importance where the matriarchal element is dominant.

Men's support of one another, the origin of which goes back to the earliest union of men in the male hunting group of primordial times, is at first dominated by feminine magic. The Great Mother as Goddess of Fertility, Food and Animals assuredly played an important role in hunting magic long before the fertility rites of agriculture. And the hunting male is always at once killing and warlike.

Thus, in its connection with the Great Mother, magical activity was both phallic and warlike; this is made strikingly evident by the

paleolithic rock drawings in which the penis of the hunting male
is connected with the imploring woman who is standing behind
him. Here the male's phallic activity toward woman is clearly
related to his warlike-hunting activity toward game. Both belong
to the sphere of fertility over which woman rules. This Great
Woman in her imploring attitude is not – as certain interpretations
of the role of woman in the primordial age would lead one to
suppose – the victim and prey of male aggression; the phallic and
warlike male is still in the service and under the domination of
woman in her fertility and nourishment aspect. Those who adhere
to the widely accepted thesis (largely a product of ecclesiastical
thinking) that the hunting peoples were originally monotheistic,
overlook the significant role of woman in this early period of mankind whose matriarchal character has not been sufficiently recognized. We have often attempted to explain what we mean by the
matriarchate. We owe a well-known but hitherto unexploited
example of the magical significance of woman in early cultures to
Frobenius:[6]

> In the year 1905 in the jungle territory between Luebo and
> the Kasai River I came upon representatives of those hunting
> tribes which are so well-known as the Pygmies. They had found
> a place of refuge in the forests of the Congo after being crowded
> out of the plateau. A few of the people, three men and one woman,
> accompanied the expedition for about a week. One day – it was
> nearly evening and by now we were the best of friends – there
> was great distress in the camp kitchen. I asked the three little
> fellows whether they might slay an antelope for us before the
> day ended. They looked on me with obvious astonishment at
> my words. Then one of them blurted out in reply that they
> would very much like to comply but as for today it was quite
> impossible since they had made no preparations. A lengthy dis-
> cussion followed with the end result that the hunters declared
> themselves ready to carry out these preparations on the next
> morning at sunrise. And so we separated. The three men then
> investigated all around and eventually went to a high place on
> the neighboring hill.
> As I was eager to learn what the preliminaries might consist of,

I rose before sunrise and crept into the bushes beside the clearing which the Pygmies had chosen for their ceremonies the previous evening. It was still twilight when the men arrived. They were not alone as the woman came, also. The men crouched on the ground, cleared a space and made it smooth. Then one man squatted and with his finger drew something in the sand. All the while the other men and woman mumbled some charms and prayers. Then waitful silence. The sun rose above the horizon. One of the men stepped to the side of the cleared space and drew an arrow in his bow. After a few minutes the sun's rays fell on the drawing. In the same moment, as quick as lightning, the following took place: the woman raised her hands towards the sun as if trying to catch hold of it and shouted sounds which to me were quite unintelligible; the man shot the arrow; the woman yelled even more; and then, weapons in hand, the men jumped into the surrounding undergrowth. The woman remaining standing for a few minutes longer and then returned to camp. As soon as she was gone I stepped out of the bushes and went to see the drawing in the smooth sand. It was the likeness of an antelope about three feet long. In its neck stuck the discharged arrow.

While the men were still away I tried to return to the hill in order to get a photograph of the drawing. But the woman kept to my side and prevented this. She urged me to give up the idea. So we marched off. That afternoon the hunters rejoined us with a handsome deer. It had been killed by an arrow through the jugular vein. The Pygmies delivered their prey and then returned to the hilltop with a few tufts of hair and a fruitpod full of antelope blood. Not until two days later did they catch up with us again. And not before evening, beside a bubbly palm wine, did I dare speak about these matters with the one among them who trusted me most. He was an already older man, the oldest at least of the three, and he told me that they had simply gone back to rub the hairs and blood on the antelope likeness, to remove the arrow and erase the picture. About the chants and their meaning I could learn nothing. But he did mention that the "blood" of the antelope would destroy them if they failed to complete these steps. Furthermore, it was

necessary to erase the picture just as the sun rose, also. He
begged me not to tell the woman of our talk. It seems that he
feared very much the consequences of his chatter for on the
next day the Pygmies left us without saying good-bye.

Another example from perhaps a still older cultural sphere, the
bear hunt, is quoted by Joseph Campbell:

> When a very young black bearcub is caught in the moun-
> tains, it is brought in triumph to the village, where it is suckled
> by one of the women, plays about in the lodge with her children,
> and is treated with great affection. As soon as it becomes big
> enough to hurt and scratch when it hugs, however, it is put into
> a strong wooden cage and kept there for about two years, fed
> on fish and millet porridge, until one fine September day,
> when the time is judged to have come to release it from its body
> and speed it happily back to its mountain home. The festival of
> this important sacrifice is called *iyomande*, which means "to send
> away," and though a certain cruelty and baiting is involved,
> the whole spirit of the feast is of a joyous send-off, and the bear
> is supposed to be extremely happy – though perhaps surprised,
> if this should happen to be the first time that he has visited the
> Ainus – to be thus entertained.
>
> The man who is to give the feast calls out to the people of his
> village, "I, so-and-so (perhaps, for example, Kawamura Mono-
> kute), am about to sacrifice the dear little divine thing from
> among the mountains. My friends and masters, come to the
> feast! Let us enjoy together the delights of the 'sending away'!
> Come! Come all!"
>
> The guests arrive and a number of prayer-sticks (*inao*:
> "message-bearers") are fashioned, some two to five feet long,
> whittled in such a way as to leave shavings clustered at the top
> in a kind of head. These are stuck beside the hearth, where the
> fire-goddess, Fuji ("grandmother, ancestress"), is ever present,
> guarding the house; and, after having been revered there, the
> prayer-sticks are brought to the place outside where the bear
> is to be killed, and again stuck in the ground. Two long, thick
> poles, known as *oknumba-ni*, "the poles for strangling," are
> then laid at their base. The men approach the bear cage; the

women and children follow, dancing and singing; and the whole company sits in a circle before the bear, while one of their number, moving very close to the cage, lets the little visiting god know what is about to happen.

"O Divine One, you were sent into this world for us to hunt. Precious little divinity, we adore thee; pray, hear our prayer. We have nourished and brought you up with a deal of pains and trouble, because we love you so. And now that you have grown big, we are about to send you back to your father and mother. When you come to them, please speak well of us and tell them how kind we have been. Please come to us again and we shall again do you the honor of a sacrifice."

The bear, secured with ropes, then is taken from the cage and made to walk around in the circle of the people. Blunt little bamboo arrows, bearing a black and white geometrical design and a compact clump of shavings at the tip (called *hepere-ai*, "cub arrows"), are let fly at him, and he is teased until he becomes furious. Then he is tied to a decorated stake, two strong young fellows seize him, a third thrusts a kind of long wooden bit between his jaws, two more take his back legs, two his front, one of the "poles for strangling" is held under his throat, the other above the nape of his neck, a perfect marksman sends an arrow into his heart in such a way that no blood spills to the earth, the poles are squeezed together, and the little guest is gone.

The bear's head is removed with the whole hide attached, carried into the house, and arranged among prayer-sticks and valuable gifts by the east window, where it is to share the parting feast. A succulent morsel of its own flesh is placed beneath its snout, along with a hearty helping of dried fish, some millet dumplings, a cup of sake or beer, and a bowl of its own stew. And then it is honored with another speech.

"O Little Cub, we give you these prayer-sticks, dumplings, and dried fish; take them to your parents. Go straight to your parents, without hanging about on your way, or some devils will snatch away the souvenirs. And when you arrive, say to your parents, 'I have been nourished for a long time by an Ainu father and mother and have been kept from all trouble and harm. Since I am now grown up, I have returned. And I have brought these prayer-sticks, cakes, and dried fish. Please rejoice!' If you say this to them, Little Cub, they will be very happy."

A feast is celebrated, there is dancing, while the woman who suckled the bear alternately weeps and laughs, along with some of the older women, who have suckled many young bears and know something of the mixed feelings of waving good-bye. More prayer-sticks are made and placed upon the bear's head; another bowl of its own stew is placed before it, and when time has been allowed for it to finish, the man presiding at the feast calls out, "The little god is finished; come, let us worship!" He takes the bowl, salutes it, and divides the contents among the guests, a small portion for each. The other parts of the beast are then eaten also, while some of the men drink the blood for strength and smear a portion upon their clothes.

The head of the bear is then separated from the rest of the skin and, being set upon a pole called *ke-omande-ni*, "the pole for sending away," it is placed among a number of other skulls remaining from earlier feasts. And for the next few days the festival continues, until every bit of the little god has been consumed.[7]

The decisive step from the matriarchate to the patriarchate is a progressive development of male consciousness and its liberation from the matriarchal world which is always a world of magic correlated with woman. But this progression is also a release of the ego from the matriarchal, moon-dominated consciousness whose negative aspect is fear of the demonic world which for the male ego is a world determined by the feminine and the unconscious.

The subordination of the man to the woman as child-bearing and as nourishing representative of the Great Mother is now replaced by a hostile and repressive attitude of man toward woman. Ethnologically this is manifested most clearly among one of the most primitive peoples, the Tierra del Fuegians, to whom we owe the following story about the replacement of the lunar matriarchate by the solar patriarchate.[8]

Some of the main ideas are outlined in my earlier reports. Disregarding these, I repeat here what Tenenesk told us that evening in the Big Hut:

In olden days there were already many *"howenh"* in our country. At that time sun and moon, stars and winds, mountains and rivers moved about the earth like human beings, just as we do today. But in those days it was women who had the say everywhere, both inside and outside the hut. They told men what work to do. Just as today it is the men who tell them what to do.

In those days the men were subservient and obeyed the women. The women told them what work to do in the hut, and the men did it. The men were compelled to remain in the dwelling hut and do everything the women told them to do: they had to keep up the fire, to roast the meat, to stretch the furs and to take care of the small children. If there was something to be discussed, only the women met, the men remained in their huts. They were not allowed to sit in the circle of the women when they discussed or deliberated on something. Only the women made decisions and gave orders, the men had to do what they were told. Thus the men were entirely dependent on the women.

But because the men were strong and numerous, the craftiest among the women were afraid they might rise up and refuse to obey. For that reason the women sat down together: they thought it over for a long time. They pondered how to keep the men in this subservient condition; they did not want them to rise up and refuse to obey. The craftiest of all the women was Mrs. Kra (Moon), the wife of Kran (Sun). She was a powerful Xon and possessed the greatest influence on all the other women. All the others were very much afraid of her, no one dared to contradict her. The women kept pondering, they pondered a long time.

Finally the women began to hold a secret meeting such as we men hold today: at a great distance from the dwelling huts they built a big hut. Here there was room for all the women. They met there in the afternoon. Day and night a few women

always stayed in this Big Hut, the grown-up girls seldom returned
to the camp. From afternoon until late at night all the women
stayed there.[9] None of the men were allowed to approach the
Big Hut. Only women met there. They kept a sharp lookout.
The men had to remain in the camp all the time.

Each of the women painted her body with special designs,
today this way, tomorrow another way. They set a painted
bark mask on their heads, their faces were completely covered.
Now no one could recognize them. Thus the women came out
of the Big Hut, singly or in pairs or in a long line, sometimes
hopping or jumping. When they could be seen outside the Big
Hut, some of the women called the men and the children out
of the dwelling huts. They looked on from a great distance.

Some of the women made their husbands believe that these
(beings) came down from heaven or stepped out of the earth
and came to the women who were gathered here in the Big Hut.
They treated both men and women with haughty self-will.
Everyone was at their mercy, they were very powerful . . .

The most influential of all was Mrs. Kra, she commanded the
other women. She also told them what tasks each was to impose
upon each man. Each woman imposed on her husband the task
that Mrs. Moon indicated. The men did it all. The women
spent almost the whole year in the Big Hut. During the day
one woman or another would return to the camp. She stayed
a short time and meted out new tasks to her husband. She also
ate the roast that he had prepared for her; for she was always
very hungry. And she sometimes slept with her husband. For
the most part the women slept together in the Big Hut; they
seldom came to the camp for the night. Each woman demanded
that a good supply of meat be kept on hand in her dwelling
hut. She said to her husband: "Xalpen in the Big Hut requires
much meat for herself!" So the men often went hunting and
brought back an abundance of game. They had to hand over
all the meat to the women in order not to make the dangerous
Xalpen still angrier.

Once the women met on a fine large plot of grass: Here they
played *kloketen* in a spacious cone-shaped hut. The men were
in the camp that was far away. They took care of the small

children and did all the work. When a *soorte* went through the camp, they wrapped themselves in their cloaks. He always treated them badly and sometimes beat them severely.

Kran, the Sun Man, was an excellent hunter and a good runner. On his wanderings he always found an abundance of game. He was almost always hunting. He brought home much meat every day; he distributed it among the other huts. A few girls came to the camp each day. They came from the Big Hut. They said to the men: "Xalpen has sent us. She desires meat!" And the men had to turn over everything they possessed. The girls always hauled a great deal of meat back to the Big Hut.

One day the Sun Man was hunting out on the cliffs. Soon he killed a large guanaco, he was a good hunter. He loaded the animal on his shoulders and turned toward the camp. Wearied by the arduous journey and the heavy load, he grumblingly threw it down. He sat down to take a short rest behind a bush. Unsuspecting he had come near the *kloketen* hut, he was sitting not far from a lagoon. Soon he saw two grown girls on the shore: they were bathing. They talked gaily and laughed a good deal. Cautiously Kran crept close to them; he wanted to listen to what they were saying. They were painted like the *keternen* who were sometimes displayed near the Big Hut. The girls practiced holding themselves stiffly upright and taking very short steps forward and backward, as Mrs. Moon had taught them to do. And they laughed a good deal. They said: "We'll soon be able to do it . . . How surprised the men will be!" And they kept giggling. They were making fun of the men. Because the men believed they were really *keternen*. They were very much amused at the slyness of the women and the men's constant fear . . . The girls went on playing for quite a long time . . .

When Sun arrived in the camp, he acted quite indifferent toward women and men, no one could suspect what a terrible thing he had just seen. Cautiously he then went to see one man after another in his dwelling hut: he told each one about the sly game the women were playing, to each one he explained how terribly they were each and all being cheated by the women. All the men now learned the truth, that there were only women in the Big Hut. That they painted their whole bodies and put a *t'olon* on their heads, so that no one could recognize them ... When the men heard this, they grew very angry, but they too hid their agitation. Kran gave them strict orders to show nothing ...

But a great unrest came over the men. The women were well aware of this. Mrs. Moon shouted over to the camp: "Keep still. Xalpen is very angry!" But these words did not calm the men. In despair Mrs. Moon confessed to the women: "Things are looking bad for us. Let us make one more attempt to frighten the men, let us quickly perform: *Xalpen ke xat!*"[10] At once the women formed two rows and stepped out of the Big Hut, one row on the right, the other on the left side of the entrance. Between the rows Mrs. Kra herself stood outside the hut. In a loud voice she called to the men to come closer, for now Xalpen was going to summon one woman after another into the Hut and eat her up. This was intended to throw the men into a terrible fright.

But meanwhile each of the men had equipped himself with a thick club. Now when Mrs. Moon said to the men in the camp: "Come a little closer; you will see how angry Xalpen is! All your women are going to be eaten up!" – they charged fiercely. They came storming up and ran much further than they were supposed to. Mrs. Kra commanded them to stop. She shouted: "Not too close, you men. Keep away from the Hut!" At this moment Sun gave a whistle, he had kept himself hidden very close to the Hut. The men understood the sign. They pressed impatiently forward. Mrs. Moon cried out in extreme fear: "Back, you men, or Xalpen will jump out!" ... The other women in the Hut had been obliged to look on. In their despair they all encouraged the moon woman: "The men are near, shout louder!" ... "Oh, oh, oh, where can we go?" But the men pushed Mrs. Kra back against the Big Hut. They finally reached the entrance and pressed inside. Entering in a dense knot, the men had pushed the Moon Woman ahead of them.

Now Kran shouted with all his might: "Strike the women

down!" And the men swing their clubs. Furiously they struck at the mass of women. Each man choked the first woman he could lay hands on. In a short time all the women lay bloody and dead on the ground. Sometimes a man found himself suddenly face to face with his wife or daughter. If possible, he let another man kill them. But some struck down their own relatives; so great was the rage of the men!

The Sun Man took a burning log from the fire. With it he struck his mighty woman. At the first blow he struck the entire tent of heaven trembled, at the second and third the quake became even more menacing. Consequently the Sun refrained from striking down his woman for fear that the whole heavens might collapse. Mrs. Kra escaped from the Big Hut and immediately fled up to the heavens.

Immediately Kran ran after his wife. But to this day he has been unable to catch her. On her face you can still see the fire spots and black scars. Sometimes the woman is red all over; that happens when she flies into a rage over the man. But to this day the men's hatred of that deceitful woman has not died down either . . .[11]

Conclusions to be drawn from this myth:

"When these ceremonies were in possession of the women, they were shrouded in mystery. The men have preserved this principle. For these ceremonies would immediately cease to be what they are if the female population were allowed to fathom their spirit and purpose.

"With this meeting the men pursue various aims. But the first and fundamental aim is never to let the males' present position of power over the females escape them. Their efforts in this direction are all the more justified in that the relation of forces is thought to have previously been the opposite. Thus the *kloketen* ceremony serves to preserve the present social system. Thence result four rules of conduct that the various groups of the population must strictly observe."

In the life of the collectivity the process of ego-development (and the increasing independence of the male) leads to the triumph of the men's societies and of the patriarchate. In the course of this process the phallic-masculine principle is manifested in the symbolism of the deadly weapon with which, as we have seen, it was already identified in the matriarchal phase. But now this masculine principle is turned against the women. To this day, accordingly, the masculine appears in the dreams of both men and of women as a "killing" principle, hostile to women.

Where the sexual act is viewed as a killing and being killed, it is always on the basis of this conflict between man and woman. The relation between man and woman is experienced as a "battle of the sexes," a conception which indicates that neither the man nor the woman is sure of himself. It is only after this phase of development has been transcended that there can be a true adult relationship between the sexes.

This warlike accentuation of the masculine is necessary both phylogenetically and ontogenetically for the liberation of consciousness and the ego from the preponderance of the matriarchate. Only the heroically fighting ego is capable of overcoming the feminine-maternal which, when it impedes the ego and the masculine principle of consciousness in their development toward independence, becomes Terrible Mother, dragon and witch, a source of anxiety.

Anxiety does not spring only from fundamental superiority of the archetypal world to the ego and especially to the ego in process of development; it also arises at the points of transition from one archetypal phase to another. Just as the whole archetypal world appears to the ego primarily as the Great Mother, so each phase to be surpassed becomes the dragon of threatening regression, which must be defeated by the hero-ego of progress. Whereever in its transition from one archetypal phase to the next the ego is forced to abandon its previous position, it is assailed by fear. As we have already stressed, there is a fundamental conflict between the development of ego-consciousness and the "inertia" or "gravitation" of the psyche, its tendency to adhere to a position once attained and developed. This tendency of psychic inertia to hold the ego fast is symbolized by the terrible clinging aspect of the mother archetype, the dragon that threatens to devour the progressive ego.[12]

In the phase of development now under discussion it is the mother archetype which in the transition to the patriarchate and the father archetype confronts the ego as a clinging negative dragon. But in other phases of development this same father archetype can also become a dragon which must be defeated when it becomes necessary to transcend the patriarchal stage of development. In any case, anxiety is a necessary symptom of centroversion, that is, of man's innate tendency to develop as a totality and, progressing from phase to phase, to overcome in each case the terrible aspect of the clinging archetypal world. Where it does not overpower the ego, this anxiety is a sign of development; it acquaints the ego with what is to be feared and so makes possible a new orientation.

For the ontogenic development, that is, for the life of the child, this means that regardless of her personal behavior, the mother, the vehicle of the archetypal image, becomes, in the transition from the matriarchal to the patriarchal world, a negative power from which the ego must turn away. Here what the Psychoanalysts have called the castration complex plays a symbolically significant role. No fortuitous personal incident between the child and its parents should be held responsible for the complex; no, it springs from the universally human and transpersonal constellation of transition from one archetypal phase to another. Thus, quite understandably, there are cases of castration complex in which no personal trauma can be uncovered, while in other instances a number of demonstrable personal traumata have not led to a castration complex. In disregard of reality, the child psyche attributes the supposed threat of castration to the person who is the vehicle of the threatening archetype. That person may, according to the child's stage of development, be its mother or father. Thus a child who has in fact been forbidden something by its mother, may turn against the father and ask him why he always forbids everything. This occurs when the child is in a phase of development in which the father has replaced the mother as vehicle of its super-ego. Similarly a good personal mother can be experienced as a witch if the personal father takes a more negative attitude toward the child than the mother at the time that the child's phase of psychic development requires it to turn away from its mother. Regardless of what actually happens, the child correlates matriarchal castration, the threat of domination by the Great Mother, with a feminine person, and patriarchal castration, the threat of domination by the Great Father, with a masculine person. Likewise in the child's dreams and fantasies an archetypal development is often represented independently of the behavior of the two personal parent figures.

For this reason the normal anxiety necessary to a child's development leads to a progressive strengthening of the ego. The unconsciously constellated archetypal phases make possible and even necessitate a development of consciousness because through the threat to the ego, the danger of ego-extinction that is present in all anxiety, they bring about a reactive consolidation of the ego.

The development of consciousness that leads to an assimilation or "splitting" of the archetypes, as well as the processes of de-emotionalization, abstraction, etc. accompanying this development, culminate in a consolidation of the ego. The consequence of all these dynamisms is that an increasing quantity of libido becomes available to the ego, which makes use of it in over-coming anxiety, in consolidating itself, and in increasing its will to world-conquest.

It has rightly been pointed out[13] that magic should be correlated with a certain stratum and phase of the collective unconscious. But a purely philosophical interpretation of the archaic, magical and mythological stratum of consciousness cannot be adequate. Grounded as it is in living human experience and in ethnology, depth psychology must take a more complex view of the relations between world-experience and the stages in the development of the ego.

The magical phase is by no means characterized by a relative lack of ego, but – as we have set forth above – by the first emergence of an accented, in fact overaccented, ego. The world to be sure is still experienced as a unitary reality determined by participation mystique, but the magical ego begins to free itself, through ritual self-establishment, from the matriarchal embrace and to achieve an autonomy and independence which take on their clearest form in the warlike and solar ego of the patriarchate.

Quite aptly, Frobenius's account of hunting magic bears the

title "Symbolism of Light." For the magical phase forms a transition between the matriarchal world and the patriarchal world of consciousness. But, though the magical ego leads to a patriarchal development, it still discloses evident ties with the matriarchal world.

In Frobenius's report, the matriarchal component is still demonstrable through the role of the woman who implements the magic both by her words and her gestures, which characteristically consists of a raising of her arms. The numinous position of woman in connection with magic is further confirmed by the man's fear that Frobenius might tell the woman that he has spoken of the magic. The fact that woman is present in all human history as positive mana figure and as witch and in the unconscious as Lady of Magic shows to what extent magic belongs to the matriarchal phase.

But Frobenius's communication about hunting magic also makes clear the connection between magic and a new phase of development. The deadly magic of the masculine is connected with the symbolism of light, especially the sun, the central figure of the patriarchal upper world of heaven. The sun as a hunter and hero who shoots arrows of light is a very widespread archetype that can be followed from the myth of the Tierra del Fuegans to the slaying, arrow-shooting Apollo and to the report from Africa in which the identification of the shooter of arrows with the sun is strikingly evident.

The human ego allies itself ritually with the archetype of the masculine-warlike Self and from this identification draws the power and the right to kill. Just as the killing power of the patriarchal hero is based, through the ritual equation "I and the father are one," on the fact that he is the son of the divine father, so the action of the magical-warlike ego is based on its connection with the superior magical power of light which here is not a god of light as such but what has been called a god of the moment. For it is not the sun as such, but the rising sun whose radiant power is preponderant over the darkness of the night it has defeated. It is the transpersonal hunting-killing principle, its symbol is the bird of prey, the eagle. Its killing, warlike function is known to us not only from Mexico but also from astrology where the sun is correlated with the lion and with the searing and killing July heat, with which in magical rites the hunter is identical. It is only thanks to this identity that he is able to kill without being destroyed by the vengeance of the shed blood of the animal with whom he is still closely linked.

The killing must therefore be annulled and the unity of the world restored through the concluding ritual of the following morning. Through the sacrifice of restitution, in which the hair and blood of the slain antelope are restored to its image, the antelope is renewed as a living figure. And the same context is known to us from innumerable early rites of a similar nature, such as the above-mentioned bear rites of Siberia and the Stone Age. It is possible that this restitution with the help of a picture drawn on the ground is based on the fact that the earth as Great Mother of Death and Regeneration regenerates the slain animal.

The withdrawn arrow is a symbol of the annulment of death, and with the effacement of the picture of the antelope at sunrise the animal is reinstated as animal lord over life and over the once again complete world. The magical rites in which the sun, as a transpersonal being, annuls death transforms the human ego into the servant and executor of a higher principle. It takes away the guilt of killing, because the human ego had as it were followed only the killing solar power, for death was invented not by man but by the powers, and the man who kills is only following the example of a transpersonal power.

At this solar stage the ego is no longer, as at the phallic stage, the executor of an unconscious, matriarchal, instinctive constellation by which it was directed; here, rather, a spiritual act is operative even when it has not yet reached the conscious level in myth. The ritual action bears witness to an identification between ego and Self, in which the Self is a superior killing Self which the active ego merely follows.

This magical activity is the adequate expression of a situation in which man is still so interwoven with the environing reality that he cannot, as he does later, oppose himself to it without difficulty. To do so, as we have seen, man requires a strengthening of the ego, which lifts him out of his psychic unawareness and inertia and out of his unquestioning embeddedness in the world, so enabling him to oppose the thou and the object with concentrated power as an ego and a subject.

When a modern man prays and goes off to war, "conscious of his just cause," hence connected and identified with transpersonal values, he effects a similar magical inner preparation. The outcome of the battle depends in part on this inner preparation just as it did with early man, and moreover such a preparation does much to enable men to withstand the horrors of killing and the danger of being killed. For only if a man – like the pygmies of Africa – is afterwards able to efface the image of his killing, to cease relating it to his ego and to give it back to the transpersonal powers, will he be spared by the blood of the slain. Consequently the absence of adequate rites and attitudes in modern man leads to an inner poisoning, for his psyche is made increasingly neurotic by his unassimilated acts of destruction.

But if the ego fortifies itself by allying and identifying itself with a transpersonal power, so that destruction and power cease to be the arbitrary attributes of a mere person and become parts of a cosmic order, the consequence is a transformation of the masculine destructive drive and will to power. Such a transformation is necessary to the development of the ego. Then, instead of being a murderer, it becomes a hunter or warrior; the function of blood shedding becomes identified with the transpersonal life of the group and the necessity of human life, and so justified.

Where the personality and the ego have ceased to follow the unconscious will of nature and are no longer wholly taken up with magical activity, but have begun to account to themselves and so come to self-consciousness, there lies the threshold of the patriarchal and solar world. But this strengthening of the ego also requires a ritual. As at the magical stage of the ego, this ritual is first enacted within the group which is experienced by the individual as his directing group-Self.

Ontogenetically, when a child is weaned, the mother of the primal relationship first assumes the role of the Self as an outer Self or relatedness-Self upon which the developing child ego leans while phylogenetically the group as group-Self assumes this role toward the individual. All rites of initiation, whether matriarchal or patriarchal, whether of boys, girls or adults, have the function of transforming the ego in its relation to the Self.

In the following we shall try to understand what psychic processes and authorities correspond to the emergence of the patriarchate. It is only at this point, where the child overcomes the matriarchate and forms a relation to the father archetype, that the sexes begin to diverge in their development and that a girl begins to differ from a boy in her psychology.

Totemism and the Patriarchal Development

In connection with the development of the patriarchal solar ego we must clarify an aspect of "totemism" which students have attempted to understand from a variety of angles. The totem as animal, plant, or other element of nature stands in a close bond with the group. This bond is based on *participation mystique* between group and totem. This *participation mystique* creates a relationship of kinship and identity between the totem and the group that reveres it. If the totem, as was originally by no means always the case, is an animal, this animal is not hunted and is eaten only under very special circumstances; the group's entire dealings with it, especially if the totem is regarded as the group's original ancestor and author, are regulated by special rules.

The essential fact about the totem is that it is not a personal but a transpersonal father figure and the founder of the group descended from it. The bond of the members with the group is confirmed by a solemn act of initiation. The mysteries of the male group are opposed to those of the female group; because they were "founded," they are spiritual mysteries and not nature mysteries like those of women. The male, totemic group is united by an upper spiritual, or – in our terminology – solar bond. This sacred bond between the parts of the group is created by the totem meal, at which on solemn occasions the totem is eaten and "incorporated." "In the light of general ethnology the totemistic mentality reveals a preference for solar conception."[14] This means that the totem is an incarnation of the spiritual, founding ancestor of which every group member is the spiritual son. This is equally true in all later religions and mysteries; the totemic group is no doubt their earliest precursor.

The totem animal as transpersonal "group-Self" may at first have a uroboric character, that is, it may present both maternal-containing and paternal-begetting features. But still in the matriarchal period, the paternal and founding aspect, which is later characteristic of the totem in its opposition to the matriarchal world, begins to come to the fore.

As long as the male group is bound together only by hunting magic, it has not yet left the matriarchal sphere. Hunting magic is by nature related to the alimentary drive, for its object, game, was in the early days the main food of the human group. Even where fertility magic, aimed at making wild animals multiply, enters in, the central aim of magic remains the food supply. Hunting and food-supply magic — the basic form of magic in the Ice Age — is the essential foundation of the totemism of a later day. The oral rites based on the alimentary drive are the earliest of rites, and all later rites and festivals connected with ritual meals taken in common are based on this early development. As we have seen, it was necessary to atone for the killing of a living creature which in primordial times was held to have been borne by the Great Mother as Mistress of the Animals and to be identical with her. This was one of the basic conceptions of the matriarchal early period with its *participation mystique*.

The men's societies already made their appearance during this early matriarchal period. They used for their own purposes rites and festivals that were originally based on the alimentary drive and intended to promote the acquisition of food. The eating of the totem animal was primarily a rite of transition, in this case the transition from the matriarchate to the patriarchate. Thus it paved the way for a new archetypal phase. Totemic men's societies are often present in a matriarchal order to which they form a counterweight.

The killing, devouring aspect of the masculine principle becomes evident in the magic stage of man as warrior. But at first this "Terrible Male" may still be a companion figure to the Great Mother and belong in part to the matriarchal sphere; the oral accent also points in this direction.

By eating the totem animal that constellates the men's society, the male group establishes an identification with the devouring Terrible Male, the beast-of-prey aspect of the Terrible Mother. This meal has a twofold function. By reinforcing the masculine principle, it forms the basis of the independence of the men's society which subsequently overcomes the matriarchate. But at the same time the identification of the group with the Terrible Male, manifested in the symbolic eating of the god and the incorporation of the totem-father, serves to transform the male into a patriarchal male and so completes the replacement of the mother archetype by the father archetype.

When as Terrible Male he turns against the matriarchate, he has freed himself from his bond with his feminine origin. But only when the male group incorporates the totem animal, which is at once founding father and spiritual ancestor, and so identifies itself with the upper masculine principle, can the solar aspect predominate. The eating of the totem animal results in an identification with an upper masculine principle which as sun combines within itself both light-consciousness and the killing aspect. Thereby the patriarchal stage is definitely achieved.

The same rite can signify both liberation from the matriarchate and the identification of the male group with the Terrible Male as a form of the father archetype, but it can also take on the significance of a parricide at a later stage when the process of development calls for the transcending of the father archetype and the devouring son turns against the devoured father.

The father figure belongs to both strata. Both the Terrible Male, who at first stands side by side with the mother and turns against her only later, and the upper heavenly father are aspects of the father archetype. This archetype is manifested both in phylogenesis and in ontogenesis, but in a historical succession of stages, in which the upper follows the lower, the solar the phallic.

We shall speak later of the specificities of the female development.[15] Here I wish only to interpolate a brief general remark relating to the development of the phallic stage which is characteristic of the ego in process of gaining independence.

In the period of the domination of the Great Mother, when the ego is still wholly dependent, the Great Mother herself is the phallus bearer. Not only mythologically but in the development of the child as well, the mother with the male genital organ is an early anxiety image. Later – as has already been set forth – the male satellites of the Great Mother become the phallus bearers; they belong to her, they depend on her and possess only a relative and ephemeral phallic activity and independence. The youthful lover and the male group subordinated to the matriarchate are characteristic of this phase. As the masculine principle achieves greater independence, the ego comes, precisely in the course of its struggle against the mother as world and unconscious, to identify with the phallic and phallic-warlike. But seen from the standpoint of later development, this masculine principle is still a lower, instinctive-sexual and active-warlike principle. It is only at the solar stage when the phallic appears as "spirit-phallus" and as source of the wind that the masculine principle achieves its supreme generative-spiritual potency. And it is only at this phase that the ego's still immature identification with the lower phallic and its related hostility to woman are overcome.

The aim of the male initiations, of which the youth initiations are best known to us, is always a kind of "Second Birth"; in a manner contrary to nature, that is, without the participation of a woman, the individual is reborn as a member of the group. In those rites where the initiate is "born" and must behave ritually like a newborn child, he is not borne by a personal mother, but by a transpersonal being, the house of initiation for example, the symbolism of which is always connected with the archetypal father figure. The initiate ceases to be a part of the personal primal relationship through which he is descended from his mother and connected with her. But he also has no relation to a lower masculine principle of sexuality. For regardless of his age the noninitiate is not held to be a man, or in any sense human. Characteristically, he is often not permitted to engage in sexual relations before initiation and never permitted to marry. Only a man who has proven his upper masculinity is held to be capable of marriage, for only such an individual is capable of withstanding the danger represented by woman. For the initiate, upper masculinity, that is the masculine values of the cultural canon, are the supreme authority; he must be capable of defending them against the assaults of his lower, instinctual masculinity. This attitude is crucial to the survival of the community. Without it the male group and its culture would disintegrate, giving way to a bestial rivalry between males.

The purpose of the tests which the initiate must withstand is to sustain his upper masculinity, his ego-stability and consciousness in contrast to his unconscious instinctual nature. The bond among men is so essential for this development that women are absolutely — and often on pain of death — excluded from male initiations.

As founding father, the totem or solar-upper masculine principle, is a begettor, but he is a spiritual, not a bodily begettor. What he begets is a male brotherhood which is engendered by a spiritual act.

Totemism is a group phenomenon and cannot be derived from a personal Oedipus situation. The problem of totemism is more complex. Even to assume that the totem is always an animal, let alone a beast of prey, is a mistake.

Freud's theory of totem and patricide is an extension of his study of phobias in which the patient, threatened by his father in animal form, eats him totemistically. His conception revolves around the final form in which the totem appears ontogenetically in childhood within the framework of the Oedipus complex and the successful or unsuccessful process of overcoming the father archetype.

Freud's misunderstanding was made almost inevitable by the fact that in ontogenesis this phenomenon is in part experienced through the personal father. In a phase of research which was concerned only with individual experience, which from consciousness had delved only as far as the personal unconscious and had not yet come to understand the archetypal, transpersonal structure of the psyche, a personal interpretation of patricide and totemism was inescapable. Such an explanation, however, covers only a part of the reality.

In the primordial age, the subject of development was the group and not the individual. The men's society, which was founded first by magical, later by totemic developments, was the sacral unit of which the individual was only a part. Through the formation of the male group and its magic, the individual ego, still weak at this stage, was strengthened and so prepared for independence. the connection, so characteristic of the patriarchal phase, between the community, ego-consolidation and consciousness becomes evident for the first time in the men's societies and in the totemism which pertains to them. In this phase – in contrast to the modern period – the individual's ego is consolidated within the group and his connection with the leader-figure and the father archetype becomes evident for the first time. Chief and medicine men are incarnations of the hero archetype; both are aspects of the totem as group-Self, which not only founds the community, but guides, initiates, and instructs it as well. "The male collectivity is the source of all the taboos, laws and institutions that were destined to put an end to the dominance of the uroboros and the Great Mother. Heaven, Father and Spirit are all masculine and belong together; they represent the victory of the patriarchate over the matriarchate."[16] The power to resist the matriarchal world arises in the male group, and the individual ego becomes a hero-ego which, because it has the power to kill, is able to overcome the mother-dragon.

The totemic identification of each man with his ancestors and of the individual with the group-Self is the foundation for the psychic consolidation of the male group and of the higher consciousness incarnated in it, which ultimately enables it to overcome the Great Mother as unconscious and as world. The solar ego has an activity which is no longer exclusively an exponent of the body-Self, but is related to the father archetype of the sun, which is both disembodied and unearthly. Only this solar ego is an "upper" ego: it experiences itself as belonging to a higher, heavenly, spiritual world and is therefore able to oppose itself to the "lower" world of the earthly, bodily and unconscious. Its final form, the solar-rational ego, is characteristic for the development of the patriarchate and of patriarchal culture.

CHAPTER SIX

The Patriarchate

To make possible an understanding of the transition in child development from the matriarchate to the patriarchate and from the magical to the solar ego and of the structure of the human psyche correlated with this transition, we must clarify the relations between the ego and the Self and between the mother and the father archetypes. First of all, let us sum up what has thus far been said on the subject.

The child living in the unitary reality characterized by *participation mystique* and an absence of polarity between inside and outside, consciousness and the unconscious, has at first no independent ego. The development of an independent ego, the rise of consciousness, and the polarization of the world, or in mythological terms the separation of the World Parents, go hand in hand and determine the next phase of development. From the standpoint of analytical psychology it is essential to note that this development and its phases are transpersonal. Just as the organs of the body develop and the central nervous system gradually grows into its functions in accordance with a pattern that is universally human, so the psyche develops in transpersonal stages. This implies that in the course of an archetypally ordered development, the ego and consciousness are sustained by the unconscious until they gain the relative autonomy characteristic of the modern adult.

We term this directedness of development by the unconscious as the containing totality — out of whose "belly" the ego-nucleus and consciousness gradually develop through centroversion. It is matriarchal, because the archetype of the Great Mother dominates the life of the child both phylogenetically and ontogenetically.

As we have seen, the development of the personality leads gradually to the independence of the ego and consciousness which liberate themselves from the shelter and clinging embrace of the unconscious and of the Great Mother. In liberating itself, the ego grows away from the unconscious which is its nurturing soil. The security and healthiness of this development depends on a successful primal relationship, that is, on a positive relationship between mother and child, which is identical with the relationship between Self and ego, the unconscious and consciousness.

The condition for a successful development is the achievement of a universally human constellation in which what was held in the mother's embrace becomes free and what was dependent becomes independent. In this phase accordingly a conflict must necessarily arise between the child as ego-consciousness and the mother as unconscious. This conflict is at first manifested as the polarizing of the world by consciousness or as separation of the World Parents, but later it is manifested by a conflict between the sexes, in which the active, self-liberating ego experiences itself— in both sexes – as masculine in its conflict with the mother archetype.

Polarization and the separation of the World Parents mean that the uroboric entity which had hitherto contained the opposites now separates into its components. The male-female uroboros becomes the Great Mother with the masculine companion figures that are subordinated to her, and as the development proceeds, these companion figures become "strugglers" and finally emerge as independent masculine figures.

In the course of this development the ego must progress from its passive directedness through the stages which – both phylogenetically and ontogenetically – strengthen and consolidate it and so secure it against flooding either by the unconscious or by the impact of the world. In all its variants the protective magic of the magical phases is a precursor of what in a later period we term the defense mechanisms of the ego, just as the magical methods of ego-concentration and ego-consolidation are preliminary stages of the ego-will which develops later.

But it is only with the emergence of the father archetype as antithesis to the heretofore dominant mother archetype that the tension between the poles of above and below, heaven and earth, consciousness and the unconscious is fully constellated. Such a tension could not arise, nor could the weak, childlike ego withstand it if a transpersonal support for this resistance were not embedded in the psyche itself.

We have pointed out that every archetype has two aspects, one "good," the other "terrible." The consequence of this ambivalence of the archetype is that the dominant archetype of each successive phase of development has a tendency to hold the ego fast. This gives rise to a conflict between centroversion, which presses on toward the next stage of development, and the self-perpetuating inertia of each dominant phase. In this situation the archetype of the next phase shows its positive aspect and that of the phase in process of being transcended shows its clinging, terrible, fear-inspiring aspect. But here we see how the Self, with its drive toward wholeness and toward the fulfillment of the human pre-disposition, manipulates the archetypes and their aspects. The ego's fear of the terrible aspect of the clinging phase proves to be purposive, for it facilitates or necessitates the transition, and indeed this fear is set in motion by the Self. In each stage of development, the Self incarnates itself in an archetype, yet does not become identical with it. Thus its manifestation changes from phase to phase; it appears first in the mother archetype, then in the father archetype, next as a group-self, then as an individual Self. This leads the ego into a fundamental conflict.

When the Self incarnates itself in an archetype, this archetype represents a supreme value for the ego. Consequently the trans-formation of the Self compels the ego, which is likewise in process of transformation, to kill what has hitherto been the supreme value: a "deicide" becomes necessary. But for the ego this inevi-tably means anxiety, guilt feelings and suffering, because from the standpoint of the older manifestation of the sacred, the mani-festation of the next higher stage of the Self is dangerous and sinful.

In consequence of this necessary conflict, human development is dependent on a creative openness which allows man to become a suffering as well as a creative and heroic being. For to complete the stages in the development of consciousness means not only to receive and identify with supreme values, but also later to abandon them and withdraw identification.

At a number of points we have stressed the importance of these transformations in the manifestations of the Self for the development of the psyche. Such a transformation occurs in the matriarchal phase when first the uroboric Mother, then the Great Mother represents the Self when the Self gradually moves into the child as it achieves independence and the child's existence depends on whether it feels accepted or rejected by its mother. Similar changes in the archetypal dominance occur in the phase of liberation from the matriarchate, and then from the patriarchate itself.

Time and time again, the Self incarnates itself and then becomes independent of the archetypal incarnation which it first assumes, then casts off and destroys.

This fundamental freedom and formlessness of the Self is of the utmost importance for our understanding of the human psyche, its dynamics and development.

In this metamorphosis of the gods that arises through the change in its manifestations, the Self is correlated with the phases in the development of the human personality. But all these manifestations are mere cloaks and images of the Self. Though the Self is incarnated and takes form in the psyche, it is, by its own nature, formless and both extra-psychic and extra-worldly. Beyond the images by which it is manifested in the collective unconscious and beyond the projection of these images on something outside, for example, on the figure of a god as an extra-phenomenal Self, there exists as it were a "Self as such," which is identical neither with its outward nor with its inner psychic images and manifestations.

Thus the differentiated stage of the human psyche in which inside and outside are polarized encompasses not only the psychic image world within, and the quasi-objective world of forms without, but also the unitary reality which precedes this stage and is independent of it and the extra-phenomenal Self as well. As the history of religion and philosophy shows, this Self can take all manner of forms in mankind; it can reveal itself as mother or father archetype, as god and as totem, as savior and as ancestor, as Tao of the way, and yet again as the quintessence in every thing.

It can appear as white light or as *En Sof*, as the unattainable infinite or as the purely formless. Or beyond all manifestations it may remain hidden.

If we approach the personality exclusively from the standpoint of the ego, we can define it as a living biopsychic individuality existing in an environment. But once we have understood that the ego can never exist and develop without the Self that underlies it, we arrive at the crucial Copernican revolution of depth psychology, which views the human personality and human life no longer from the standpoint of the ego but from that of the Self around which the ego revolves as the earth revolves around the sun. Then we realize that the ego-Self axis is the foundation of the personality. Then we understand the dynamics of human life as a unity in which conscious and unconscious processes, "inner" psychic contents and "outward" world contents form an indissoluble whole.

At least insofar as the first half of life is concerned, we can describe the development of the individual and his confrontation with life as the development of an inner factor with and against an outward factor, and we can discuss the continuous changes in these relations between inside and outside. But we must always remain aware that the center which directs this development and confrontation is situated neither in a place we can designate as within nor in a place we can designate as without, but must be localized in the extraneous region of the unitary reality, in other words, beyond the separation effected by our polarizing consciousness into inside and outside, world and psyche. This directing factor has no place; we are incapable of localizing it. The Jewish designation of God as *Maqom*, Place, refers perhaps to this extraneous, paradoxically unlocalised place in which the process takes place – through the "in," which at first seems necessary for the orientation of our consciousness, is inapplicable.

The central point represented by the Self partakes of neither of the two antithetical positions of later psychic development; the Self is neither in the psychic nor in the physical world. It lies, as we say but should not say, outside this polarization. The limits to our power of formulation and communication become immediately apparent because it is not accurate to describe the unitary reality as something outside. It is just as much inside as outside, just as

much between as beyond. In relation to the Self, we find ourselves in the situation of iron filings spread over a surface and
endowed with a consciousness capable of apprehending only two
dimensions. Suddenly we feel that we are being directed by a
magnetic-Self, but we must also recognize the impossibility of de-
fining this presence in the dimensions of our consciousness. We
can describe its reality only in terms of paradox. No understanding
of the creative as a basic human phenomenon or of individuation
as the Self-realization of the individual within his culture is possible without an insight into the roles played by the changing
manifestations of the Self and by the Self-as-such which is independent of these manifestations.

Under the pressure both of nature and of the collectivity the
individual must, as a matter of course, look upon the archetype
relevant to his phase of development as an incarnation of the Self
and as his supreme, directing value. Thus in the matriarchal
phase to regard the father archetype as a supreme value passes
for sacrilege, while under the patriarchate, conversely, it is sacrilege to regard the mother archetype as a supreme value. Thus –
though Catholic dogma is beginning to undergo a change in this
respect – a Jew or Protestant takes it for granted that the supreme
deity is a father-God and God of Heaven, and regards the idea
of replacing or complimenting this image by that of a supreme
goddess as pagan, heretical and altogether impossible. And it
strikes him as almost equally impossible to recognize the "atheism"
of Buddhism or on the contrary the plethoric divine figures of
Hinduism as a mode of the "formlessness of the divine."

The transformation of the Self which in the various phases of
development clothes itself in the various archetypes, is a universally human phenomenon; it corresponds to a natural aptitude in
man. Nevertheless, as we have seen, this development takes place
in a specifically human environment and is dependent on it. This
is particularly clear in the case of the father archetype which in
contrast to the mother archetype is always connected with the
individual cult of the male group and with its canon of supreme
values. The development of the stages of consciousness and the
concomitant development of the ego are a process which is
normally so dependent on the collectivity that we find rituals in

almost all human groups. They make possible and facilitate the transition from one phase to another, for by identifying himself with the traditions, myths, rites and religion of the group the individual achieves an understanding of his existence and of his function in the collective. Such initiations apply not only to the youth, but also to the older people, man and woman alike, and transitions of children from phase to phase are enacted ritually by the parents who subject birth, release from the mother, the separation of the sexes, and the formation of sex groups to a collective, ritual order. As long as these transitions between phases are accented as necessary developments by the group's rites of initiation, the fulfillment of man's specific predisposition is provided for.

Whereas in modern man these collective rites no longer exist, and the problems relating to these transitions devolve upon the individual, his responsibility and understanding are so overburdened that psychic disorders are frequent. This is the case not only in childhood but also in puberty, in marriage and mid-life, at the climacteric, and in the hour of death. All these stages in life were formerly numinous points at which the collectivity intervened with its rites; today they are points of psychic illness and anxiety for the individual, whose conscious awareness does not suffice to enable him to live his life.

This situation is further exacerbated by the fact that it is no longer sufficient for a modern man to adapt himself to the collective; at the same time he must develop as an individual. In modern times there can be no rites providing for the development that leads from general adaptation to the collective to the self-realization of individuation, or at all events no such rites exist as yet. The problem of individuation, the development of the uniqueness of the individual, the urgency of such especially for the second half of life has been set forth by Jung, leads to psychic conflicts between individuation and collective adaptation. Depth psychology is only beginning to gain an understanding of these conflicts.

Whereas in the first phase of human development the Self is manifested in the mother archetype as directing nature, the situation changes when it assumes the role of the father archetype which is bound up with the perpetually changing culture of the group and of the epoch in which the group lives. Conflicts develop which affect the development of both group and individual and can cause profound disorders not only in adults but in children as well. The relation between Self, father archetype and super-ego discussed in the next section has a direct bearing on these conflicts.

The Father Archetype and the Masculine Principle

Both the father and mother archetypes are parts split off from the original uroboric archetype which still contained the totality of the opposites combined within itself. For this reason the earliest forms of both archetypes always involve a uroboric element. As uroboric mother, the mother archetype is also paternal and masculine, while the uroboric father archetype is also maternal and feminine.

When we speak of a uroboric masculine principle, we have in mind a group of traits which symbolically combine the masculine and the feminine. The patriarchal godhead is unthinkable without the sheltering, protective character which belongs essentially to the symbolism of the maternal, regardless of whether this feature is primary or whether the patriarchate has taken it over from the matriarchate. When we say "safe in Abraham's bosom," we are imputing a positive maternal trait to the patriarchal principle, whereas the devouring character of Moloch, one of the terrible masculine gods, embodies the symbolism of the Terrible Feminine, the "negative hole."

In the later differentiation of the masculine principle, however, the uroboric traits recede and – as in all archetypal developments – the duality and ambivalence of the archetype come to the fore. The ambivalent masculine principle in which positive and negatives stand side by side is activity and motion, aggression and penetration, fecundation and destruction in one. Heaven and sun, lighting and wind, phallus and weapon are its most conspicuous symbols.

The symbol of heaven is, to be sure, a symbol of the spiritual world, but heaven as the abode of the gods is an abode not solely of the good, but also of the terrible, which as fate and destiny, as a godhead that flings lightning and arrows, embodies the upper masculine principle in its life- and death-giving potency. Thus the

masculine sun which belongs to this heaven is not only the life
that confers warmth and light, but is also a beast of prey, a lion,
the symbol of searing heat, of dazzling, blinding light and of
overpowering assault. The solar hero as an arrow-shooting god
embodies the basic symbolism of this archetypal masculine principle in its unity of creative fecundation and of destruction; he
can be fecundating in destruction and destructive in fecundation.
Accordingly, the fecundating phallus is not only a symbol of
generation, but also frequently enough, as penetrating weapon a
symbol of killing. Thus Shiva, the dancing Indian god, is expressive
of a fecundating, yet aggressively destructive dynamic that has
been a symbol of the archetypal masculine since primordial
times, since long before men discovered the fecundating motion
of the male seed and the fecundating aggression with which it
penetrates the resting feminine ovum.

But in its ambivalence of fecundation and destruction this
masculine principle also combines an upper spiritual aspect with a
lower aspect pertaining to the earth and the instinctual side of the
unconscious psyche. But the spiritual aspect which opposes the
unconscious, the earth, and the feminine as lower nature, is itself
nature, as the symbol of the sun and the related symbolism of the
daytime sky, of light and the upper elements show. Originally
world and psyche, as well as spirit and nature, were experienced
as a polarized unity. It was the subsequent decadence of western
thinking that first led men to see an opposition between spirit and
nature and to confuse spirit with consciousness and reason, or
even with intellectual thinking.

Like the symbols of the spiritual aspect of the upper masculine
principle, light and lightning, storm and rain, the symbols of the
lower, earthly aspect – the fire of the volcanic depths and the
water of rivers and brooks – imply a combination, characteristic
of the masculine principle, of motion and aggression, fecundation
and destruction. The animal symbols of this erupting masculine
power are not confined to the beasts of prey; its fecundating and
aggressive power is also symbolized by bull and stallion, ram and
he-goat. (It is worth noting that for this reason the bull fight
is an automatic symbol of the conflict between the upper and the
lower aspects of the masculine principle.) The masculine sexuality

and aggression pertaining to the lower masculine principle can be symbolized by the earthly elements and by animals. But far more significant is the male's collective experience of himself as spirit, as related to heaven and light, as upper in contrast to the feminine principle and all lower things. This experience is the foundation of the patriarchate; on it, as upon a supreme value, masculine culture is grounded.

The upper masculine principle in its connection with heaven is manifested most clearly in the father archetype, whose prefigurative conception, which must be counted among the earliest uroboric symbols of mankind, shows in its very formlessness an essential characteristic of the spirit. This formlessness is an expression of the mysterious dynamic of life itself, which is symbolized in the uroboric circle of inchoate existence. "The initial movement, the procreative thrust naturally has an affinity with the paternal side of the uroboros and with the beginning of evolution in time, and is far harder to visualize than the maternal side."[1] The invisibly moving, formless but formative principle as creative wind, creative breath and creative word is one of the earliest symbols. The Egyptian god Amon, the "breath of life," is an incarnation of this divine-masculine creative power. Concerning the connection between this god of the creative sun and the god Amon-Re, Henri Frankfort writes:

In reality it was a truly creative thought which realized the potentialities of a combination of the concept of the creator-sun with that of Amon, the "breath of life," "the hidden one," who, as one of the Eight of Hermopolis, was part of uncreated chaos.

We have seen how theological speculation had at an early age apprehended chaos as four pairs of deified concepts. One of them, Amon, occupied an exceptional position; he was recognized as a god of some importance already in the Old Kingdom, and as a personification of the wind he represented a dynamic element. Just as Ptah could, by being equated with the Ogdoad, be considered the First Cause, the divine person from whom the sun was an emanation, so, among the figures of the Eight, Amon could be viewed as the First Cause, especially since, as breath, unseen, he could be apprehended as the basis of all life. Hence the phrase: "Amon, the venerable god who came into being first; he is that breath which stays in all things and through which one lives forever." The same thought is expressed in the Luxor temple in a design in which Amon holds the sign of life toward King Amenhotep III with the words: "My beloved son, receive my likeness in thy nose."

The theological argument establishing Amon as the First Cause takes into account that the Creator is the sun, Atum: "Amon who came forth from Nun. He leads mankind. Another of his forms is the Ogdoad. The begetter of the Primeval Gods giving birth to Re. He completed himself as Atum." And Amon is really felt to combine the characters of sun and wind: "To thee belongs what thou seest as light, what thou passest through as wind."[2]

This early mythological and theological development is based on the archetypal image of the sun-phallus as source of the wind, which Jung discovered in the fantasy of a psychotic[3] and also in the Egyptian magic papyrus describing the mysteries of Mithras, and which unmistakably recurs in the Christian symbolism of the Middle Ages. I have in mind the symbolism of the Annunciation in which the fecundating dove of the Holy Ghost flies into a tube emanating from a deity represented as the sun, and disappears under Mary's skirt.

The sun-phallus in which the formless creative principle takes on figure and form is not a chthonian-creative principle of lower fertility but represents a numinous power, the spirit-wind, which draws its fecundating energy from the daytime sky and spirit-sun. This fecundating spirit-wind is an invisible mover. This invisible mover and fecundator is among the earliest experiences of mankind; it harks back to the matriarchal world which did not yet know that men were the agents of procreation. In matriarchal times this creative masculine principle correlated with the feminine was manifested as moon-spirit and as spirit-wind, which fecundates women as it does the tortoise, earth symbol of the Great Mother, and the vulture,[4] both of which passed in Egypt as ancient symbols of the Great Mother and were believed to number only females in their midst.

The invisible spirit-wind as mover of the world and the unconscious is one of the earliest human symbols. Psychologically speaking, it corresponds to the emotional side of the spirit, the spirit which in ecstasy seized upon man and ravishes him. In the solar principle we already discern a later principle of light and knowledge, the daytime world of heaven as a higher spiritual sphere. The sun-phallus as the source of the wind contains both aspects of the spirit, the emotional flash that moves us and the clarity which enlightens us. Wherever an invisible mover is discerned in symbolism, it relates to this primary spiritual-emotional dynamic of living existence. In other words, the spirit was first manifested in emotional seizure; it irrupted, penetrated and overpowered.

This *numinosum*, however, captivated not only woman, who maintained an attitude of openness to it and as seeress and priestess received the god, but man as well. True, the Dionysian element, with its irruption leading from the realm of instinct to ecstatic intoxication of the soul and spirit, was largely the concern of women, and the phallic mysteries were for the most part situated at the dividing line between below and above. But it is precisely this captivation by the upper masculine principle that distinguishes the prophetess and seeress as Sophia from the maenad and witch.

For matriarchal consciousness this upper spiritual aspect is procreative; it seizes upon the receptive consciousness of woman and overpowers her entirely. This same principle of the directing spirit plays a decisive role in the animus psychology of modern woman. The animus is the masculine, spiritual component in woman herself, toward which the feminine ego is receptive. But when the irrupting spiritual aspect is a transpersonal, archetypal factor exceeding the animus which is a part of the feminine personality, the woman as a whole becomes the receiver. But in both cases, regardless of whether the woman's ego or the whole woman is receptive, a woman can, in her biopsychic sexual character, identify herself with the irruption.

But when a man is exposed or exposes himself to such an irruption of the spirit, something different happens. Here the receptive factor is part of the man, what analytical psychology terms the anima, the feminine side of man. But this receptive factor, open to the incursion of the god, is not – as in woman – identical with his ego or with the totality of his personality. Consequently, even when masculine ego-consciousness is overwhelmed by the incursion of the *numinosum*, it does not lose its creative, understanding and consciousness-promoting activity. This power to resist the *numinosum* and keep a certain distance from it, which we find in such high degree in the prophets of the Old Testament, enables men to assimilate and elaborate the irrupting spirit in a way that is not possible for women.

The experience that "I and the Father are one," transmitted by the tradition and mysteries of the men's societies, expresses the close bond between the irrupting solar father archetype and the son-ego, but at the same time shows that for all his immersion in the archetype the son preserves his own identity.

This fundamental difference in psychic structure underlies the difference between creative men and women. Whereas woman is captivated as a whole and so tends to undergo a change of personality, that is, to be transformed from nature to spirit, man attains to the spiritual creativity of works and culture, the characteristic hallmarks of the patriarchate. And this creative achievement of the patriarchate, in which consciousness plays the leading part, is often possible without a transformation of the personality.

However, where a creative man does not complete the psychic differentiation characteristic of the patriarchal world, he may — especially if he is an artist — combine the feminine with the masculine mode of experience. Then his work is inseparable from the transformation of his personality, and this is invariably true in the case of great art.

The earlier in human culture such captivation occurs in man, the more radical it is and the more it transforms his personality. The mantic behavior of such mana personalities as shamans, medicine men, seers and poets is still close to the matriarchal world with its unconscious dominant. With the progressive development of consciousness toward the patriarchate, this feminine component recedes, but never disappears entirely.

Here we discern a phenomenon which probably did much to promote the formation and systematization of consciousness. The manifestation of an archetype exerts a fascination on the ego. Emotional captivation accounts for only a part of this fascination, for fascination also presupposes an archetypal content capable of exerting overwhelming power. An *idée fixe*, dogmatic obsession with an archetypal content, is necessarily exclusive. From the standpoint of our modern consciousness we generally regard this phenomenon as purely negative. But it is probable that it also had another, positive effect on the development and stabilization of consciousness, which are what concerns us here. There is an essential relation between the archetype's exclusive domination of consciousness and the development of form in the sense of delimitation and clarification. The revealed content exerts so overpowering an impact on consciousness and is so brightly illumined that it occupies the center of consciousness and blinds it to other impressions.

Because it bars the way to all contents that are unrelated or opposed to it, such an exclusive revelation helps to consolidate consciousness by concentrating it on one focus or archetypal revelation, and this concentration upon one content furthers the consolidation and stabilization of the ego. A consciousness that is just beginning to be systematized and stabilized is always in danger of being flooded by contents of the unconscious and so disintegrated. For this reason, concentration, defense and systematization are fundamental necessities for an early consciousness. It is only for the later free-moving ego of modern man, situated in a broad, highly-developed consciousness capable of containing many contents, that possession and dogmatic fixation become a danger.

In early times, just as the fascination of the archetype was consciousness-promoting, so the individual possessed by the archetype exerted upon his group a fascination that served to consolidate it and give it form and content. An individual fascinated by an archetypal content might found a group and endow it with rites of initiation which consolidated it and at the same time set it apart from other groups.

We have intentionally formulated this context in very general terms. But now the question rises: if every archetype works in this direction – and we know that by and large every archetypal content has this fascinating effect on the ego and consciousness – what has this fascination to do with the specific archetype of the upper masculine principle and the spirit?

We have spoken above of a spirit-instinct in animals and in

primitive man, by which we meant an ordering principle which determines their unconscious behavior and so molds their reactions toward the members of their species and their environment. This order is transpersonal; in animals it preserves the species through instincts governing breeding and care for the young. Moreover it includes an extraneous knowledge which far exceeds the experience of the individual, for it is the basis of a planning which extends to times and places of which the individual can have no direct experience. Even where this behavior becomes an ordered ritual which imposes itself on the individual as a higher power, the individual animal, though its conduct may show slight variations from the norm, does little more than enact this order medially.

There are certain correspondences between this behavior on the part of animals and the ritual behavior of early man. In both cases the mover exerts a fascination and an exclusive power; and in both cases there is an emotion that seizes upon the whole personality. In animals this emotion is the attunement which maintains the behavior directed and ordered by instinct.

The term spirit-instinct refers to a higher sense of order which imposes itself with the help of emotions and drives. It makes possible a ritual action with a form of its own and a transpersonal meaning. This ritual action embodies an extraneous knowledge and manifests the light of nature which perhaps has knowledge of the circumstances that the future offspring will find at a time when the parent generation, executor of the ritual, has ceased to exist.

In man, even in early man, where it is an ego still living largely in a medial bond with the matriarchal consciousness that is captivated by the unconscious constellation, the situation is fundamentally different.

If we speak here not of instincts but of archetypes, it is because — and here we presuppose the fundamental observations of C. G. Jung — they not only lead man to a mode of action, but also, because he is ego *and* consciousness, affect him in another way, namely, they are *manifested* to him as images or symbols: the revelation appears to him, or he hears it as a voice. Image and language-symbols are phenomena that presuppose a seeing and

hearing consciousness. Here it is immaterial whether these phenomena are manifested within the psyche or in the world outside,
or in which of the two they are localized by the human individual.

In animals as in men the instinct that organizes behavior is an
ordering principle, but wherever we speak of medial behavior we
mean that the individual, whether animal or man, becomes the
instrument of an agent that imposes itself. In the human realm the
situation changes when the ego and consciousness enter in. Now
the unconsciously directing principle expresses itself; it speaks to
man. It bespeaks him for its own intention and makes a demand
upon him. This claim has a compelling character. There is
nothing voluntary about a fascination by the archetype, for the
archetype not only speaks but calls; the called one has a "calling";
he is prophet, a herald and proclaimer of the demand raised by
the speaking archetype.

For this reason the constellated archetype that irrupts into the
consciousness of man always has a significance, a meaning. In
accordance with the tendency to psychic wholeness discovered by
Jung, the emerging content has a compensatory effect; it supplies
what is lacking to ego-consciousness, to its conception of the world,
and its behavior. In other words it provides new meaning. It has
significance for the individual – and in the case of a creative individual also for the collectivity to which he belongs. Thus it becomes
incumbent upon the ego, especially upon the solar ego, not only to
execute an archetypal command, but to interpret and understand it as well.

To speak of the compensatory function of the archetype that
brings revelation implies that its emergence is directed by the
totality of the psyche, by the Self. The Self is capable of setting any
archetype in motion. It is a superordinate authority which, like
the organization, dynamic and compensatory of the biopsyche
dependent on it, operates autonomously, without the intervention
of ego-consciousness. But this directing authority has a vector that
is directed toward consciousness and the ego, to which it not only
communicates, but also reveals itself. This vector compels ego-
consciousness – and this is what we call fascination – to turn
its attention toward the emerging archetype, to take note of
it and assimilate it. The effective captivation and exclusive

concentration are consequences of this compulsion exerted on consciousness by the psyche and Self.

When we speak, in connection with animals or man, of an autonomous directedness by the instincts without the participation of ego-consciousness, we are speaking of a lower, purely natural process. But wherever a human being is "spoken to," there is meaning, and the authority from which this meaning emanates is experienced as higher because it is invariably connected with a source of illumination whose central symbols are heaven and the sun. And this moving and illuminating, violently captivating and fecundating, penetrating and transforming principle is experienced in man as the spiritual aspect of the masculine archetypal principle. By virtue of its symbolism, every archetype, regardless of content, partakes of this spiritual aspect, this living dynamic which expresses itself as a meaningful and significant reality. The center of this speaking movement is a formless mover, such as the wind of the breath. Regardless of the direction of its movement, or the content of its illumination, it is a creative spirit. And the center of this spiritual aspect, as manifested in the psyche, is the Self which transcends the archetypes and unlike them does not possess a form of its own, but according to the occasion makes use of the most divergent forms. The partner of this Self is the patriarchal solar ego which is captivated and fecundated by the spirit expressed in the Self, but then sets itself apart from it to interpret, understand, configure and fulfill it.

Whereas the solar-masculine principle, manifested as the spirit principle of the upper world, is experienced by woman as the numinous "other," it is experienced by man as his own, as his authentic possession, his Self. There is a mystery-identity between this archetypal manifestation of the Self and the masculine ego: "I and the Father are one." In psychological terms, this identity is reflected in the fact that the ego-Self axis is the fundamental constellation of the personality.

In the development of the male, the consolidation and stabilization of the ego which enable it to resist flooding by the unconscious and the world are brought about by a link with the upper creative Self, the spiritual and creative father archetype. It goes without saying that in this relationship with the ego the Self takes on a patriarchal symbolism. On the one hand, the Self has the fecundating spiritual character of the upper masculine principle, and on the other hand the ego experiences itself as a derivative of the Self, as its son-like image and correspondence; it is appointed by the Self and originates in it. The above-mentioned rites, in which men collectively experience and celebrate their origin in a creator god, totem or divine ancestor, are expressions of the fundamental experience of the initiated ego that knows itself.

The hostility of the solar ego to the lower feminine world of the mother-dragon goes hand in hand with its attachment to the higher masculine spirit world. As unconscious and as world, the mother-dragon assails the ego, which also has a lower masculine component of its own.

In the thus constituted patriarchal world, the ego-Self axis is no longer symbolized by the relationship between ego and mother, but by that between ego and father. In psychological terms, this means that the male no longer feels himself to be conditioned by the lower earthly power of instinct, but unlike other living creatures experiences himself as a higher spiritual being who, as it says in the Bible, became a living soul when the divine breath was breathed into him.

The secret of the masculine order[5] and the core of its mysteries is that this upper masculine-spiritual principle is invisible, just as the wind — *ruach* — is a mover but cannot be seen. This invisibility, especially when contrasted with the evident visibility of the feminine earth and blood mysteries of menstruation, pregnancy and child-bearing, compels the man to keep secrecy and to exclude women from their mysteries. Another reason for this is that invisibility can so easily be mistaken for nonexistence and so often is mistaken for it by the earth-bound mind of women and men alike.

The belief of certain anthropologists that the male mysteries are a fraud perpetrated on women is based on the same misunderstanding. The invisibility of inwardness of the masculine spirit-principle — as wind-sound-logos-voice — is an essential attribute of this spirit, which in its religious, ethical, artistic and scientific form comes into conflict time and time again with visible reality whose archetypal representative is the Great Mother as nature and as the visible, tangible world.

This conflict between above and below, spirit and nature, the invisible and the visible world, is one of the motives for the struggle of men against women in the patriarchal world. Psychologically, it is intensified by the fact that this world to be combated is also present in the man himself, whose lower instinctual masculinity partakes of it. And another reason for this conflict is the danger that the feminine principle represents for man, not only because man projects his own lower aspect upon women, but even more so because the male unconscious is naturally subject to the fascination of woman who in all her forms – mother and sister, anima and beloved, wife and daughter – keeps the non-spiritual aspect of man in constant motion both psychologically and biologically.

As it increases in independence, the male group gradually takes over the functions which were originally handed over to it by women and then subjects the women who originally directed the group to their patriarchal yoke. One reason why this progress is necessary is no doubt that with the progressive development from the family group to the larger group, the tribe and the stage, the instincts attuned to the natural environment prove more and more unequal to the tasks of life, so that legislative, cultural acts become necessary.

Man's culture-creating faculty is a predisposition of the human species, and just as we must regard consciousness as a creative product of the unconscious, so the human tendency to create culture and laws is a drive which is demonstrably present wherever men exist; this drive must be classified as what we have called spirit-instinct. Among the earliest human beings known to us we find ritual actions and the tendency to form a society. This society becomes gradually more conscious, and the religious, cultic-ritual legislation that is so pronounced in early cultures moves progressively away from the originally unconscious totality-regulation that we ascribe to the Self.

Thus there arises a masculine world with a patriarchally-accented collective consciousness whose content, to be sure, varies from epoch to epoch and from group to group, but which everywhere has as its center the directive factor of tradition, culture and the development of consciousness.

The father archetype which is originally a manifestation of the

Self is at first by no means identical with the lawgiver god of the later patriarchal canon, who subsequently becomes man's super-ego. Earlier than the lawgiver aspect of the father archetype is the all-embracing figure of the father-god, whose features, characteristically, are not always exclusively masculine.

At first the accent is not only on his creative spirit-and-light aspect, but also on an archaic uroboric factor that embraces the opposites. Precisely because this father-god works invisibly, in contrast to the mother archetype which is gradually devaluated and reduced to the level of lower nature and matter, he attracts to himself the positive components of the maternal manifestation of the Self, whereas the matriarchal principle comes to be looked upon merely as the beginning of consciousness and history, as *prima materia* and chaos, primordial water or egg, as the time of the beginning and place of origin.

Just as in the Biblical story of creation man no longer springs from woman but Eve from Adam, so, conversely, the father archetype has maternal traits in patriarchal cultures. The nourishing, protecting and comforting aspect of the mother archetype is encompassed in the image of the father-god, though this does not modify the patriarchal, anti-feminine character of the culture. On the contrary, the reduction of the originally directing goddess to the rank of a mere wife is a form of the patriarchal dethronement of the feminine principle. This is the trend in patriarchal marriage: little by little the wife is deprived of her rights; the husband sets himself up as her protector and provider, so restricting the feminine sphere more and more.

But in the course of the patriarchal development this partly uroboric figure of the father archetype, still bearing feminine features, diminishes in importance. The female in the male is diminished. The nature-bound aspect of the father archetype recedes and its cultural, ethical, sociological and political significance comes to the fore.

In contrast to the mother archetype whose nature content remains relatively unchanged, the father archetype presents a certain formal aspect quite apart from its founding and lawgiving content. Its content changes with every culture; it always gives laws, but the content of these laws varies. In his lawgiving the god always creates and imposes orders of life that restrict nature: this is archetypal; but the type and content of the order, the character of what is ordained, permitted and forbidden varies with the time and culture. In so far as the projected image of the father-god is saturated with the contents of the cultural canon of the moment, the father-god archetype may emerge with the founder or tribal god appointed by the individual culture or group. Then the father-god becomes a principle determining the collective consciousness and ceases to be an autonomous content of the unconscious. This gives rise to a development in which the creative-spiritual nature of the solar-ambivalent father archetype splits off from its form- and law-giving function. By law we here mean every traditional norm that the group observes, regardless of whether its giver is an ancestor, a god, or someone else.

In the course of development the god-image now becomes largely identified with the culture-conditioned super-ego and the numinous god-image of the father archetype is devaluated. Whereas originally the father archetype combined masculine and feminine, positive and negative traits and for that very reason had a mysteriously overpowering character to the human ego, now, in the course of the patriarchal development, this primordial character of the numen gradually recedes and the divine principle becomes an unambiguous god of ordering, law-giving reason, a representative of the good, the true and the just.

The polyvalent father archetype is largely reduced to the level of a law-giver-god and, like its counterpart in the individual consciousness, the superego with its injunctions and prohibitions becomes a component of the collectivity's traditional conscious values. The unity of lawgiver-god and super-ego becomes the highest authority of the collective consciousness, expressing the immersion of the personality in its particular cultural canon.

Thus as the patriarchal world develops, the experience of society is interposed between man's direct experience and the nature inside and outside him. The individual's duty ceases to be primarily what nature or his psyche require of him, but is imposed by the demands of the collective. More and more the collective relieves the individual of the need for direct confrontation with nature, but the price paid by the individual for this alleviation is that his confrontation with his fellow men becomes more difficult because it is governed by collective morality. The duties and obligations of this cultural world are represented by the culture-promoting super-ego. Now for better or worse man's guides cease to be his natural instincts and become the social traditions of the fathers.

But this patriarchal cultural front is in lasting conflict with man's nature; it brings about an intra-psychic tension between the natural and the cultural sides of man. For this reason the law of the super-ego in every cultural canon is manifested as hostile and superior to nature, because it is the higher, spiritual demand of a traditional duty. The arbitrary and mutually contradictory character of the ethical demands of the various cultural canons that mark human development – from cannibalism and head-hunting to self-mutilation and harakiri – shows that the demands of the super-ego are not conditioned by nature but in each case pre-suppose the unique historical development of a particular group.

But in the relationship between ego and super-ego every demand of the super-ego is, for the ego, vested in the authority not only of objectivity, but precisely of the spirit of consciousness. The reason for this is the connection, fundamental to the patriarchal world, between the super-ego and the father archetype, the sun and consciousness. The lawgiver-god or the lawgiving ancestor as an objective, outward authority and the super-ego as an inner subjective authority were originally identical. But even later, when they ceased to be experienced as a unity, the connection between them remains demonstrable. Through the introjective process of "eating the god," in which the individual "incorporates" this superior authority, the outward god as representative of the collective tradition is introjected to become the inner authority of the personality.

In the earliest stages of human development no ethical distinction is made between inside and outside, between heteronomy (determination by the outward collectivity) and autonomy (determination by automorphism). The individual lives in the group, he merges with it and is only minimally differentiated from it. Lawgiver-god, tribal ancestor and commanding inner authority are still one; individuality and the individual's personal and unique development are not yet accented, and the individual's Self is still largely integrated with the group Self.

In this phase, accordingly, the group is intolerant of deviations from the collective norm. Collective consensus was taken for granted and in extreme cases deviations from it were punished by expulsion, which under primitive conditions meant death. This is most clearly illustrated by the rigor of the initiations and their progressively increasing demands on the individual who in the course of them became a full representative of the collectivity and its consciousness.[6]

At this stage, where the inside is still outside, the individual received everything from the collectivity, in whose symbolism he was embedded. The development of the individual at this stage seems to involve only outward adaptation, because the collective consciousness included everything that was necessary for the existence of the individual. Through this subordination to the cultural canon of supreme values, the patriarchate enabled the individual to adapt at once to society and to the development of consciousness. Both orientations were experienced as adaptation to an outward principle which determined reality. In this sense, Freud's outward-oriented principle of reality is still patriarchal.

In addition to the two components we have mentioned, on the one hand the father archetype as the specifically human predisposition for law as opposed to nature and on the other hand the fathers of the collective tradition of each particular culture, there is a third: the individual figure of the personal father. But even this seemingly personal figure is in high degree molded by the cultural canon,[7] which tells the father what kind of father to be. To this the father's individuality can bring only insignificant modifications – at least in the epochs and cultures determined by a cultural canon . . .

Concluding Remarks

The author did not live to complete the present work. It ends in the middle of the section concerning the relation between the

Self, the father archetype and the super-ego and it does not reach the stage of development at which the girl child requires separate treatment.

By way of giving at least a general idea of the specific character of the feminine development, we shall cite a few excerpts from earlier works by the author:

"Superego formation and the opposition between super-ego and Self are among the general factors in the development of the patriarchal consciousness. The third form of guilt feeling, the patriarchal guilt feeling, is connected with the super ego . . ."

"For a girl, as Freud noted, the shift from her first object of love, her mother, and the transition to her father, is harder than for a boy, whose love is directed from the start toward the opposite sex and remains so. An analogous difficulty of no less significance is the difference of sex symbolism in a girl's experience of her Self. For both sexes, boy and girl alike, the first, formative experience of the Self is bound up with the mother. The girl preserves this bond. In other words, a woman can remain in the primal relationship, unfold within it and come to herself without having to depart from the maternal-uroboric sphere of the Great Mother. As long as she remains in this sphere, she remains childlike and fails to grow up as far as the development of consciousness is concerned, but she is not alienated from herself. The basic affinity between the primal relationship and the process of coming to oneself gives her from the very start the advantage of a natural wholeness, which the male lacks . . ."

"The relationship between mother and child is one of mutual identification, and the consonance between the process of finding herself in which a girl child learns to experience herself as a woman and the primal relationship in which the mother experiences herself as a woman leads to a primary intensification of all the relations that spring from identification. Here again the girl differs from the boy, for whom relatedness is essentially a confrontation . . .

"Let us briefly consider the consequences for the culture of man in general, but particularly of modern man, of the following parallel and opposing processes: patriarchal development of consciousness, release from the primal relationship, acquisition of a relationship with the object of love, and transformation of the sexual symbolism of the Self.

"The dissolution of the unitary reality, the development of consciousness and the resulting life in a polarized world of subject and object, inside and outside, are identical with the division of the personality that we have termed the separation of systems . . .

"The super-ego is not, like the Self, an individual authority of the personality, it is a later introjected collective authority which endeavors to impose the demands of the fathers, that is of the collectivity, on the individual by violence. Adaptation to this collective conscience, which is made possible only by the violence characteristic of the super-ego and the individual's repression of his own nature, leads, in the collectively guided development of the individual, to the formation of the 'persona' and the 'shadow,' authorities of the personality which are necessary to and characteristic of patriarchal culture if not of all culture . . ."

"The patriarchal development of consciousness leads by an undeniable inner process to 'matricide,' to the greatest possible negation, exclusion, devaluation and repression of matriarchal elements, that is, those determined by the unconscious, and ontogenetically in the failure, which has persisted to our own day, to recognize the crucial significance of the primal relationship and the pre-Oedipal world, the world of the separation of the World Parents . . ."

"Once the matricide has been carried out, a man must, to employ a paradoxical formulation, look for and find a new home and place of origin in an anti-nature that corresponds to his nature.

"The alienation of the Self, that is, its shift from the maternal to the paternal principle, which in boys is a necessary symptom of the process to which we have referred as the change of the Self's sex, leads to the belief inherent in every patriarchal view of the world that one is really not of this world and does not belong to this world . . ."

"In the modern world, where she is no longer subjugated and no longer prevented from participating in the life of the collectivity, woman is led from childhood on to develop her contradictory psyche. In other words, the development of her consciousness forces woman into a certain Self-alienation. More is demanded of her than of a man. Whereas all that is expected of a boy is manliness, a woman is expected to be both manly and womanly. Unquestionably this involves a complication for woman . . ."

"A further consequence of the fundamental situation of woman is that in so far as conscience (super-ego) is shaped by the values of the patriarchal collectivity, it can find no full resonance in a girl, since, as an expression of the patriarchal culture, it often contradicts the values of the feminine Self. In the identification of her ego with patriarchal consciousness, a woman never feels entirely 'herself' . . . But her suffering is legitimate and her 'dual' nature is pathological only if measured against the naïve totality and oneness of the primal situation, which must be abandoned in any case . . ."

For purposes of clarification we wish to point out that although Neumann speaks of mankind in general, his investigations of the human psyche starting from the post-embryonic uterine period relate principally to men living in a Western and in particular a Judeo-Christian culture.

The author's last manuscript of the present work has been published almost unchanged despite the repetitions that are only natural in a rough draft. This, however, has served to bring out the intensity of the author's thinking.

Notes

Chapter 1

1. Portmann, Adolf, "Das Tier als soziales Wesen" in *Eranos-Jahrbuch* XVLL, 1947.
2. In the following we always speak of the "mother", though in certain unusual cases another person may assume the mother's function.
3. Neumann, Erich. *The Origins and History of Consciousness,* Princeton, New Jersey, Princeton University Press, 1954.
4. On the Self, cf. below.
5. *The Origins and History of Consciousness.*
6. *The Origins and History of Consciousness.*
7. Neumann, "Mystical Man," in *The Mystic Vision,* Bollingen Series XXX, Vol. 6, Princeton University Press, 1968.
8. Scott, W. C. M., "Some Embryological, Neurological, Psychiatric and Psycho-analytic Implications of the Body Scheme," in *Int. J. Psycho-Anal., 19,* 3, 1948.
9. *The Origins and History of Consciousness.*
10. Neumann, "Mystical Man."
11. Freud, Sigmund, "Papers on Metapsychology," in *The Standard Edition of the Complete Psychological Works of Sigmund Freud,* Vol. XIV, London, Hogarth, 1964.
12. Bowlby, John, *Maternal Care and Mental Health,* Monograph Series 2, World Health Organization, 1951.
13. Sullivan, Harry Stack, *The Interpersonal Theory of Psychiatry,* New York, W. W. Norton, 1953.
14. This problem was to have been treated in a second volume of the present work.
15. Brody, Eugene B., and Redlich, Frederick C., *Psychotherapy with Schizophrenics,* A Symposium. London, Baily Bros. and Swinfen, 1952, p. 60.
16. Rosen, John Nathaniel, *Direct Analysis,* New York, Grune, 1955.

17. This was to be discussed in greater detail in a projected section of the present work.

18. Neumann, "Psyche and The Transformation of the Reality Planes," *Spring*, Analytical Psychology Club of New York, 1956. Eranus-Jahrbuch XXi, 1952. The reader is also referred to Hagenbrechner's interesting work, *Para-Psychologie und Para-Psychiatrie, Neue Wissenschaft*, Jg. 6, Heft 8/9, Zurich, 1956, in which he informs us among other things that roughly 85% of all cases of spontaneous telepathy occur between mother and child.

19. Evocation of the Archetype. See Index.

20. Here we shall not be concerned with the disturbances brought about by the mother's personal behavior, the intrusion of the patriarchal canon into the primal relationship, etc.

21. Tinbergen, N., *The Study of Instinct*, London, Oxford University Press, 1951.

Chapter 2

1. *The Origins and History of Consciousness*, Index: "Body."

2. We can only mention here the possible bearing on the phenomenon of schizophrenia that the failure to transfer the Self into the child's body might have.

3. Jung, C. G., "Psychic Conflicts in a Child," *Collected Works*, Princeton University Press, 1954, Vol. 17, par. 1 ff.

4. *The Origins and History of Consciousness*.

5. Bowlby, *Maternal Care and Mental Health*.

6. Neumann, Erich, *The Great Mother*, Bollingen Series XLVII, Princeton, New Jersey, Princeton University Press, 1955.

7. Cassirer, Ernst, *The Philosophy of Symbolic Forms*, I, New Haven, Yale University Press, 1953, p. 201.

8. *The Great Mother*.

9. Neumann, "Psyche and the Transformation of the Reality Planes," *Spring*, Analytical Psychology Club of New York, 1956.

10. *The Origins and History of Consciousness*

11. Piaget, Jean, *The Child's Conception of the World*, London, Routledge and Kegan Paul, 1951, p 167.

12. Klein, Melanie, *The Psychoanalysis of Children*, London, The Hogarth Press, 1950, p. 208.

13. Such an interpretation is correct only if the child fails to progress beyond this stage at an age when he should normally have a rational consciousness.

14. This primary identification of world and mother becomes clear in the child's later, magical attitude toward the world — which also comes from the primal relationship. The child learns only gradually to distinguish between its mother's relatively certain response to its magical cry of distress (for it is she who represents the world) and its far more doubtful fulfillment by the outer world, which does not by any means respond directly to the magical needs of the distressed child.

15. Graver, Gustav Hans, *Zeugung, Geburt und Tod. Ein psychoanalytischer Vergleich.* Bern, Humber, 1930.

16. Jensen, *Hainuwele,* Frankfurt/Main, Klostermann, 1939 and *Das religiöse Weltbild einer frühen Kultur,* Stuttgart, Schröder, 1948.

17. *The Great Mother.*

18. Klein, p. 284.

19. Portmann.

20. Briffault, Robert, *The Mothers,* New York, Macmillan, 1931.

21. Portmann, p. 95.

22. We shall speak of the social consequences of a disturbed primal relationship in connection with misdirected development of the ego.

23. Neumann, Erich, "Art and Time", Bollingen Series XXX, Vol. 3, Princeton University Press.

24. *The Origins and History of Consciousness,* Appendix I, "The Group and the Great Individual," p. 421; Appendix II, "Mass Man and the Phenomena of Recollectivization," p. 436.

25. We should not venture to maintain that this paradox "results" from the genesis of the soul. We merely believe that the nature of the soul is reflected in its genesis. But perhaps it may be said that disturbances in the development of the Self "result" from the human fact of the primal relationship.

26. Fenichel, Otto, *The Psychoanalytical Theory of Neurosis,* New York, W. W. Norton, 1945.

27. Fenichel, p. 479.

28. Fenichel, p. 86.

29. Szondi, Leopold, *Experimentelle Triebdiagnostik,* Bern, Huber, 1947.

30. The fact that the Self is the center not of the unconscious but of the entire psyche does not modify this context.

31. The importance of this constellation for the understanding of depersonalizations and of certain parapsychological phenomena is evident but cannot concern us here.

32. The same applies to experiences that had never before reached the ego.

33. Neumann, "Psyche and the Transformation of the Reality Planes."

34. Neumann, "Mystical Man."

35. Cf. D. T. Suzuki's publications on the subject.

36. The question of whether moon mythology preceded sun mythology or whether the two existed side by side from the start is irrelevant from the psychological or archetypal point of view. Psychohistorically, the unconscious and the feminine psyche correlated with it are "earlier," the consciousness and logos principle of the masculine world came "later."

37. Kerényi, K., *Gods of the Greeks*, London, Thames and Hudson, 1961, p. 16ff.

38. Neumann, "The Moon and Matriarchal Consciousness." Analytical Psychology Club of New York, Spring, 1954.

39. Neumann. "The Moon and Matriarchal Consciousness."

Chapter 3

1. Buber, Martin, *Des Baal-Schem-tov Unterweisung im Umgang mit Gott*, Berlin, Schocken, 1935.

2. Buber, *Die chassidischen Bücher*, Hellerau, Jakob Hegner, 1928, p. 548.

3. Quoted in Weiss, Edward and English, Oliver Spurgeon, *Psychosomatic Medicine*, London, Philadelphia, Saunders, 1943, p. 23.

4. Szondi believes that the ego of this stage, which is not identical with the Self, "takes no position." But it seems to us that every reaction and every independent expression amount to "taking a position."

5. Huizinga, Johan, *Homo Ludens*, Boston, Beacon Press, 1950.

6. Kardiner, Abram, *The Individual and his Society*, New York, Columbia University Press, 1944, and Mead, Margaret, *Sex and Temperament*, New York, Wm. Morris, 1935.

7. Klein, p. 193 ff.

8. Erikson, Erik, *Wachstum und Krise der gesunden Persönlichkeit*, Stuttgart, Klett, 1953.

9. This difficult dual situation is alleviated by the collectivity which places the personality within a fixed cultural canon that orients it and relieves the personality of certain important problems and conflicts.

10. It is self-evident that asocial traits and a negativized ego do not make so-called "social behavior" impossible. Here again compensations, socializations and sublimations can help to bring about a balance. Moreover, what today passes as social behavior is not at all what

psychology means by it. Thus for example the development of aggression with its competitive drive and the repression of automorphism are in many places regarded as social ideals. It is not yet recognized that this tendency breeds pathological forms of the personality, the accentuation of which leads to militaristic and class-struggle ideologies or to a philosophically camouflaged nihilism expressive of an isolated negativized ego that has lost access to the world and the Self.

11. Portmann.

12. The same is probably true of the non-human organisms which with their instinct and extraneous knowledge live in archetypal fields.

13. Here I should like to refer only in passing to another, more fortunate way in which a negative primal relationship can be overcome still in childhood, namely, through an intensified compensatory relationship with the father. This development is typical of hero mythology. Herakles is a striking example. Persecuted by the "snakes of the goddess," that is, by the Terrible Mother. But his primary bond with his father, the god Zeus, triumphs; he strangles the snakes and thus while still an infant embarks upon his heroic struggle against the power of the Terrible Mother. But it is clear that only the intervention of the gods could liberate the child hero from the negative sphere of the Terrible Mother.

14. Freud, "The Ego and the Id," in *The Standard Edition of the Complete Psychological Works*, Vol. XIX.

15. Ibid., p. 37: "According to the hypothesis which I put forward in *Totem and Taboo*, they (religion, morality and social feeling) were acquired phylogenetically out of the father complex: religion and moral restraint through the process of mastering the Oedipus complex itself, and social feeling through the necessity for overcoming the rivalry that then remained between the members of the younger generation. The male sex seems to have taken the lead in all these moral acquisitions; and they seem to have then been transmitted to women by cross inheritance."

16. Briffault, *The Mothers*.

17. Freud, "The Ego and the Id," p. 37.

18. Ibid.

Chapter 4

1. Jung, C. G., "The Relations between the Ego and the Unconscious," *Collected Works*, Vol. 7.

2. Jung, C. G., "The Psychology of the Transference," *Collected Works*, Vol. 16.

3. Spitz, René Arpard, *Die Entstehung der ersten Objektivbeziehungen*, Stuttgart, Klett, 1957.

4. Ibid.

5. Graber, Gustav Hans, *Zeugen, Geburt und Tod*.

6. Jensen.

7. Malinowski, Bronislaw, *The Sexual Life of Savages*, New York, Halcyon House, 1929, p. 444.

Chapter 5

1. Here it should be stressed that the phases of ego development that we distinguish are structural phases of the personality and not distinct successive stages in time.

2. Róheim, Géza, *Magic and Schizophrenia*, New York, International Universities Press, 1955.

3. But unquestionably, as we must stress time and time again, all the stages we have mentioned merge and overlap and can be clearly distinguished only in the abstract.

4. For this reason, we often find in male neuroses related to a tie with the Great Mother that ego development has stopped at the magic-phallic stage. Here the necessary transition of the patriarchate and to independent manhood often takes the form of a fantasy of a "permanent phallus," that is, the patient believes that his sex organ should be in a state of permanent erection. The continuity of upper solar manhood, that is, the necessity of a continuously thinking and acting consciousness is confused with lower phallic manhood. To the same context belongs the Don Juan neurosis, in which active protest against the Great Mother, who is at once shunned and sought for, is experienced through the permanent phallus of ever-changing relations with women.

5. Cassirer, Ernst, *The Philosophy of Symbolic Forms*.

6. Frobenius, Leo, *Kulturgeschichte Afrikas*, Wien, Phaidon, 1933, p. 127 f. Translated from the German by Beverly Dunlap.

7. Campbell, Joseph, *Masks of the Gods*, New York, Viking Press, pp. 334–338.

8. Translated from Gusinde, Martin, *Die Feuerland-Indianer*, Berlin/Wien/Leipzig, Zsolnay, 1946.

9. Because at dusk spirits begin to appear more frequently.

10. Gusinde, *Die Feuerland-Indianer*, p. 922.

11. *Loc. cit.*, p. 601.

12. For a detailed discussion of this matter, see Frankenstein, Carl, "Structural Factors in the Anxiety of the Child," *Acta Psychologica* XII 5–6, 1956.

13. Whitmont, Edward C., "Magic and the Psychology of the Compulsive States," *The Journal of Analytical Psychology*, Vol. II, No. 1, London, 1957.

14. Koppers, Wilhelm, "On the Origin of the Mysteries," Bollingen Series XXX, Vol. 6, Princeton University Press, 1968.

15. Cf. "Concluding Remarks."

16. *The Origins and History of Consciousness*.

Chapter 6

1. *The Origins and History of Consciousness*.

2. Frankfort, Henri, *Kingship and the Gods*, Chicago, University of Chicago Press, 1962, p. 160 f.

3. Jung, C. G., *Collected Works*, Vol. 8, pars. 317–319.

4. Briffault, *The Mothers*, II, p. 402.

5. Bettelheim, Bruno, *Symbolic Wounds, Puberty Rites and the Envious Male*, London, Thames, 1955.

6. The rigor is sometimes compensated by a certain laxity in the execution. We know, for example, that among the early Jews, whose canon provided that the merest trifles were punishable by stoning or some other form of extermination, the death penalty was virtually never carried out.

7. Mead, Margaret, *Sex and Temperament in Three Primitive Societies*.

Glossary

In chapter 1 of *The Child*, Erich Neumann calls for a new terminology that will clarify the distinctive approach of analytical psychology to the theory of personality development. This brief glos-
sary, prepared by Charles T. Stewart, M.D., has been added to the
present edition to provide the reader with a convenient summary
of several key terms used in Neumann's text. For further definitions of Jungian terminology, the reader is directed to "Definitions"
in *Psychological Types*, vol. 6 of *The Collected Works of C.G. Jung*
(Princeton: Princeton University Press, 1971), and to *A Critical
Dictionary of Jungian Analysis*, edited by Andrew Samuels, Bani
Shorter, and Fred Plaut (London and New York: Routledge and
Kegan Paul, 1986).

SELF   Neumann states: "Analytical psychology attributes to the
   Self, as the totality of the individual, the quality of a datum given
   a priori and unfolding in the course of life" (p. 19). And central
   to Neumann's view of child psychology is the interconnection
   between the development of the ego and the development of
   the total personality: "The total personality and its directing
   center, the Self, exist before the ego takes form and develops
   into the center of consciousness; the laws governing the development of the ego and consciousness are dependent on the
   unconscious and the total personality, which is represented by
   the Self" (p. 9). Thus, each phase of the life cycle begins when
   a constellation of the Self manifests itself in an archetypal unit
   that initiates and then directs a particular stage of development:
   "In this metamorphosis of the gods that arises through the
   change in its manifestations, the Self is correlated with the phases
   in the development of the human personality" (p. 183). The
   archetype constellated out of the Self during each stage of de-

velopment captivates and directs the ego through its numinous emotional quality, which "represents a supreme value for the ego" (p. 182).

AUTOMORPHISM and CENTROVERSION   These terms refer to functions of the Self. Their definitions again reflect the importance of the relationship between the development of the ego personality and the development of the total personality: "We give the name of centroversion to the psychic function of the totality, which in the first half of life leads, among other things, to the formation of a center of consciousness, which position is gradually assumed by the ego-complex" (p. 9). "By *automorphism*, on the other hand, we mean the specific and unique tendency of every individual to realize his potentialities" (p. 68). Neumann further differentiates the concepts of centroversion and automorphism in the following way.

> Whereas the concept of centroversion applies to the interrelation of the personality centers, the concept of automorphism embraces the development not so much of the psychic centers as of the psychic systems: consciousness and the unconscious. It concerns their relation to one another; for example, the compensatory relation of the unconscious to consciousness, and also the processes that take place only in the unconscious or only in consciousness but serve the development of the personality as a whole. (pp. 9–10)

Centroversion also contributes to formation of the ego-Self axis: "Centroversion is a universal tendency, present in every human psyche; it leads to the formation of the ego and of the ego-Self axis, to the accentuation of ego-centrality in the first half of life and to a reversal of this trend in the second half" (p. 68).

EGO-SELF AXIS   It requires an individual effort to bring the relationship between the ego and the Self, the ego-Self axis, into perspective.

> If we approach the personality exclusively from the standpoint of the ego, we can define it as a living biopsychic individuality existing in an environment. But once we have understood that the ego can never exist and develop without the Self that underlies it, we arrive at the crucial Copernican revolution of depth psychology, which views the human personality and human life no longer from the standpoint of the ego but from

the Self around which the ego revolves as the earth revolves around the sun. Then we realize that the ego-Self axis is the foundation of the personality. (p. 184)

The ego-Self axis is "the spinal cord of individual automorphism and, later on, of a stable ego and ego-consciousness" (p. 44) and as such is "the center of a complex of parallel and opposing processes which take place between the directing totality center on the one hand, and consciousness and the ego center on the other" (p. 45). The ego-Self axis undergoes development.

The ego-Self axis comes into being when the ego is established as a derivative of the Self, when it moves away from the Self. This moving away attains its culmination in the first half of life when the psyche separates into conscious and unconscious systems and the ego achieves an apparent autonomy. In the individuation process characteristic of the second half of life, the ego and the Self move back together again. But normally, quite apart from these age-conditioned shifts in the psychic center of gravity, the ego-Self axis is always in motion, for it is affected by every change in consciousness. Not only in sleep and dreams, but in every psychic process the relations between consciousness and the unconscious and between the ego and the self, are modified. (p. 47)

Throughout the life-cycle the ego-Self axis is "the basis for the tendency to compensation and balance between the ego and the unconscious and also between the world and the individual" (p. 124).

CONSTELLATION The activation of an archetype (or complex). When discussing the constellation of archetypes during child development, Neumann emphasizes the mutual nature of this process: "When two human beings are united by a powerful bond, their mutual appetency forms a bilateral connection between them, releasing corresponding archetypes in the psyches of each other. So it takes two individuals to effect or set in motion these transpersonal factors of archetypes" (p. 85). Confirmation of this mutuality is found in instances of disturbed primal relationships: "Once we have grasped this interhuman reality and the 'two-footedness' of the archetype, it will be clear to us that an archetype cannot be evoked by any spontaneous process within the psyche—otherwise the mother archetype would emerge in infants abandoned by their mothers and they would develop instead of dying or succumbing to idiocy" (p. 86). Neumann then observes that in man "these reactions are also provoked in accordance with the system that largely dominates the animal world: an instinctive process set up by a specific 'stimulus pattern'" (p. 24). Once the archetypal image is evoked in the psyche, it first initiates and then directs a stage of development as it "sets in motion a complex interplay of psychic functions in the child, which is the starting point for essential psychic developments between the ego and the unconscious" (p. 24).

Index

Index

Other C.G. Jung Foundation Books
from Shambhala Publications

Depth Psychology and a New Ethic, by Erich Neumann. Forewords by C.G. Jung, Gerhard Adler, and James Yandell.

From Freud to Jung: A Comparative Study of the Psychology of the Unconscious, by Liliane Frey-Rohn. Foreword by Robert Hinshaw.

The Golden Ass of Apuleius: The Liberation of the Feminine in Man, Revised and Expanded Edition, by Marie-Louise von Franz.

A Guided Tour of the Collected Works of C.G. Jung, by Robert H. Hopcke. Foreword by Aryeh Maidenbaum.

Knowing Woman: A Feminine Psychology, by Irene Claremont de Castillejo.

In Her Image: The Unhealed Daughter's Search for Her Mother, by Kathie Carlson.

Power and Politics: The Psychology of Soviet-American Partnership, by Jerome S. Bernstein. Forewords by Senator Claiborne Pell and Edward C. Whitmont, M.D.

The Wisdom of the Dream: The World of C.G. Jung, by Stephen Segaller and Merrill Berger.

Woman's Mysteries: Ancient and Modern, by M. Esther Harding. Introduction by C.G. Jung.

*Published in association with Daimon Verlag, Einsiedeln, Switzerland